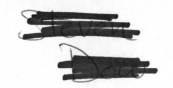

A COMMENTARY ON

PLATO'S MENO

A COMMENTARY ON
PLATO'S MENO

JACOB KLEIN

THE UNIVERSITY OF CHICAGO PRESS

Chicago and London

The University of Chicago Press, Chicago 60637
The University of Chicago Press, Ltd., London

© 1965 by The University of North Carolina Press
All rights reserved. Originally published 1965
University of Chicago Press edition 1989
Printed in the United States of America

98 97 96 95 94 93 92 91 90 89   5 4 3 2 1

Library of Congress Cataloging in Publication Data

Klein, Jacob, 1899–1978.
  A commentary on Plato's Meno / Jacob Klein.
    p.   cm.
  Reprint. Originally published: Chapel Hill : University of North
Carolina Press, 1965.
    1. Plato. Meno. 2. Socrates. 3. Virtue. I. Title.
B377.K55   1989   89-34929
170—dc20   CIP
ISBN 0-226-43959-3

♾ The paper used in this publication meets the minimum requirements of
the American National Standard for Information Sciences—Permanence of
Paper for Printed Library Materials, ANSI Z39.48-1984.

NOTE

This book was to have been written some thirty years ago. I was prevented from writing it by rather unusual circumstances. From 1936 on, I have had, however, many opportunities to talk to friends and students, in America as well as in Europe, about some of the points made in the book.

Except for the Introductory Remarks, Sections V, VII, 1, 2, and the notes, I have transliterated all Greek words and sentences into Latin script to make the running commentary more accessible to readers who do not know any Greek.

The final version of the book owes a great deal to the care of Eva Brann.

J. K.

CONTENTS

A COMMENTARY ON

PLATO'S MENO

"Eek Plato seith, who-so that can him rede,
The wordes mote be cosin to the dede."

Chaucer, The Canterbury Tales, *The Prologue*

INTRODUCTORY REMARKS

1.

In the past, for long stretches of time, writing commentaries was a way of expounding the truth. It still may be that. But how about commentaries on Platonic dialogues? Must they not be based on a variety of preconceptions and predecisions, on a vast area of questionable assumptions and anticipations, perhaps more so than any other venture of our understanding? And is not, therefore, such an undertaking almost self-defeating? Whatever else it might require, it certainly demands, above all, awareness of the gravity of this problem.

What considerations, then, should guide the writing of a commentary on a Platonic dialogue?

First there is the conviction that a Platonic dialogue is not a book claiming to speak for itself. This conviction was, and still is, shared by many. Inferring from a remark in Aristotle's *Poetics*[1] that a "Socratic" dialogue is akin to a mime, and nourished by information derived mainly from Diogenes Laertius[2] and Athenaeus,[3] historians and commentators have tried to see Platonic dialogues as dramas, philosophical mimes, philosophical comedies and tragedies, or at least to establish what their relation to mime, comedy, and tragedy is. One and a half centuries ago Schleiermacher set the tone. This is what

1. 1447 b 9–11 (cf. fragment 61, 1486 a 9–12).
2. III, 18.
3. XI, 504 b; XIV, 620 d – 622 d, *et al.*

4 he had to say[4]: ". . . if anywhere at all, it is here [in Plato's philosophy] that form and content are inseparable; each sentence can be properly understood only where it is placed, within the connections and limitations that Plato provided for it."[5] What distinguishes a genuine Platonic dialogue is "the form and composition in its entirety."[6] For a Platonic dialogue is "a whole in itself";[7] the "almost indispensable pattern" of its "form" is precisely the "dialogic clothing." Its intent is to imitate oral instruction. A "special peculiarity" serves this purpose, to wit, "that mimic and dramatic quality through which personages and circumstances become individualized and which, as everybody admits, spreads so much beauty and grace over Plato's dialogues."[8] Yet Schleiermacher also characterizes that mimic peculiarity as an "admixture" (Beimischung).[9]

This theme of the "dramatic quality" of the dialogues has never been quite abandoned.[10] But it is curious to observe

4. F. Schleiermacher, *Platon's Werke*, 1st ed., 1804–10, quoted from the 3rd ed., 1855–61, and the 2nd ed., 1862, of the *Republic*, I, 1, Einleitung.

5. P. 14: . . . wenn irgendwo, so ist in ihr [der Philosophie des Platon] Form und Inhalt unzertrennlich, und jeder Satz nur an seinem Orte und in den Verbindungen und Begränzungen, wie ihn Plato aufgestellt hat, recht zu verstehen.

6. P. 28: die Form und Composition im ganzen.

7. P. 14: ein Ganzes für sich.

8. P. 29: jene mimische und dramatische Beschaffenheit, vermöge deren Personen und Umstände individualisiert werden, und welche nach dem allgemeinen Geständnis soviel Schönheit und Anmuth über die Dialogen des Platon verbreitet.

9. *Ibid.* Cf. the Introduction to the *Republic*, III, 1, p. 9. (See also Introduction to the *Protagoras*, I, 1, p. 153; Introduction to the *Apology*, I, 2, pp. 128 f.; Introduction to the *Gorgias*, II, 1, pp. 5 f; Introduction to the *Phaedo*, II, 3, p. 9; Introduction to the *Euthydemus*, II, 1, p. 273.)

10. The following list is far from complete:
F. Thiersch, "Über die dramatische Natur der platonischen Dialoge," *Abhandl. d. philos.-philol. Classe d. Kön. Bayerischen Akad. d. Wissenschaften*, Bd. 2, 1837.
Ph. W. van Heusde, *Initia philosophiae Platonicae* (1827–36), 2nd ed., 1842, pp. 97–99, 175–95, 299–311.
C. A. Brandis, *Handb. d. Gesch. d. griech.-röm. Philosophie*, 1844, II, 1, pp. 151 ff.
H. von Stein, *Sieben Bücher z. Gesch. des Platonismus* (3 Teile), 1862–75, esp. I, 9–57.
Ed. Zeller, *Die Philosophie der Griechen in ihrer geschichtlichen Entwicklung dargestellt*, 4th ed., 1889, II, 1, pp. 569 ff.
R. Hirzel, *Der Dialog*, 1895, esp. I, pp. 199–259.
H. Reich, *Der Mimus*, 1903, pp. 354–413, esp. 409 ff., 900.
U. von Wilamowitz-Moellendorf, *Platon*, 1919, II, pp. 21–31.
W. C. Greene, "The Spirit of Comedy in Plato," in *Harvard Studies in Classical Philology*, Vol. XXXI (1920).

how little light the various attempts to cope with it throw on the actual drama aimed at in any given dialogue. One of the reasons for this failure can be indicated plainly.

We shall consider, by way of example, views expressed in René Schaerer's book, where the main problem is precisely to find the right approach to an understanding of Platonic dialogues. "Whatever the point of view from which one considers the Dialogues, they are ironical," writes Schaerer,[11] and there can hardly be any disagreement about that. For, to begin with, irony seems indeed the prevailing mode in which the Socrates of the dialogues speaks and acts. It is pertinent to quote J. A. K. Thomson on this subject. With a view not only to Thrasymachus' utterances in the *Republic*[12] Thomson says[13]: "When his contemporaries called Socrates ironical they did not mean to be complimentary."[14] "The old Irony of the tragic or comic reversal of fortune they perfectly appreciated. But this new kind, which had a trick of making you uncomfortable if you took it as a joke and of getting you laughed at if you took seriously? People did not like it, did not know what to make of it. But they were quite sure it was Irony. They called it so, and it is because they so called it that Irony has its modern meaning."[15] This meaning implies in any event that for a statement or a behavior to *be* ironical there must be *someone* capable of *understanding* that it is ironical. It is true, a self-possessed person may derive, all by himself, some satisfaction from speaking "ironically" to someone else who

J. A. K. Thomson, *Irony: An Historical Introduction,* 1926, esp. p. 169.

P. Friedländer, *Plato I,* English version, 1958, esp. chap. V, pp. 122, 124, and chap. VIII.

R. Schaerer, "La question platonicienne, Étude sur les rapports de la pensée et de l'expression dans les Dialogues," *Mémoires de l'Université de Neuchâtel,* T. X, 1938, esp. pp. 157 ff., 174, 190, 207, 218–34.

H. Kuhn, "The True Tragedy: On the Relationship between Greek Tragedy and Plato," in *Harvard Studies in Classical Philology,* Vol. LII (1941), Vol. LIII (1942).

A. Koyré, *Introduction à la lecture de Platon,* 1945.

P. Merlan, "Form and Content in Plato's Philosophy," *Journal of the History of Ideas,* VIII (1947).

R. G. Hoerber, "Plato's Euthyphro," *Phronesis,* 3 (1958), "Plato's Lysis," *Phronesis,* 4 (1959), "Plato's Meno," *Phronesis,* 5 (1960).

11. *Op. cit.,* p. 233: Quel que soit l'angle sous lequel on les considère, les *Dialogues* sont ironiques.

12. 337 a (cf. *Symp.* 218 d, e; *Soph.* 268 a 7).

13. *Op. cit.,* p. 166.

14. Cf. *op. cit.,* pp. 3–4 (also Aristotle, *Nic. Eth.* II, 7, 1108 a 19–23; IV, 7, 1127 a 20 ff.; Theophrastus, *Characters,* I).

15. *Op. cit.,* p. 168.

does not see through the irony at all. In this case, the speaker himself is the lonely observer of the situation. But this much can be safely said of Socrates as he appears in a Platonic dialogue: he is not ironical to satisfy himself. Everything about Socrates' irony depends on the presence of other people who are capable of catching the irony, of hearing what is not said. A dialogue, then, presupposes people listening to the conversation not as casual and indifferent spectators but as silent participants. That this condition is actually fulfilled is sometimes obvious, sometimes explicitly mentioned. And it certainly obtains whenever Socrates himself is the narrator of the dialogue. Hirzel[16] had occasion to note about the latter case: "The main point is that Socrates and not Plato himself is telling the story and his telling it cannot be conceived without envisaging a circle of listeners gathered about him with whom he previously had been engaged in conversing." Usually it is not important to know how many people are listening and who they are. (In some cases it may well be.) But it is of prime importance to realize that we, the readers, belong to them and belong to them in the sense of silently active participants. In fact, we are the only ones in those dialogues where other listeners are precluded (and not even cicadas allowed). Paul Friedländer's remark[17] "The dialogue is the only form of book that seems to suspend the book form itself" could perhaps be elaborated on as follows: a (Platonic) dialogue has not taken place if we, the listeners or readers, did not actively participate in it; lacking such participation, all that is before us is indeed nothing but a book.

Schaerer, to revert to his statement quoted above, assumes exactly the opposite: "The readers of the Dialogues constitute an audience similar to the one which surrounded the two contestants, forming a living hedge, but passively so: the discussion is not intended for them, it has its own justification within itself."[18] And "the spectator as such enjoys the contest

16. *Op. cit.*, p. 212, note 1: Die Hauptsache ist, dass nicht Platon selber, sondern Sokrates erzählt und dessen Erzählung nicht gedacht werden kann ohne einen Kreis um ihn versammelter Zuhörer, mit denen er vorher im Gespräch gestanden hat.
17. *Op. cit.*, p. 166.
18. *Op. cit.*, p. 44: Les lecteurs des *Dialogues* forment un public analogue à celui qui entourait d'une haie vivante, mais passive, les deux adversaires: la discussion ne leur est pas destinée; elle trouve en elle-même sa raison d'être. . . . One of the main points in Schaerer's book is the complete autonomy and sovereignty which he ascribes to the Logos. Ultimately, the Logos alone is the active character of the dialogue, the only individuality which counts

merely the way one enjoys good sport."[19] This view seems to express with admirable clarity a tacit assumption shared by the vast majority of commentators and reflected in their attitude of detached, if "historically" interested, spectatorship. Could that assumption be justified by Socrates' own testimony in the *Apology*? People who listen to his refutations enjoy this experience, says Socrates with wonderful restraint, "for it is not unpleasant."[20] Is there not more to it? "Considered from the philosophical point of view," writes Schaerer,[21] "the Dialogues are dramas in which the destiny of the human soul is at stake." Yet the assumption made explicit by Schaerer places the listener, the reader and, therefore, the commentator, together with his philosophical point of view, outside the arena of combat. Where is he then?

It seems that it is not enough to talk about the dramatic character of Platonic dialogues "from the outside." We have to play our role in them, too. We have to be serious about the contention that a Platonic dialogue, being indeed an "imitation of Socrates,"[22] actually continues Socrates' work. This again is by no means a novel view.[23] There is immediate

---

(le seul personnage actif du dialogue, l'unique individualité qui compte, p. 38).

19. P. 45, note: . . . le spectateur, en tant que tel, ne retire de la joute qu'un plaisir sportif.
It is only fair to note that Schaerer himself contradicts these statements when he says (p. 202): "We see that, at all events, Plato strives to provoke an impulse of dissatisfaction in the soul of the reader. . . . The dialogues are . . . open works (On voit que Platon s'efforce, dans tous les cas, de susciter en l'âme du lecteur un élan d'insatisfaction. . . . Les *Dialogues* sont . . . des œuvres ouvertes . . .).

20. ἔστι γὰρ οὐκ ἀηδές – *Apol.* 33 c 4.

21. P. 233: Jugés du point de vue philosophique, les *Dialogues* sont des drames, où se joue le sort de l'âme humaine.

22. Regardless of whether Socrates speaks or is silent or is not even present at all. (Cf. A. Diès, *Autour de Platon*, 1927, I, 161–65, 181.)

23. Cf. Schleiermacher, *op. cit.*, I, 1, p. 15, and p. 16: Plato's main point must have been "to guide each investigation and to design it, from the very beginning, in such a way as to compel the reader either to produce inwardly, on his own, the intended thought or to yield, in a most definite manner, to the feeling of having found nothing and understood nothing. For this purpose it is required that the result of the investigation be not simply stated and put down in so many words . . . but that the reader's soul be constrained to search for the result and be set on the way on which it can find what it seeks. The first is done by awakening in the soul of the reader the awareness of its own state of ignorance, an awareness so clear that the soul cannot possibly wish to remain in that state. The second is done either by weaving a riddle out of contradictions, a riddle the only possible solution of which lies in the intended thought, and by often injecting, in a seemingly most

plausibility in it. And yet its consequences are hardly ever accepted. These are that we, the readers, are being implicitly questioned and examined, that we have to weigh Socrates' irony, that we are compelled to admit to ourselves our igno-

strange and casual manner, one hint or another, which only he who is really and spontaneously engaged in searching notices and understands; or by covering the primary investigation with another one, but not as if that other one were a veil, but as if it were naturally grown skin: this other investigation hides from the inattentive reader, and only from him, the very thing which is meant to be observed or to be found, while the attentive reader's ability to perceive the intrinsic connection between the two investigations is sharpened and enhanced." (. . . jede Untersuchung von Anfang an so zu führen und darauf zu berechnen, dass der Leser entweder zur eigenen inneren Erzeugung des beabsichtigten Gedankens, oder dazu gezwungen werde, dass er sich dem Gefühle, nichts gefunden und nichts verstanden zu haben, auf das allerbestimmteste übergeben muss. Hierzu nun wird erfordert, dass das Ende der Untersuchung nicht geradezu ausgesprochen und wörtlich niedergelegt werde . . . , dass die Seele aber in die Notwendigkeit gesetzt werde, es zu suchen, und auf den Weg geleitet, wo sie es finden kann. Das erste geschieht, indem sie über ihren Zustand des Nichtwissens zu so klarem Bewusstsein gebracht wird, dass sie unmöglich gutwillig darin bleiben kann. Das andere, indem entweder aus Widersprüchen ein Räthsel geflochten wird, zu welchem der beabsichtigte Gedanke die einzig mögliche Lösung ist, und oft auf ganz fremdscheinende zufällige Art manche Andeutung hingeworfen, die nur derjenige findet und versteht, der wirklich und selbstthätig sucht. Oder die eigentliche Untersuchung wird mit einer andern, nicht wie mit einem Schleier, sondern wie mit einer angewachsenen Haut überkleidet, welche dem Unaufmerksamen, aber auch nur diesem, dasjenige verdeckt, was eigentlich soll beobachtet oder gefunden werden, dem Aufmerksamen aber nur noch den Sinn für den inneren Zusammenhang schärft und läutert). (See also *op. cit.,* pp. 30 and 34.)

Cf. furthermore Brandis, *op. cit.,* pp. 154 f. and 159 f.: ". . . did not Plato assume that the reader, through his spontaneous participation in the recorded investigation, would be able to supply what was lacking in it, find its true center and subordinate everything else to that center so that, by developing the train of thought begun in the dialogue, he would successfully solve its apparent contradictions; did not Plato assume that such a reader, but only such a reader, would convince himself of having reached real understanding . . . ?" (. . . setzte Plato nicht voraus, dass der Leser durch selbsttätige Teilnahme an der aufgezeichneten Untersuchung das Fehlende zu ergänzen, den wahren Mittelpunkt derselben aufzufinden und diesem das übrige unterzuordnen vermöge, damit die Lösung der scheinbaren Widersprüche durch fernere Entwickelung der eingeleiteten Gedankenreihe ihm gelinge; aber auch nur ein solcher Leser die Überzeugung gewinne zum Verständnis gelangt zu sein. . . ?). This passage is quoted approvingly by Zeller, *op. cit.,* p. 577.

See also Friedländer, *op. cit.,* p. 166; É. Bourguet, "Sur la composition du «*Phèdre*»," *Rev. de métaph. et de morale,* 1919, p. 341; Schaerer, above, note 18; P.-M. Schuhl, *L'œuvre de Platon,* 1954, p. 10: "Platon . . . exige du lecteur une collaboration active, la meilleure des disciplines."

rance, that it is up to us to get out of the impasse and to reach a conclusion, if it is reachable at all. We are one of the elements of the dialogue and perhaps the most important one. A commentary can, at best, lend voice to this element and do no more.

This is not to say that the dialogues are void of all "doctrinal" assertions. On the contrary, this further consideration ought to guide our understanding of the dialogues: they contain a Platonic "doctrine"—by which is not meant what has come to be called a "philosophical system." The dialogues not only embody the famous "oracular" and "paradoxical" statements emanating from Socrates ("virtue is knowledge," "nobody does evil knowingly," "it is better to suffer than to commit injustice") and are, to a large extent, protreptic plays based on these, but they also discuss and state, more or less explicitly, the ultimate foundations on which those statements rest and the far-reaching consequences which flow from them. But never is this done "with complete clarity."[24] It is still up to us to try to clarify those foundations and consequences, using, if necessary, "another, longer and more involved, road,"[25] and then accept, correct, or reject them—it is up to us, in other words, to engage in "philosophy."

That is why that layer of preconceptions and predecisions, mentioned in the beginning, must, of necessity, weigh so heavily on us. Our role as participants in the dialogue is fundamentally not different from that of Plato's own contemporaries who may have listened to somebody reading them aloud. There is no question that we share with them views commonly held by many people at all times. But there is this difference: between them and us there is the immense philosophic—and philological—tradition of the ages which stems, for the most part, from Socrates' and Plato's teaching. It is not in our power to remain untouched by it. And as much as this tradition may help our understanding, it may also obstruct and distort it. We can try to avoid at least two pitfalls: (a) to become obsessed by the view that the chronology of the Platonic dialogues implies a "development" in Plato's own thinking and that an insight into this development contributes in a significant way to the understanding of the dialogues themselves; (b) to attempt to render what is said and shown in the dialogues in petrified terms derived—after centuries of

24. πάσῃ σαφηνείᾳ – Soph. 254 c 6.
25. ἄλλη . . . μακροτέρα καὶ πλείων ὁδός – Rep. IV, 435 d 3 (cf. VI, 504 b, d).

use and abuse—from Aristotle's technical vocabulary. In one respect, however, the philological and historical work which began with the Alexandrians and reached such amazing heights and depths in the nineteenth and present centuries remains indispensable to us: it provides the means, limited though they may be, of restoring some of the immediate intelligibility which so many allusions, situations, names, proverbs, and puns in the dialogues must have had for Plato's contemporaries. We should not forget that, in most cases, there is a direct link between the possibility of restoring their intelligibility and their being widely familiar in their own day. It is the familiar that Plato is bent on exploiting.

2.

What has been said so far is open to the objection that, book or no book, a Platonic dialogue is a written work, and to be able to participate in it means, first of all, to face a *written* text. How can we participate in it then? And are we not, moreover, reminded by Plato himself, in the much quoted closing exchanges of the *Phaedrus,* that a written text cannot be quite relied on? This objection has to be met.

There, in the *Phaedrus,* Socrates compares (276 b-d) any writing to the quick raising of potted plants, which may well be an enjoyable undertaking and may even serve a purpose on festive occasions,[26] but cannot be understood as serious business like the artful and time-demanding activity of a prudent farmer who wants the seed he plants to bear fruit. Writing is a playful thing, is for amusement's sake ($\pi\alpha\iota\delta\iota\hat{\alpha}\varsigma$ $\chi\acute{\alpha}\rho\iota\nu$), although this kind of play and amusement, Phaedrus and Socrates agree (d-e), is incomparably higher in dignity than any other kind. Written words must (277 e 6) of necessity ($\dot{\alpha}\nu\alpha\gamma\kappa\alpha\hat{\iota}o\nu$) have a great deal of playfulness ($\pi\alpha\iota\delta\iota\grave{\alpha}\nu$ $\pi o\lambda\lambda\acute{\eta}\nu$) in them. Why "of necessity"? We gather an answer from the *Phaedrus* itself, and the *Sophist.* As Phaedrus puts it (276 a 8 f.),[27] the written word may be justly called a sort of

26. Cf. 265 c 8 f. and the context. (See R. Hackforth's translation of the *Phaedrus,* 1952, p. 132, note 2.)
27. It is possible that Phaedrus, an "expert" in these matters, quotes Alcidamas at this point, just as the entire passage uses terms and imagery "borrowed" from the contemporary controversy about the merits and demerits of "speech-writing." It is one thing, however, to find traces of this controversy in the *Phaedrus* and quite another to understand what is said in the context of the dialogue. Cf. L. Robin in his edition of the *Phaedrus* (*Platon, Œuvres com-*

image (εἴδωλον ἄν τι λέγοιτο δικαίως) of the spoken word, the one that is alive (ζῶν καὶ ἔμψυχος) and, as Socrates suggests (276 a 1 f.; 278 a 6), is alone legitimate or authentic (γνήσιος). The written word "imitates" the spoken word. But "imitation" (μίμησις) is the source of the highest kind of "play" (παιδιά). The Stranger in the *Sophist,* where the mode of being of "Image" becomes a crucial problem, asks (234 b 1–3): "Can you think of any more artful and more graceful kind of playing than the imitative one?" And Theaetetus replies: "Certainly not," adding cautiously that this kind covers quite a variety of manifestations. Written words, then, are necessarily playful and, under propitious circumstances, most exquisitely so, because it is their very character to imitate. But this character makes them also unreliable. For, as Socrates says in the *Phaedrus* (275 d): "You would think that they spoke as if they understood something, but whenever, from a desire to learn, you ask them about something which they say, they do nothing but repeat always one and the same thing."[28] They cannot, therefore, defend themselves against misunderstanding and abuse (275 e 5; 276 c 8 f.). Furthermore, they cannot and do not discriminate among those to whom they speak. Any author who holds that there could be much solidity (μεγάλη βεβαιότης) and clarity (σαφήνεια) (277 d 8 f.; cf. 275 c 6) in his written work deserves to be blamed for that, regardless of whether there is anyone to voice the blame or not.[29] In brief: a written text is necessarily incomplete and cannot teach properly.

It is to be observed that most of the conversation between Phaedrus and Socrates about writing rests on the agreement (258 d) that writing of speeches is not, as some people think or pretend to think (257 d ff.), shameful in itself (ΣΩ. Τοῦτο μὲν ἄρα παντὶ δῆλον, ὅτι οὐκ αἰσχρὸν αὐτό γε τὸ γράφειν λόγους. ΦΑΙ. Τί γάρ;). They agree, therefore, that one must examine the problem: what manner of writing is good and what manner bad? (τίς οὖν ὁ τρόπος τοῦ καλῶς τε καὶ μὴ γράφειν; cf. 259 e 1–3). The discussion which immediately follows this agreement (259 e – 274 b) bypasses that problem, however, and seems to deal more with the arts of the spoken word until Socrates reverts (274 b 6) to the original question by saying:

---

plètes, Coll. d. Univ. de France, "Les Belles Lettres," 1933) pp. CLXIV ff. and Friedländer, *op. cit.,* pp. 110–13, 357, note 6. See also below, note 33.

28. Cf. *Protag.* 329 a 2–4, 347 e 3 f.
29. Cf. also *Epist. VII,* 344 c f.

12   "There remains the matter of propriety and impropriety in writing, that is to say the question: how is it brought about that writing can be good (καλῶς) and how that it can be improper (ἀπρεπῶς)? Isn't that so?" Phaedrus: "Yes." But here again the conversation swerves away from that very question. It finally reaches a twofold conclusion. On the one hand, the doubt cast on the written word is said to refer to *any* composition (σύγγραμμα), written by anyone in the past or to be written by anyone in the future, be it on matters of law and politics or on forensic or private affairs or on whatever else (περὶ ἑκάστου), be it in verse or in prose (277 d 6–8; e 5–7; 278 c 1–4; 258 d 9–11). That doubt seems, therefore, to cast its shadow on the Platonic dialogues too, including the *Phaedrus* itself. On the other hand, nothing but the awareness or the lack of awareness on the part of the author that his writing must necessarily be deficient in solidity and clarity decides whether the writing is to be called proper or improper (277 d 1 ff.). The only distinction made among the written products themselves seems to be that "the best ones" (278 a 1), in addition to being playful, can serve as "reminders" (ὑπομνήματα – 276 d 3), that is, can remind those "who know" of what the written words are really about (275 d 1: τὸν εἰδότα ὑπομνῆσαι περὶ ὧν ἂν ᾖ τὰ γεγραμμένα – cf. 278 a 1: εἰδότων ὑπόμνησιν and 275 a 5: ὑπομνήσεως φάρμακον). But it is never, explicitly at least, stated what kind of writing or which of the writings are the "best" or what manner of writing would be most proper to its "reminding" function.

One wonders whether what is said about good speaking might not be applicable to its "image," to good and proper writing also. The prescriptions given later about good speaking (264 c; 269 c – 272 b) *do* actually apply to writing, although Socrates mentions this only casually (272 b 1; 277 a/b). The advice given at the end of the dialogue to Lysias and to other speech-writers (as well as to the poets and lawgivers), and finally the prophecy about Isocrates do refer directly to their written work. Now, Phaedrus and Socrates agree that spoken words can be clear, complete, and worthy of serious consideration provided they come from one who "knows" (εἰδώς – 276 a 8; cf. e 7) –who knows about things just and noble and good (276 c 3, e 2–3, 277 d 10 f., 278 a 3 f.) –and who also knows, as Socrates insists, how to "write" or "plant" these words in the souls of the learners (276 a 5–6; e 6 f.; 278 a 3), that is, possesses the "dialectical art" (276 e 5 f.; cf. 276 b 6 f., 265 d, 266 b, 273 e 1–3, 277 b) as well as the "art of leading souls" (*psychagôgia*) [30] which enables him to deal discriminatingly with those souls and even to remain silent whenever necessary (276 a 6 f.; e 6, cf. b 7; 277 b 8 ff.; cf. 229 e – 230 a, 270 e – 272 a, 273 d 8 f.). Only when these conditions are fulfilled can the words be adequately defended and supported (276 a 6; e 7 f.), only then may examining and teaching of what is true (ἀνάκρισις καὶ διδαχή – 277 e 9, 276 c 9) take place. Can all this be said of good writing also?

It cannot be said if the written text is to be taken in its dead rigidity. It can be said if the written text gives rise to "live" discourse under conditions valid for good speaking. This two-fold answer is reflected in the ironic ambiguity of any Platonic dialogue and, especially, of the *Phaedrus*.

It might be helpful at this point to look at the composition of the *Phaedrus* as a whole. The dialogue is framed, as it were, by two figures, one at the beginning and one at the end.[31] The first one is Lysias, the famous speech-writer, who appears on the scene in the most suitable mask: he is the scroll in Phaedrus' left hand. He remains present in this guise throughout the dialogue. The second is Isocrates, the no less famous speech-writer, who is conjured up by Phaedrus and given stature and dignity by Socrates turned prophet (278 e 10 ff., cf. 242 c 3–5).[32] We get only a glimpse of him. One emerges a past master of bad writing, the other full of promise of becoming a writer of truly superior standing and perhaps even going beyond that to greater things.[33] Between these two extremes (ἄκρα – 264 c 5) young Phaedrus, the ardent lover of speeches (228 a f., 242 a–b), is confronted by another "lover

30. This term is not specifically Socratic or Platonic, as has been pointed out often enough. In Socrates' use of it the more familiar connotations (cf. Homer, *Odyssey XXIV*, 1 ff.), at any rate, cannot be ignored, and Aristophanes, for one, does not miss this point (*Birds*, 1553–55).
31. Cf. L. Robin, *Phèdre*, 1933, p. XIV.
32. *Theaet.* 142 c 4 f. and *Phaedo* 84 e 3 ff. (also *Charm.* 169 b 4–5).
33. The passage about Isocrates has provoked innumerable comments. The reconstruction of the "historical" relation between Plato and Isocrates is of little help for the understanding of the figure of Isocrates in the dialogue. Robin, *Platon*, 1935, p. 26: ". . . the dialogues offer clear evidence of a kind of composition which transforms factual data to such an extent that the historian cannot derive any certainty from them with regard to anything with which those data are associated in the dialogue" (. . . les dialogues offrent des témoignages manifestes d'une composition par laquelle les données de fait sont transfigurées, au point de ne fournir à l'historien aucune garantie par rapport à tout ce dont elles sont, dans le dialogue, l'accompagnement). See also Hirzel, *op. cit.*, pp. 181 ff. and P. Wendland, "Die Aufgaben der platonischen For-

of speeches" (ἀνὴρ φιλόλογος) (228 b–c, 230 d–e, 236 d–e) with the problem of Speaking and Writing—and so are we.

Three speeches are heard, one written by Lysias and read by Phaedrus, the other two spoken by Socrates who keeps attributing their authorship variously to somebody he cannot remember (235 c/d) or to the local deities, the Nymphs and Pan, and the cicadas (238 c/d, 241 e, 262 d, 263 d), or to Phaedrus (242 d/e, 244 a), or to Stesichorus (244 a). The two speeches spoken by Socrates are, at any rate, painstakingly elaborate and, if they are not to be taken as written speeches, can hardly be conceived as improvised unless, indeed, inspired or dictated by divine or superior powers. The theme of "writing," throughout the dialogue, appears in fact more important than the one of "speaking." After Socrates finishes his Palinode—the great middle part (264 c 4) of the dialogue which takes place while the sun goes through its highest course—it is the problem of writing, and only by implication that of speaking, which is immediately taken up.

There is a definite change in the tenor of the dialogue after the speeches are done with. Phaedrus, who before the Palinode was quite certain (243 d 8 – e 1) that he could prevail upon Lysias to write another speech competing with the one Socrates was about to deliver, is very doubtful now (257 c) whether Lysias would consent to join the contest.[34] Has he not already been abusively called a mere "speechwriter"? Phaedrus agrees with Socrates that the real problem is to distinguish good from bad writing and that this problem should be put before Lysias, Phaedrus considering himself the latter's mouthpiece,[35] and he is more than willing to launch into the discussion of the problem. It is here that Socrates calls Phaedrus' attention to the cicadas over their heads. He tells a story about their origin: they were once human beings, even before there were Muses; now, in their present form, so says Socrates, they are supposed to report to the Muses and to

---

schung," *Nachrichten v.d. Kön. Gesellsch. d. Wissenschaften zu Göttingen, 1910, Geschäftliche Mitteilungen,* Heft 2, p. 112.

As far as Isocrates in the dialogue is concerned, Schaerer has said (*op. cit.,* pp. 178–80) all that needs to be said.

34. According to Hermias (*Hermiae Alexandrini in Platonis Phaedrum Scholia,* ed. Couvreur, Bibliothèque de l'École Pratique des Hautes Études, Sciences historiques et philologiques, Fasc. 133, 2me partie, 1901, p. 209), this is because Phaedrus does not believe that Lysias will be turned by Eros towards Philosophy (257 b). Hermias' implication is that Socrates has succeeded in persuading Phaedrus.

35. Cf. 264 e 3: "... τὸν λόγον ἡμῶν."

tell them who among men honors whom among the Muses; they are watching him and Phaedrus now at noontime, says Socrates, and if they see both talking to each other and not asleep—like sheep and most men—they may be pleased and report accordingly. Why does Socrates tell this wondrous story of the cicadas' origin and nature at this moment? Is it not done to underscore that, from now on, Phaedrus and Socrates, instead of exchanging elaborate speeches, that is, written or dictated words, will in leisurely and sober fashion converse about speechmaking and speechwriting and thus restore to the spoken word its proper and unchallengeable function?[36] In what follows we do indeed witness how those speeches are criticized and analyzed, how the beginning of Lysias' written text is made to repeat itself twice, word for word (262 e; 263 c – 264 a); we hear Socrates interpreting freely the speeches he himself made, assuming the role of their "father" (275 e 4), that is, supporting and defending the truth in them, adding to them, omitting the doubtful and changing their wording; we observe Socrates and Phaedrus bearing down on various books which purport to teach the art of speaking; we see them, in short, engaged in a serious conversation, which Phaedrus, the "lover of the Muses" (257 a 4–6; 259 b 5), describes, without apparently knowing what he is saying, as "somewhat bare" (ψιλῶς πως – 262 c 8).[37] It is important to see that all this *action* clearly anticipates Socrates' *later words* about the relation between the spoken and the written word.

Yet at the crucial point, when the discussion seems to revert to the problem of good and bad writing, it is again interrupted by another story. Socrates suddenly asks (274 b 9): "Do you know (οἶσθα) in what way you would best please divinity in the matter of words, either in making speeches or speaking about them?" Phaedrus replies: "I certainly do not. Do you?" Socrates: "A tale (ἀκουή), no more, I can tell from hearsay, a tale that has come down from our forefathers—as to the knowledge of the *truth*, it is *theirs*." And Socrates

---

36. Cf. Robin, *Phèdre,* p. XXXVII, where it is said, though from a different point of view, that "le mythe des Cigales est comme le pivot du *Phèdre.*"

37. Not "poetical" enough in Phaedrus' understanding (cf. 257 a 4–6). The implication that this "bareness" has can be seen from *Theaet.* 165 a 2 and *Symp.* 215 c 7. Cf. also *Statesman* 258 d 5, where the word "ψιλός" characterizes *genuine* sciences, and Aristotle, *Poetics* 1447 a 29.

adds: "But should we ourselves find this truth, would any human fancy (δόξασμα) about it still be of any concern to us?" Phaedrus: "A ridiculous question!" Urged by Phaedrus to report what he heard, Socrates proceeds to tell the story of Theuth and Thamus, in which writing is revealed as bringing about a great deal of forgetfulness and as substituting external marks, "reminders" at best, for genuine recollection "from within." We cannot help feeling, nor can Phaedrus help pointing out (275 b 3 f.), that this "Egyptian" story has been appropriately made up by Socrates himself for the occasion. To Phaedrus' admiring and mocking compliment about the ease with which Socrates is able to invent any "foreign" tale he wishes, Socrates replies in mocking indignation: In former times people were content to listen to oracular sayings of mere oaks and rocks, provided these spoke the truth, but nowadays young people in their sophistication, and among them, of course, Phaedrus, look less to what is true than to the personality and the origin of the speaker. Phaedrus is stung; he gives in and rallies to Thamus' opinion about writing, as related by Socrates, an opinion or a fancy that only a moment later Socrates himself calls an oracle (μαντεία).

No doubt, Socrates has chosen a proper way of leading Phaedrus' soul, as he has done throughout the dialogue. But are we to follow Phaedrus? Do we not see how closely interwoven the seriousness and the playfulness of the conversation was? Socrates himself, towards the end of the dialogue, lets it be understood that he and Phaedrus have been "playing" (278 b 7: οὐκοῦν ἤδη πεπαίσθω μετρίως[38] ἡμῖν τὰ περὶ λόγων). What he *says* (277 d 6 ff.) —collecting himself before elaborating upon his "Egyptian" story—about the necessary lack of solidity and clarity in any writing is contrived by Plato so as to be anticipated by what *happens* in the dialogue. Shall we forget that the answer to the question as to what constitutes good and proper writing has been deliberately and playfully withheld? Should we not seek the answer by ourselves, mindful of Socrates' emphatic distinction between Hearsay and Truth? And is not the answer to that question to be gathered, if not from the words, then from the action which the—written—dialogue "imitates"?

---

38. From Ficino onwards, most translators, notably Schleiermacher, Jowett, Robin, understood μετρίως as meaning "enough." But it also seems to preserve the meaning of "fittingly," "as it should have been done," i.e., with the appropriate seriousness. C. Ritter and R. Hackforth have apparently tried to render both meanings.

A properly written text will tend to transform the unavoidable deficiency of writing into a lever of learning and understanding. By imitating a discussion the character of incompleteness can be accentuated: as we all know, the movement inherent in any discussion, if it does not reach an end in complete agreement or complete clarification (which may happen but rarely happens), is the best inducement for its continuation. A properly written text will have, therefore, to initiate this movement and keep it alive by stringing it along decisive questions and partial or ambiguous answers. This, in itself, is nothing but an outgrowth of Socrates' veiled way of speaking. But beyond that, answers can be given in a written text by the very action it presents. That is what usually happens in Platonic dialogues and what constitutes their dramatic or mimetic quality. This also confers on the dialogues the quality of completeness as against their unfinished (aporetic) character in terms of the verbal argument.[39] The dramatic answers may not refer directly to the questions asked but may refer to those implied in, or intimately connected with, them. Furthermore, these answers may or may not be perceived, depending on the intensity of our attention and participation.[40] More often than not the dramatic answer anticipates the corresponding verbal argument; sometimes the dramatic answer accompanies the argument; sometimes the argument is underscored and put in relief, as it were, by what happens in the dialogue after the argument has been completed. All this reflects the character of Socrates himself, whose life and death speak still louder than his words.[41] The power of words, however great, is limited.[42] Words can be repeated or imitated; the thoughts conveyed by the words cannot: an "imitated" thought is not a *thought*. But only actions of men, irrevocable as they are, lend themselves to genuine "imitation," in life, on the stage—or in words.

39. Cf. the entirely different point of view of Schaerer, *op. cit.*, pp. 89 f., 135 ff., 169.
40. Cf. Schleiermacher, *op. cit.*, I, 1, pp. 16–17, and above note 23; also Schuhl, *op. cit.*, pp. 10–11, 59 f., 68.
41. Cf. Friedländer, *op. cit.*, p. 60. See Xenophon, *Memorab.* IV, 4, 10 (Socrates speaking to Hippias): ". . . Don't you think that deeds provide evidence more worthy of consideration than words?" (. . . ἢ οὐ δοκεῖ σοι ἀξιοτεκμαρτότερον τοῦ λόγου τὸ ἔργον εἶναι;) and the context; also *Apol.* 32 a 4–5, c 8 – d 2, and the *Phaedo* in its entirety.
42. *Epist. VII*, 343 a 1: "the feebleness of words" (τὸ τῶν λόγων ἀσθενές).

The dramatic and mimetic modes vary from dialogue to dialogue. But one can discern at least three different mimetic devices in them. One is that of ethological mimes,[43] that is, of imitations of actions in which the speakers reveal themselves both in character and in thought, κατά τε τὸ ἦθος καὶ τὴν διάνοιαν, to use Aristotle's phrase,[44] in which they show their souls "naked," to quote Plato himself.[45] Another is that of doxological mimes, in which the falsity or rightness of an opinion is not only argued in words but also manifested by the character, the behavior, and the actions of the speakers themselves. The third one is that of mythological mimes,[46] inasmuch as the drama of the dialogue presents, interprets, or replaces a myth (quite apart from the myths told by Socrates and others in the course of a conversation). But in each case the medium, the vehicle, the spur of the action is uniquely the spoken word, the *logos*, by which Socrates lived and still lives. All depends not only on what, but on how, under what circumstances, where, and in what context something is being said. Within the dialogue, the *logos* thus has *two* functions. One is mimetic, the other argumentative. Their interplay provides the texture into which we, the listeners or readers, have to weave our thread. That is how the drama itself, the "deed," the "work," the *ergon* of any of the dialogues, which is "in words" (λόγῳ) only, can encompass both, the dialogue's mimetic playfulness and its argumentative seriousness.

There is kinship between the two, between Play and Seriousness, one the "sister" of the other;[47] their common origin could perhaps be rightly described as a certain detachment from "reality." There are two ways of achieving such detachment, the way of "pretending" and the way of "wondering." In the playful act of pretending, which underlies *any* playing, the claim of "reality" to its matter-of-course genuineness is implicitly being challenged. It is from this challenge that any playing derives its charm and its fascination. On the other hand, any act of wondering amounts to ascribing pretensions to "reality," to seeing it suddenly as possibly not being what

43. This is the point H. Reich insisted upon, with too much vigor, some misunderstanding, and some exaggeration. See *op. cit.*, especially pp. 375, 390 ff. More to the point J. A. K. Thomson, *op. cit.*, p. 169.
44. *Poetics*, 1449 b 37 ff.
45. *Charm.* 154 d – e; *Lach.* 187 e – 188 a; *Theaet.* 162 b 3, 169 a 6 – b 4. (Cf. *Gorg.* 523 c – e, 524 d.)
46. Reich's understanding of the term is different (cf. *op. cit.*, pp. 404 and 239 f.).
47. *Epist. VI*, 323 d 2.

it pretends to be, in other words, to weighing the possibility of its being but an "image." For the extraordinary mode of being of an image is precisely to be what it is not. In the serious, if primitive, act of wondering we exert the fundamental faculty of *eikasia*,[48] a specific human privilege by virtue of which we are able to see an image *as* an image. In terms of the pattern of the divided line in the *Republic*,[49] this faculty of *eikasia* bears the same relation to our perceiving and accepting the visible world, as it presents itself to us, that our natural reasoning power, our *dianoia*, which is always bent on understanding the visible world, bears to our thinking what can *only* be thought. Neither *dianoia* nor *eikasia* are autonomous: each depends on something immediate and more comprehensive. But each has the tendency to separate itself from its soil; hence the danger of both dialectical perversion and mimetic self-sufficiency. It is the latter which is on trial in the tenth book of the *Republic*[50] and which is attacked throughout Plato's work. It is no other than the attitude of the chained men in the Cave as long as they do not turn their heads.

A dialogue usually moves on both the mimetic and the dianoetic levels simultaneously, although at a different pace. If we give due attention to the playfully mimetic aspect of the dialogue, the faculty of *eikasia* may be doubly aroused in us, and this can lead to our serious dianoetic participation in the unfolding drama, "beginning with the very first words of the dialogue."[51]

48. *Rep.* VI, 511 e 2; VII, 534 a 5.
49. *Rep.* VI, 509 d 6 ff.
50. 602 c ff.
51. Friedländer, *op. cit.*, p. 233; see also p. 366, note 8 (cf. Plato, *Rep.* II, 377 a 12; *Laws* VI, 753 e 6 ff., Aristotle, *Nic. Eth.* I, 7, 1098 b 6 f., *Sophist. Elench.* 34, 183 b 22 f.). Plato's care for the text and especially for the "beginnings" of dialogues seems to be implied in what we are told by Dionysius Halicarnassensis, Περὶ συνθέσεως ὀνομάτων, 208/209 (*Opuscula* II, 1 [Usener-Radermacher], p. 133), and by Diogenes Laertius III, 37 (with reference to Euphorion and Panaetius) concerning the beginning of the *Republic*, and in the anoꞁymous commentary on the *Theaetetus* (Diels-Schubart, 1905), p. 4 (cf. p. XXV, also F. M. Cornford, *Plato's Theory of Knowledge*, 1935, p. 15) concerning the beginning of the *Theaetetus*.

It is necessary to emphasize that Paul Friedländer was the first in recent times to refuse to separate the allegedly "ornamental" parts of Platonic dialogues from their philosophical substance (cf. especially *op. cit.*, pp. 161, 232). Attempts, antedating Friedländer's work, to point to the inseparability of "form" and "content" in Platonic philosophy (for example, H. von Stein, *op. cit.*, I. P. Wendland, *op. cit.*, pp. 100 ff., also J. Stenzel, *Literarische Form und philosophischer Gehalt des platonischen Dialogs*, 1916, in *Studien*

Under the spell of the cherished and bottomless modern notion of "art" there is a prevailing tendency to peel the so-called artistic and poetic skin off the philosophical meat of the dialogues or, conversely, to exalt their "poetry" regardless of the truth they might or might not contain. This tendency to isolate the "artistry" of a work and to render it autonomous parallels closely that of the professional rhetoricians Plato is always attacking.[52] The "art"-seeking eye does not seem to see that the deliberate and elaborate artfulness in the composition of the dialogues is imposed on them by their intent. It grows out of the Socratic task which the dialogues set for themselves and out of nothing else. This task is to provide the conditions under which we, the readers, can be induced to reflect upon our lives with the utmost sobriety. This task is formidable enough, for a reflection of this kind, if serious and persistent, is "madness."[53]

4.

It is possible, then, and indeed necessary, whatever the difficulties, to "participate" in a Platonic dialogue which we face as a written text. There is still, however, a grave problem to be considered: the written text, according to Thamus and to Socrates in the *Phaedrus,* can do no more than offer a "reminder" to those who already "know." Who are they, these "knowers"? According to Socrates again, the writer stores up such "reminders" for his own old age and *also* for anyone who "follows the same track" (καὶ παντὶ τῷ ταὐτὸν ἴχνος μετιόντι – 276 d 4; cf. 266 b 5–7). Presumably, then, both the writer and his "followers" are the knowers. And that will include us, if we are willing "participants."

Both classes of "knowers," taken conjointly, are referred to in the *Phaedrus* on two other occasions, when the superiority of the spoken word is proclaimed by Socrates. "I think a far nobler seriousness . . . is achieved when—by applying dialectical art and choosing a fitting soul—one plants and sows words founded on knowledge (μετ' ἐπιστήμης), words which are able to support themselves as well as him who planted them and which do not remain barren but contain seeds, whence they

---

zur Entwicklung der platonischen Dialektik von Sokrates zu Aristoteles, 2nd ed., 1931, esp. pp. 133–36) remained merely "programmatic" or superficial.

52. Cf. *Phaedr.* 260 b, d.
53. Cf. Aristophanes, *Frogs* 1491–99. The verb used here is παραφρονεῖν.

grow up again, differently in different persons, and thus are able to perpetuate this seed undyingly . . ." (276 e 4 – 277 a 3). "Words such as these ought to be considered legitimate children: first the speaker's word, if found by the speaker in himself (πρῶτον μὲν τὸν ἐν αὐτῷ, ἐὰν εὑρεθεὶς ἐνῇ[54]), and then those words which may have grown up in other souls in proportion to their worth, words which are the children and at the same time the brothers of the first one" (278 a 5 – b 2). Among the "knowers," we may conclude, belongs first the speaker or the writer who has gotten hold of the truth "about things just and noble and good"[55] in himself; if he is himself the writer, he thus can recognize this truth in his own writing without difficulty; and among the "knowers" belong secondly those of the listeners or readers who "follow the same track." Although they "know" in some way, they still have the effort of full discovery before them. Their being "reminded" by a written text is only the beginning of the maturing of the seed, and the author who knows will enjoy seeing the tender plants grow up (276 d 5).

Surely the dithyrambic words of the Palinode (249 b 5 f., e 4 f.) supply the background for these contentions. But it does not seem enough to appeal to Socrates' "mythic hymn" (265 c 1) for an understanding of the emphasis that is put in the *Phaedrus* on the speaker and writer who "know" and on the merely "reminding" function of a written text. It is tempting to interpret this emphasis as Plato's justification of, and even apology for, his own writing or his "compelling urge" to write, as against Socrates' uncompromising dedication to the spoken word. Indeed, the theme of the poet in Plato struggling with the thinker in him, that is, with his better— or worse—Self, is ever-present in modern literature. It is no less tempting to infer that the dialogues are exoteric writings as against Plato's own oral and esoteric teaching in (and outside) the Academy. Not a few writers on Platonic philosophy have succumbed to this temptation.[56] It is even tempting to envisage friends, pupils, or "followers" of Plato attending a reading of a Platonic dialogue somewhere in Athens and be-

---

54. Cf. Hackforth, *op. cit.*, p. 162, note 1.
55. See p. 12.
56. Harold Cherniss' (*The Riddle of the Early Academy*, 1945, pp. 2 ff., 11 ff., 75) devastating criticism of the way this position is arrived at is irrefutable. But is there any good reason to believe that Plato could not have made known some of his views to other people and even have discussed them in the Academy? (Cf. *op. cit.*, p. 68.)

ing happily reminded by what they hear of something they understand much better than the other, uninitiated listeners. There may have been some of these indeed. All these biographical and historical considerations, however, lead away from the problem which writing poses, lead away, that is, from a genuine and universal problem which is not confined to Plato's peculiar circumstances and which is more acute than ever in our time. Above all, no light is thrown by those considerations on Socrates' contention in the *Phaedrus* that the good writer "knows" just as the good speaker does.

It is Socrates' "knowledge," to all appearances, which gives to his words, spoken by himself or reported by others, so much weight and produces such a profound effect on his hearers, as Alcibiades' outburst in the *Symposium* attests.[57] Does the Socrates of the *Republic* play the role of a man who does not "know"? Is not knowledge on the part of the speaker—or speakers—presupposed in the *Laws*, when the Athenian suggests that the writing down of conversations such as he is engaged in at the moment might provide the best material for the education of the young?[58] Again, is it not presupposed that Socrates knows when, according to the *Theaetetus*, a conversation between Socrates, Theodorus, and Theaetetus, narrated by Socrates to Eucleides, impressed the latter so much that he decided to put it in writing and gradually succeeded in accomplishing this task with the help of Socrates himself?[59] Must not indeed the "antidote" ($\phi\acute{\alpha}\rho\mu\alpha\kappa o\nu$) of "knowing" ($\epsilon\emph{i}\delta\acute{\epsilon}\nu\alpha\iota$)[60] be present in the mimetic playfulness of any Platonic dialogue? Must not Socrates know? And also, in varying degrees, the strangers from Mantineia, Elea, Locri, Athens? Does not Plato, the writer, know?

But is not, on the other hand, the professed ignorance of Socrates the very nerve of the Socratic conversation and of its enduring impact? Does not the very structure of most Platonic dialogues reflect Socrates' assertion of his ignorance? This assertion is the lever which Socrates constantly uses to compel other people to examine with him, in common and from the level of common ignorance, the understanding which underlies his and their lives. Socrates' self-knowledge, his knowledge of his ignorance, is his unique "human wisdom."[61]

57. 215 d 3–6.
58. 811 c – e.
59. 143 a.
60. *Rep.* X, 595 b 6 f.
61. *Apol.* 23 a 7.

It is this assertion of his ignorance which charms, annoys,
and captivates everyone he approaches. Could Plato, the writer,
then, ever assume the role of a "knower"?[62] Could a Platonic
dialogue, the genuine "image" of a Socratic conversation, destroy the integrity of Socrates' wisdom?

It is true, neither those with whom he converses nor we, the
witnesses of these discussions, are quite prepared to take Socrates' assertion of his ignorance at its face value.[63] We are inclined to call it "ironic." The *Phaedrus* and the tenth book of
the *Republic* explicitly support and justify this disbelief. Socrates must "know" more than he ever admits. And is there
any way to exclude Plato, the writer, from the rank of "knowers"?

The problem which we face, that of the genuine or pretended ignorance of the "knower," is no other than the
Delphic problem of self-knowledge, self-control, or *sophrosyne*
as discussed by Critias and Socrates in the *Charmides* (164
c ff.).

Critias insists that a man who "knows himself" (γιγνώσκει
αὐτὸς ἑαυτόν) must possess the knowledge which not only
knows "the other knowledges" but also—and mainly—knows
itself (ἐπιστήμη or γνῶσις αὐτὴ ἑαυτῆς) and that precisely such
knowledge constitutes *sophrosyne* (166 c 2–3; e 5–6; 168 a 6–9).
Socrates does *not* challenge this statement—more precisely,
does not challenge its converse, to wit, that a man who possesses that which "knows itself" (τὸ αὐτὸ γιγνῶσκον) will "know
himself" (αὐτὸς αὐτὸν γνώσεται) (169 e 6–7), but he wonders
about the statement's implication. Knowledge which knows
itself must also know its opposite, ignorance, that is, absence
of knowledge (ἀνεπιστημοσύνη – 166 e 7; 167 c 1–2; 169 b 6–7),
and this means that *sophrosyne* consists both in knowing that
one knows and in knowing that one does not know, as the
case may be. This in turn means, according to Socrates, that
sophrosyne consists in knowing that one knows what one knows
and also in *knowing* that one knows *what* one does not know
(167 a 6–7; b 2–3; 169 e 7–8). Critias does not see any diffi-

62. Cf. Schaerer, *op. cit.*, p. 251: "One can . . . contend that Plato
did not write anything in the sense in which one says that Socrates
did not know and did not say anything" (On peut . . . affirmer
que Platon n'a rien écrit, au sens où l'on dit que Socrate ne savait
rien et n'a rien dit). Cf. *Epist. VII*, 341 c 4–5; *Epist. II*, 314 c 1–4.
63. *Apol.* 23 a 3–5; Xenophon, *Memorab.* I, 2, 36 (Charicles speaking):
"But you, Socrates, you are in the habit of asking questions to
which you know the answer most of the time" (ἀλλά τοι σύγε, ὦ
Σώκρατες, εἴωθας εἰδὼς πῶς ἔχει τὰ πλεῖστα ἐρωτᾶν).

culty in this: he claims that these statements amount to the same thing (170 a 1). And yet how is it possible at all to know what one does not know?

Socrates mentions his being apprehensive of the matter for the first time immediately after Critias has stated (166 c 1–3) that all other knowledges are knowledges of something other than themselves, but that *sophrosyne* alone is both knowledge of the other knowledges and "knowledge of itself." Critias does not believe that Socrates could fail to notice this and accuses Socrates of merely trying to refute him, while neglecting the very thing the argument, the *logos*, is about. Socrates denies this and asserts that his only purpose is to find out whether he is right in what he himself is saying, out of fear he might, without noticing it, believe he knew something, while he knew it not (φοβούμενος μή ποτε λάθω οἰόμενος μέν τι εἰδέναι, εἰδὼς δὲ μή – 166 d 1–2).

This exchange presents us with an example of the twofold function of the *logos*, the argumentative one and the mimetic one. What Critias says is far from wrong perhaps, but the possible rightness of his statement is at best "in words" only: his possibly being right does not mean, as we see a short while later, that he, in fact, possesses *sophrosyne* and understands what he is saying. What Socrates, on the other hand, has to say about his "fear" manifests "in deed," manifests shiningly, Socrates' own *sophrosyne*.[64]

Socrates proceeds to "refute" Critias' statement. This refutation consists in comparing knowledge that knows itself (a) with a set of human faculties which seem to preclude their ever making themselves their own object: vision (ὄψις) does not see itself, hearing (ἀκοή) does not hear itself, and analogously no other sensing power (αἴσθησις) and also no desiring (ἐπιθυμία), no willing (βούλησις), no loving (ἔρως), no fearing (φόβος), no opining (δόξα)—so it seems, at least—can ever make itself its own object (167 c 8 – 168 a 5); (b) with a set of relations between multitudes and magnitudes of all kinds, relations which quite obviously cannot be made to apply to themselves: the "greater" cannot be greater with respect to itself, the "double" cannot be the double of itself, the "heavier" than itself, the "older" not older than itself, and so on (168 b 5 – d 3). How, then, can knowledge know itself?

64. Just as the indecisive statement which Charmides makes, blushingly, in answer to Socrates' question whether he, Charmides, possesses *sophrosyne* (158 c 7 – d 6) reveals that he, indeed, possesses it.

There follows a recapitulation of sorts (168 d 3 – 169 a 7) of the same argument; the impossibility of self-application in the case of everything which belongs to the second set is clear beyond doubt (παντάπασιν ἀδύνατον – 168 e 6) ; as to the first set, a curious "addition" (ἔτι – 168 e 9) is inserted by Socrates: "motion" which moves itself (κίνησις αὐτὴ ἑαυτὴν κινεῖν . . .), "heat" that heats itself (θερμότης [αὐτὴ ἑαυτὴν] κάειν . . .); and Socrates further adds that the possibility of "application-to-itself" in the case of everything which belongs to this—significantly enlarged—first set would be disbelieved by some but perhaps not by others (τοῖς μὲν ἀπιστίαν <ἂν> παράσχοι, ἴσως δέ τισιν οὔ).

There is indeed some ground for not disbelieving that possibility. Is not "self-motion" precisely that which characterizes "Soul," *psyche,* as described—from a different point of view and in a quite different mood—in the Palinode of the *Phaedrus* (245 5 – 246 a 3) [65]? Is not Critias, while "defining" *sophrosyne,* talking indirectly—and quite rightly so, though without noticing it—about the Soul? And does not Socrates again manifest *his sophrosyne,* his self-knowledge and self-control, by disclaiming his ability to decide the question whether "application-to-itself" can be found anywhere and especially whether *sophrosyne* is characterized by it? It is up to Critias, the son of Callaeschrus, Socrates submits, to show that there can be something of that kind.

Critias is confounded. He is ashamed to admit his confusion before the audience of old and young men who watch the conversation as we do. He conspicuously his lack of self-control, his lack of wisdom, his *aphrosyne.* His own words seem to mock him. He has to be rescued by Socrates who suggests that, for the time being, they concede jointly the possibility of knowledge knowing itself as well as its opposite and that they turn to the second question which seems to come up unavoidably in the wake of Critias' statement: what benefit would we derive from such knowledge, if it were possible?

The lengthy exchange on this subject (170 a 6 – 174 b 8) leads to the result that no benefit at all would be forthcoming, even if *sophrosyne* knew how to distinguish in all cases those who know from those who do not. Critias is constrained to admit that only knowledge of what is good and what is evil

65. τὸ αὐτὸ κινοῦν – 245 c 7; τὸ ὑφ' ἑαυτοῦ κινούμενον – e 3 (cf. *Tim.* 89 a 1–3); for τὸ ἀεικίνητον (c 5) see Hackforth, *op. cit.,* pp. 65 f.

would be really beneficial to us (174 b 10). But *sophrosyne*, being merely the knowledge of knowledge and of ignorance, would not do us any good.

Socrates does not accept this result. On the contrary, *sophrosyne* seems to him (175 e 5–7) some great and beneficial good (μέγα τι ἀγαθόν). The confirmation of Socrates' belief would require, however, the closing of a gap in the argument. It would be necessary to show that knowledge of knowledge and of ignorance is *inseparable* from knowledge of what is good and what is evil. It is not Critias alone who would be hard pressed to plug this gap.

In this same connection, Socrates finds occasion to remark (175 c 3–7) that, notwithstanding all the difficulties which Critias' *logos* presents, his and Critias' "generous" concession in the face of its paramount difficulty amounts to agreeing to the possibility of *knowing*, in some way or other (ἀμῶς γέ πως), *that* which one knows one does *not* know. What is at the heart of the argument is Socrates' own knowledge of his ignorance, is Socrates' highest—and peculiar—manifestation of his *sophrosyne*.

There are two ways of understanding how that which is not known can nevertheless be taken as somehow known. One is the account given in the myth of Recollection as presented— more or less elaborately and somewhat differently—in the *Phaedrus,* the *Philebus,* the *Phaedo,* and the *Meno:* that which is not known to us is present, though hidden, "within" us and can be brought out through the correlative processes of "reminding" and "recollecting." The other way of overcoming our incredulity in this matter is the acknowledgment of the validity of the proposition that *there must be knowledge which we do not possess.*

This acknowledgment involves at least two factors. First, there must be the insight that the knowledge we *do* possess lacks ultimate and secure foundations. It may not be possible for men to attain them, but the very anticipation of a never completely erasable residue of ignorance points to knowledge as something all-embracing and, therefore, *whole*. Secondly, there would be the affirmation that only knowledge in its wholeness can securely guide our actions so as to make them indubitably beneficial and good. In this sense the knowledge of our ignorance may indeed be intimately linked to a postulated knowledge of an all-embracing good on which everything that we call "good" depends.

Is not this the knowledge of the "knowers" in the *Phaedrus?*

And is not Socrates, in pretending *not to know,* as much
"playful" as he is "serious" in his *knowledge* of the immense
distance which separates him from the goal he wishes to attain? Is not thus Socrates' "human wisdom," his assertion of
his ignorance, the very germ from which both elements of a
Platonic dialogue, its mimetic playfulness and its dianoetic
seriousness, spring forth?[66] Inasmuch as a dialogue engulfs
us, its readers—provided we are willing to "follow the same
track"—it seems to demand that we share in Socrates' im-
moderate moderation.

5.

Platonic dialogues are not, in general, samples of the "dialectical art." There are dialogues which abound in strictly
"dialectical" exchanges. But not all argumentative parts of the
dialogues have this strictly dialectical quality, since the arguments used are more often than not arguments *ad hominem,*
that is, dictated by the exigencies of *psychagogia,* in accordance with the (unwritten) rules of a genuine rhetorical art.
Furthermore, the conversation is never completely detached
from its mimetic complement. This holds not only for the
dialogues assigned by a wide consensus to Plato's earlier life
period but also for the later ones. It might be useful to examine briefly a conspicuous example in the *Theaetetus.*

The *Theaetetus* cannot be considered apart from the *Sophist* and the *Statesman.* Unquestionably, these three dialogues
form a unity. The *Sophist* "continues" the *Theaetetus* and
the *Statesman* "continues" the *Sophist.* The links between
these dialogues are not external or superficial.[67] The composition of the *Theaetetus,* in particular, seems directly dependent
on the central piece of the trilogy, the *Sophist.* The question
raised in the *Theaetetus,* "what is knowledge?" is dealt with

66. Is not a Platonic dialogue as much a dissembling (εἰρωνική) imitation as it is one which inquires knowingly (μετ' ἐπιστήμης ἱστορική
μίμησις)? (Cf. *Soph.* 267 e 2, 268 a 7.)
67. Ed. Munk, *Die natürliche Ordnung der platonischen Schriften,* 1857,
p. 423 f., says rather convincingly: "If an author has written a work
composed of several connected parts, he wants us to read these
parts as connected with each other, it being irrelevant whether
he wrote them at one stretch or at different times" (Hat ein
Schriftsteller ein Werk in mehreren zusammenhängenden Teilen
geschrieben, wobei es gleichgültig ist, ob er die Teile hinter einan-
der, oder zu verschiedenen Zeiten verfasst hat, so will er auch, dass
man sie im Zusammenhange lese). In Munk's view, p. 421, we
have to consider Eucleides as the recorder of the *Sophist* and the
Statesman also.

thematically not in the *Theaetetus* but in the *Sophist*. But the two "beginnings" (ἀρχαί) that come to the fore in the *Sophist*, The Same (ταὐτόν) and The Other (θάτερον), cast their shadow, as it were, on the entire structure of the *Theaetetus*.

The *Theaetetus* is clearly divided into three parts, of which the first one is, in purely quantitative terms, by far the largest, larger than the second and the third taken together. Each of these parts puts before us, in a "typically" different way, one of the types of error of which our *dianoia* is capable, and the first of these is more fundamental than the other two. The first is the error of self-contradiction; the second the error of mistaking something for something else; the third is the error of treating one and the same thing as if it were not one and the same. In the first case, the gravest of all, the very distinction between the Same and the Other is denied or lost sight of; in the second case, something "other" is mistaken for the "same"; in the third case, something in its sameness is not seen as the "same."[68] The common ground of these errors is the "similarity" of the two principles, their all-pervading nature[69] which they share with the all-comprehensive genus "Being."[70] This similarity has an immediate mimetic counterpart in the similarity of the two interlocutors, Socrates and Theaetetus, who not only look strikingly alike (143 e) but also show, irrespective of their age, a remarkable affinity "with respect to virtue and wisdom" (145 b 1 f.; 144 a 3 ff.; 148 b 3 f.; 155 d 1 ff.; 185 e 3–5). Indeed, the "Same" and the "Other" are playfully made to face each other, to mirror each other, in the *Theaetetus* (cf. 144 d 8 f.) —a memorable event that Eucleides thought worthy of recording.

What characterizes the action of the first lengthy part of this doxological mime are the repeated, and finally successful, attempts on Socrates' part to draw Theodorus, the mathematician, into the discussion. Already at the very beginning of the investigation (146 a) Socrates, while expressing his eagerness to converse and almost apologizing for his own "love of discourse" (φιλολογία), addresses Theodorus in particular. Theodorus refuses to participate on account of his age and his being unaccustomed to this sort of thing (146 b). After the first round of the argument, in which Theaetetus' tentative identification of knowing and sensing is linked with the

---

68. Cf. *Soph.* 253 d 1–4.
69. Cf. *Soph.* 255 e 3–7; 256 a 7–9.
70. *Soph.* 259 a 5 ff.

doctrine of Protagoras (as well as with the "doctrines" of Homer, Epicharmus,[71] Empedocles, and Heracleitus) and seems to fall to the ground, Theodorus, the friend of Protagoras (161 b 8, 162 a 4, 168 c 3, e 7, 171 c 8, 183 b 7, cf. 170 c 6 f.), is stirred up (161 a 5–6). But in spite of Socrates' prodding he is not willing to join the contest, wants to remain a spectator (. . . οἶμαι ὑμας πείσειν ἐμὲ . . . ἐᾶν θεᾶσθαι – 162 b 5 f.) and refers Socrates back to Theaetetus. A third time Socrates taunts Theodorus, as one of the "guardians" of Protagoras' "orphan" (164 e 4 f.), to come to the latter's defense. And for the third time Theodorus refuses. He rejects Socrates' gibe by pointing out that the guardianship is not his but somebody else's (namely Callias'[72]), for he, Theodorus, had turned rather quickly from "bare words" (ἐκ τῶν ψιλῶν λόγων) to mathematics and is obviously not the man to come to Protagoras' aid. He would be grateful if Socrates himself were to do that. There also seems to be some reluctance on Theodorus' part to become the victim of a Socratic refutation, which he apparently considers a disgrace (165 b 1). He is not attracted by Socrates' peculiar "midwifery" (cf. 150 b 9 – c 3).

In the argument which follows, Socrates, as he did briefly once before (162 d–e), assumes the role of Protagoras himself. It is this "imitation of Protagoras," comparable to the sudden emergence from Hades of Protagoras' head "as far as to the neck," its making a proud and skillful speech, and its quick disappearance afterwards (171 d) —it is this mimetic performance of Socrates (166 a 2 – 168 c 2) —that turns the scale.

Through the mouth of Socrates, Protagoras objects to Socrates' using a "little boy's" fright in attacking his, Protagoras', view (166 a). And later on, Socrates, in the role of his own self, reminds Theodorus of that reproach (168 c 8 ff.). Since Theodorus is the only older person in the crowd around Socrates, it would follow, says Socrates, that nobody except him and Theodorus are to exchange questions and answers, if Protagoras' demand for a serious consideration of his doctrine is to be satisfied. After putting up some last resistance (168 e 4 f.), Theodorus gives in (169 a 6 – c 6) and joins the discussion. Socrates' *psychagogia*, which in this case, as on many other occasions, used the art of *mimesis* itself, has borne fruit.

In Protagoras' speech which comes out of Socrates' mouth it is reasserted that the distinction between "true" and "un-

71. Cf. Diog. Laert. III, 10–11.
72. Cf. *Protag.* 336 d 7 f. (also 337 d 6 f.).

true" is not to be made. The distinction between "good" and "evil," however, is to be maintained. He is a wise and good teacher who is able, by means of words, to make his pupils— and entire cities—change from a worse to a better condition. But "be not unfair in the questioning" (μὴ ἀδίκει ἐν τῷ ἐρωτᾶν – 167 e 1). If you avoid this pitfall, your interlocutors will not abandon you, will attribute their state of perplexity not to you but to themselves,[73] and will try to change themselves by taking to philosophy. If, on the other hand, you merely play and try to bring your opponent to fall by all possible means, instead of being serious and helpful in your arguments, you will not lead your interlocutors to philosophy but, on the contrary, make them hate this whole business when they grow older.

In making Protagoras utter this warning, the "imitation of Protagoras" seems to reverse itself; the imitated one and the imitator exchange their roles. Is it Protagoras or is it Socrates who is saying this? Did not Theodorus abandon Protagoras and philosophy, turn from "bare words" to mathematics? And does he not now, under the impact of Socrates' conversation and speech, return to this idle pursuit? He does indeed; he replaces Theaetetus at this point and, after continuing the discussion of the Protagorean doctrine for quite a while (169 d – 172 b), he follows Socrates into a lengthy and solemn consideration of no less a subject than that of the "philosophical life" (172 c – 177 b), before reverting, at the end of his intervention, to the Protagorean topic itself (177 c – 183 c).

That central part of Socrates' conversation with Theodorus, which happens to coincide with the middle part of the entire dialogue, is usually referred to as a "digression" or "interlude," in agreement apparently with its characterization by Socrates as a "side issue" (πάρεργα λεγόμενα – 177 b 8).[74] But is not this "digression" an essential part of the drama played out in the first part of the *Theaetetus?* What is playfully *enacted* through Theodorus' behavior before and after Socrates' "imitation of Protagoras" is the self-refutation of Protagoras. The self-contradictory character of his doctrine is revealed in *deed* (ἔργῳ) before it is formulated in *words* (171 a 6 – c 7), which words Theodorus thinks deal a little too harshly with his friend (171 c 8). Theodorus does not realize, it seems, that his own inactivity and subsequent activity are much more damaging to the status of his friend's opinions.

73. Cf. *Soph.* 230 b 9.
74. Cf. the context of *Symp.* 222 c 6 and of *Euthyd.* 273 d 3.

Socrates' "imitation of Protagoras" makes Protagoras lose his identity in accordance with the latter's own stated view (166 b 7 ff.) and makes him assert something which in fact—and again in conformity with his own doctrine—is decisively, and comically, reversed by what happens to Theodorus in the dialogue. Thus is the mimetic self-refutation of Protagoras accomplished. But this consistent inconsistency characterizes not only Protagoras (or Heracleitus) but also our faculty of sensing, our *aisthesis,* as Socrates implied at the very beginning (152 a), immediately after Theaetetus had submitted his first tentative definition of knowledge for a common consideration. The final dianoetic refutation of the identification of knowledge and sensing (184 b – 186 c) is indeed founded on the contradictory character (ἐναντιότης – 186 b 6 f.) of our sensing in all its various "affections" (παθήματα – 186 c 2, d 2). The "obstacle" (ἐναντίωμα) is brought to our attention and is removed only with the help of our reasoning power, our *dianoia,* which is the power of distinguishing by "comparing" one thing with another (186 b–c). Not before this power comes into play can we begin to approach Being and Truth. It is precisely this stage that Socrates and a changed Theodorus had reached in the preceding so-called "digression." It could be reached because the Protagorean self-contradiction had in fact been already removed from Theodorus' soul.

To point up the "dramatic" quality of Platonic dialogues, reference is invariably made to the *Euthydemus* because this dialogue shows a particular liveliness, is full of excitement and brusque changes of pace. But the decisiveness of an action does not depend on the amount of excitement or movement with which it is accomplished. The serenity of the drama presented in the *Theaetetus* bears witness to that.

PART ONE
AMATHIA

1.

The title of the dialogue, "Meno," is well authenticated by Aristotle's unmistakable references to it.[1]

Why is this title chosen? Obviously, an answer, if there is any, cannot be given now. It might gradually emerge as the dialogue, and with it the commentary, proceeds.[2]

Who is Meno? A preliminary answer to this question is that the answer can only be found in the dialogue itself, since Meno is one of the personages who speaks and acts in it, and it is *this* personage we are interested in. The dialogue is hardly written to satisfy our—otherwise legitimate—historical curiosity. The usual confusion, however, between Meno in the dialogue and the "historical" Meno is not simply due to bad scholarly habits or thoughtlessness. The name "Meno"— as most names in Platonic dialogues—conveys a more or less vivid image to the mind of the listener or reader *before* the dialogue begins. Plato's contemporaries, at least those who might have been interested in the Dialogues, knew through gossip, slander, candid reports, reliable information, or even direct contact "about" most of the dialogues' personages. We, on our part, can reconstruct the images of those personages to some extent from whatever sources are available to us, and it is fair to assume that there is some correlation between the explicitness of the written sources and the vividness of the connotations that certain names had in their own time. This,

1. *Prior Analytics* II, 67 a 21; *Posterior Analytics* I, 71 a 29.
2. This general remark seems necessary: we have to ask, in every case, what significance the title of a Platonic dialogue might have, for it does not appear to be chosen haphazardly. The title seems sometimes to state plainly, sometimes merely to hint at, and sometimes even to conceal altogether, the main theme of the dialogue or one of its important aspects. The claim, often casually made, notably with regard to the *Phaedo,* the *Theaetetus,* and the *Parmenides,* that Plato wished to set a "monument" to somebody he highly respected or to show his particular "affection" for a particular person, is not sufficiently founded and somewhat naïve. It is not applicable, in any case, to most of the dialogues.

and nothing else, justifies the recourse to the "historical" accounts given of those personages.

In the case of Meno, our main source is Xenophon.[3] Through Plutarch[4] and Photius[5] some of Ctesias' testimony reaches us also. Ctesias, who served as physician to King Artaxerxes II, was an eyewitness of at least some of the events in Asia involving Meno. A third source is Diodorus Siculus[6] (first century B.C.), who seems to follow Ephorus (fourth century B.C.) who, in turn, appears to rely on Xenophon and Ctesias.[7] These sources agree on Meno's character and disagree, or seem to disagree, only on the question of Meno's death.

Xenophon, in his portrait of Meno, contrasts him with two other leaders of the Greek armies, Clearchus and Proxenus; the former an outstanding soldier and lover of war, severe and rough, able to command but apparently not inclined to obey, generally clever and yet not cunning enough at the decisive moment; the latter ambitious politically, a pupil of Gorgias, desirous of ruling and of commanding but not very good at it, endowed with a great sense of justice and nobility. The stature of both, in Xenophon's account, is far below that of Cyrus. But compared with Meno, their excellence shines. Meno appears as a totally unscrupulous man, eager above all to accumulate wealth and subordinating everything else to that end, consciously putting aside all accepted norms and rules of conduct, perfidious and treacherous, and perfectly confident in his own cunning and ability to manage things to his own profit.

Whether Plato, when he wrote the *Meno,* had or had not read the accounts of Xenophon or of Themistogenes (whom Xenophon mentions elsewhere and who may or may not be identical with Xenophon himself[8]) or of Ctesias seems rather irrelevant. Various episodes involving the Greek mercenaries and their generals, Meno in particular, in the struggle between the Great King and his brother could not help becoming common knowledge.[9] Meno was certainly a well known

---

3. *Anabasis* II, especially 6, 21–29.
4. *Life of Artaxerxes,* 18.
5. *Biblioth.,* cod. LXXII, Bekker 43 b – 44 a, or *Ctesiae fragmenta,* ed. C. Müller, pp. 57 f. and 75, in Dindorf's edition of Herodotus (1844).
6. XIV, 19 and 27.
7. See Ed. Schwartz' summary in Pauly-Wissowa, *Real-Enz., s.v.* Ephorus.
8. See Pauly-Wissowa, *Real-Enz., s.v.* Themistogenes.
9. Cf. Xenophon, *op. cit.,* II, 1, 17; 4, 4.

public figure[10] at the beginning of the fourth century, a "Thessalian Alcibiades," in Jowett's phrase.[11] Fame, be it of a glorious or an infamous kind, does not need—especially at that time in Greece—the channel of the written word to run its course. There can hardly be any doubt that Meno's image as that of an archvillain was fixed in the minds of Plato's contemporaries, regardless of whether this image did or did not do justice to the "real" Meno. And we, on our part, can hardly escape the impact of Xenophon's description of that peculiarly gifted man.

An ancient tradition, a focal point of which seems to be Herodicus the Babylonian (second century B.C.),[12] speaks of "jealousy" (zêlotypia) between Plato and Xenophon.[13] One of the examples adduced to show their rivalry and dissension is the allegedly different characterization of Meno in the *Anabasis* and in the *Meno*. Xenophon is said[14] to be hostile to Meno (he certainly is!), while Plato is supposed to praise him.[15] To quote Düring: "The whole story of this ζηλοτυπία is a typical literary invention based on misinterpretations and half-truths, grouped around a kernel of truth and supported by a series of disconnected quotations, which are sometimes even touched up to be made more convincing." As to Meno, even if we take his figure in Plato's dialogue as an "historical" portrait, we find some *explicit* statements there (for example, 78 c 4 – d 3, 86 d 6 f.) which show rather agreement between Plato and Xenophon's estimation of that gentleman.[16]

Be that as it may, to see who Meno *in the dialogue* is and what part our preconceived image of him plays in it, we have to watch the drama closely. The question who *this* Meno is might even be a central one for our understanding of the

10. Cf. Xenophon, *op. cit.*, II, 6, 28: ". . . ἃ δὲ πάντες ἴσασι . . . ."
11. Introduction to *Meno, The Dialogues of Plato,* 3rd. ed., 1892, II, 10.
12. See Ingemar Düring, *Herodicus the Cratetean: A Study in Anti-Platonic Tradition,* 1941, Kungl. Vitterhets Historie och Antikvitets Akademiens Handlingar, Del. 1:2, esp. pp. 54 ff., 157 ff.
13. Herodicus in Athenaeus 504 e – 505 b (reproduced by Düring, *op. cit.,* pp. 24 f.); Aulus Gellius XIV, 3 (a judicious account); Diogenes Laertius III, 34; Marcellinus, *Vita Thucyd.* 27 (Schol. to Xenoph., *Anabasis,* II, 6, 29). Modern literature on the subject, mentioned by Düring, *op. cit.,* p. 55, note 1, is listed extensively by J. Geffcken, *Griechische Literaturgeschichte* II, 1934, Anmerkungen, p. 7, note 38.
14. Diog. Laert. II, 50.
15. In recent times, E. Bruhn, Χάριτες *für Leo,* 1911, revived the story in a modified form. (Cf. Wilamowitz, *Plato* II, p. 144).
16. Cf. E. S. Thompson, *The Meno of Plato,* 1901, pp. XIX f.; Friedländer, *Platon* II, 1957 (German edition), p. 255.

dialogue. We should not overlook the "example" which Socrates gives early in the conversation and in a casual manner while bringing up an apparently more important and more comprehensive problem: ". . . or does it seem to you possible that someone who does not know at all (*to parapan*) who Meno is could know whether he is beautiful, or wealthy, or again high-born, or else the reverse (*tánantia*) of these?" (71 b 4–7).

2.

[70 a 1–4]   The dialogue begins abruptly with Meno asking Socrates: "Can you, Socrates, tell me, is human excellence (*aretê*) something teachable? Or, if not teachable, is it something to be acquired by training? Or, if it cannot be acquired either by training or by learning, does it accrue to men at birth (*physei*) or in some other way?"

There are two aspects of that question and of the way it is put which strike us, the listeners or readers, immediately.

1. That a question concerning human excellence should be put by Meno, the notoriously vicious Meno, to Socrates, on whom we tend to look as a memorable example of virtue, although—be it in Athens before and after 399 B.C. or anywhere else today—we do not quite understand his ways and might even entertain some doubts as to his wholesomeness and integrity, is startling and comical.

The suddenness of the question heightens its comical character. Nothing appears to precede it. Meno, on a visit in Athens, had met Socrates the day before, as we learn later (76 e), but the question he is asking now does not seem to have any relation to what may have been discussed then. All we hear about that previous encounter is that it gave Meno the opportunity to announce that his stay in Athens could be only one of short duration. (The abruptness of Meno's initial question and of the dialogue's beginning, however, may have also another and perhaps more serious significance which escapes us, at least for the time being.)

2. On its own merits, the question is not one to be lightly dismissed. Nor is it confined to a particular time-period or civilization. We are constantly confronted with it, although the terms in which it is phrased vary. We wonder how a man of acknowledged stature in public life acquired the outstanding qualities he appears to have, whether they are due to his

teachers, to his training, to his family upbringing, or whether
they just show his native "genius" or are a "gift of heaven."
We may ask the same question on meeting a man whose moral
integrity we admire, although his private station precludes
others from knowing about it.[17] We discuss the problem of
what kind of education, if any, might change or influence the
character of a child. We are, in short, concerned in one way
or another, with what gives people marks of excellence, what
makes them possess *areté*.

There is, however, another aspect to Meno's question, not
immediately apparent, but ascertainable from other literary
sources as well as from subsequent statements in the dialogue
itself.

The same kind of question, couched in similar terms, but
usually restricted to a specific virtue, justice or prudence, for
example, and, on the other hand, applied to all kinds of skills,
seems to be a recurrent topic in Plato's time.[18] The three factors involved— (a) nature (*physis*), (b) practice, exercise, cul-
tivation (*empeiria, meleté, epimeleia, to gymnazesthai*),
(c) instruction, teaching (*paideusis, didaxis*) —are, of course,
always mentioned. The phrasing of Meno's question indicates
that Meno is very much conversant with the current debate
on that subject, and, indeed, we learn from him later in the
dialogue (80 b 2–3) that he himself has made innumerable
speeches to many people on the theme of human excellence,
speeches with which he was well satisfied.

In asking his question, Meno is well aware that there is no
ready answer to it. Opinions vary as to the source of excellence
in individual men and, in particular, as to whether that excellence can or cannot be taught—as Meno himself has occasion to point out (95 b 1–5).

17. Cf. *Apol.* 30 b 4, *Gorg.* 527 b 6 and *Rep.* IX, 592 a 4, X, 599 d 5–6:
ἰδίᾳ καὶ δημοσίᾳ (also V, 473 e 5) ; *Apol.* 20 b 4–5: . . . τῆς ἀνθρωπίνης
τε καὶ πολιτικῆς [ἀρετῆς]; *Phaedo* 82 a 11 f.: τὴν δημοτικὴν καὶ πολι-
τικὴν ἀρετήν . . . ; *Tim.* 87 b 1–2: ἰδίᾳ τε καὶ δημοσίᾳ (also 88 a 4).
18. Cf. Isocrates, *Contra Soph.* 14–18, 21; *De permut.* 186–92, 274–75;
Alcidamas, *De Soph.* 3–4. (We also find the theme in Democritus,
Diels-Kranz, 7th ed., frs. 33, 56, 183, 242, and in Critias, Diels-
Kranz, 7th ed., fr. 9.) The Platonic dialogues themselves raise this
question persistently, notably in connection with Protagoras (cf.
especially *Protag.* 323 d 6–7); see also, in particular, *Phaedr.* 269
d 4–6 and *Meno* 85 b–d; furthermore, Xenophon, *Memorab.* III,
9, 1–3, and finally Aristotle, *Nic. Eth.* I, 9, 1099 b 9–11; II, 1, 1103
a 23–26; X, 9, 1179 b 20–31, and *Polit.* VII, 13, 1332 a 38–40.
(Cf. Thompson, pp. 57–58; P. Shorey, "Φύσις, Μελέτη, Ἐπιστήμη," in
*Transactions and Proceedings of the American Philological Asso-
ciation*, Vol. XL (1909), 185–201; R. G. Hoerber, "Plato's Meno,"
Phronesis, 5 (1960), 83–84.)

We also learn from Meno (79 e 7 – 80 a 2) that he is not unfamiliar with Socrates' reputation as that of a man who curiously excels in the question-answer game, continually raising difficulties for others as well as for himself. Meno wants to be told about the manner in which excellence accrues to men. But the very wording of his question implies that it is meant as a challenge to Socrates, the "quibbler"[19]: "Tell me, if *you* can. . . ."

3.

[70 a 5 – 71 a 7]   Socrates does not take up the Thessalian's challenge: he does not answer the question at all. Instead, he brings up—rather abruptly, too—Thessaly's former and present status, contrasting it with that of Athens. The Thessalians, formerly reputed for their horsemanship and their riches (*eph' hippikéi te kai ploutôi*),[20] says Socrates, have now acquired the reputation of wisdom also, while in Athens the contrary state of affairs prevails, wisdom having apparently emigrated from Attica to Thessaly.

The irony is quite transparent: Thessaly's reputation is that of a disorderly and licentious country;[21] its conversion to wisdom is credited by Socrates to the teaching of Gorgias and to the latter's influence especially on the Aleuadae, one—and the most important—of Thessaly's ruling families, otherwise known as having sided with Xerxes before and during the Persian invasion and thus betrayed Hellas;[22] the enchantment that Meno's graces exert on his lover Aristippus, a powerful member of the Aleuadae, is brought, through verbal juxtaposition (*ho sos erastês—erastas epi sophiai*), into close parallel to the enchantment that Gorgias' wisdom exerts on the Thessalians in general and the same Aristippus in particular.

The irony is compounded by the immediately following example given by Socrates to describe the dearth of wisdom in Athens. Nobody, says Socrates, nobody in Athens would react to Meno's question in any other way than by asserting that, far from knowing the manner in which human excellence comes into being, he did not even know what, all in all, hu-

---

19. Aristophanes, *Frogs* 1491–99.
20. Cf. the notes by St. George Stock, *The Meno of Plato*, 3rd ed., 1935, Notes pp. 5 f., and Thompson, pp. 59 f.(7).
21. *Crito* 53 d 3 f.: ἐκεῖ γὰρ δὴ πλείστη ἀταξία καὶ ἀκολασία.... (cf. Friedländer, *Platon* II, p. 256).
22. Herodotus VII, 6; 172; Pausanias VII, 10, 2.

man excellence was. It is probably fair to assume that, except
for Socrates, actually no one in Athens would make such an
assertion. Later in the dialogue (92 e – 93 a) , we hear Anytus
—an Athenian as good as any, even though his reputation
may have been somewhat tarnished[23]—claim that any reputable Athenian citizen could teach a man lessons in human excellence, and the implication seems to be that any reputable
citizen would know what the subject matter of those lessons is.
In point of "wisdom" "Thessaly" and "Athens" seem indeed
interchangeable terms.

Beneath the ironical clothing there are several points which
attract our attention.

1. Meno is introduced as a Thessalian and linked, through
the mention of Aristippus, with the Persians and the Persian
dynasty.[24] This link is confirmed later (78 d 2 f.) by Socrates'
characterizing Meno as the "hereditary friend of the Great
King" (*ho tou megalou basileôs patrikos xenos*) . Whoever
Meno might be in the dialogue, he is indeed *also* the man
known to us from other sources.

2. In describing Gorgias' teaching, Socrates, in his choice of
words (*to ethos hymas eithiken*) emphatically stresses the
point that Gorgias inculcated in his pupils the *habit* of answering any question in a fearless and lofty manner, "as befits
those who know (*eidotas*) ."

3. The kind of question Meno is raising leads back to another, more comprehensive, question, to wit: what is that
thing which we call "human excellence" (*aretê*) ?

4. This latter question is tied by Socrates to the theme of
the wisdom (or lack of wisdom) of a city and the wisdom
(or lack of wisdom) of its citizens. Athens, in particular, comes
to the fore at the very beginning of the dialogue.

Towards the end of his little speech Socrates identifies him- [71 b 1 – 8]
self explicitly with his (imaginary) fellow citizens, inasmuch
as he too claims to be ignorant about what human excellence,
all in all (*to parapan*) , is. "And it is the same with me too,
Meno" (*Egô oun kai autos, ô Menôn, houtôs echô*) , are his
words. We note this ironic explicitness, keeping in mind
that, in all likelihood, Socrates alone among his fellow citizens would confess to his ignorance on that point. This ignorance, Socrates claims, makes it impossible for him to know
anything that might be pertinent to human excellence—the

23. Cf. Aristotle, *Athenian Constitution* XXXIV, 3 and XXVII, 5.
24. Xenophon, *Anabasis* I, 1, 10; 2, 1; II, 6, 28.

way, for example, it comes into being: for "how could I possibly know what is pertinent to something, if I do not know what it is?" (*ho de mê oida ti estin, pôs an hopoion ge ti eideiên?*) And it is right here that Socrates illustrates that impossibility by taking Meno himself as a case in point.

The "example" adduced by Socrates, with its suggested parallel between "human excellence" and the man Meno, is both ironic and ambiguous. Apart from containing a comical challenge to our preconceived image of Meno, it plays with the diversity of words which convey the meaning of "knowing" and with the range that this meaning itself encompasses.

If not to "know" (*gignôskein*) who Meno is means never to have been introduced to him or never to have heard of him, the "example" is not a valid one. For, even if we do not "know" what human excellence is, we are not unfamiliar with the praise of excellence; we have often enough heard other people speak of "excellent" men, and we ourselves have, often enough, joined the chorus or stood aloof, expressing disapproval; we are, however vaguely, acquainted with human excellence, even if we do not "know" (*eidenai*) what it is.

If, on the other hand, not to "know" who Meno is means that, although acquainted with him in some way, we do not have sufficient insight into his character, do not know who he "really" is, we still might "know" a great deal about him and be able to tell about his looks, his habits, his qualities, his faults. But then again, the "example" would not at all show the impossibility of saying anything pertinent about a thing, if "what" it is escapes us, would not show the impossibility of knowing *hopoion ti esti*, if we do not know *ti esti*.

[71 b 9 – c 2] Meno, however, does in no way dispute that impossibility and does not raise any question about Socrates' "example." He merely appears startled by Socrates' confession of ignorance. Does Socrates really not know what human excellence is, he asks. And he adds, with a sweeping gesture—as we imagine—over the heads of the people who form his retinue and are witnessing the conversation on the spot: "shall we spread *that* news about you [which must be known here, in Athens] back home, *too?*"

No doubt, Socrates' professed ignorance and inability to provide a fearless and lofty answer to a question he himself raises—the question, "what is human excellence?"—are in stark contrast with what Meno, thanks to Gorgias' teaching, has been accustomed to practice himself and to expect others to do. Is that the reason why Meno is so startled or pretends to be so startled? He should not be surprised in view of Socrates' reputation with which he is not unfamiliar. Or is it, more directly, because Socrates reveals an astonishing lack of knowledge in a "simple" matter that concerns everybody, the matter of human excellence? Perhaps. Or may not Meno's surprise be ultimately based on the tacit inference that, since Socrates confesses to this lack of knowledge and blames himself for it (*emauton katamemphomai* – 71 6 2 f.) , he thereby confesses to not being virtuous? Such a confession would indeed be astonishing. We do not often hear people readily and seriously admit their own badness or viciousness.

But if this be Meno's inference, he must tacitly assume that human excellence, as it manifests itself in a person, depends altogether on that person's knowing what it is; he must, in other words, assume the validity of the famous Socratic dictum that human excellence is knowledge, that knowledge, therefore, brings about excellence. To be sure, he would not be the only one to do that. Do we not, often enough, hear parents, for example, ask their naughty child indignantly, if thoughtlessly: "Don't you know how to behave?" implying that the child's knowledge should prevent the child from being naughty? If Meno then drew that inference, and if there be truth in his tacit assumption that "human excellence is knowledge," Meno would be in possession of that truth, he would *know* what *aretê* is. Again, if it be true that human excellence is knowledge and if Meno were in possession of that knowledge, how could we reconcile Meno's knowing what *aretê* is with his reputed viciousness?

Upon Socrates allowing that not only his ignorance should be reported but also his opinion that he never met any one who knew what human e llence was, Meno asks whether Socrates did not meet Gorgias when the latter was in Athens. "I did," says Socrates. And Meno: "Well then, did he not seem to you to know?" [71 c 3–7]

Socrates' reply is as follows: "I have not the best of memories,[25] Meno, and therefore I can not tell you now how he struck me then. But perhaps indeed he, Gorgias, knows and you (*kai sy*) , as well (*te*) , [know] what he, Gorgias, said. Remind me then of what he said; or, if you please, say it your- [71 c 8 – d 3]

25. Cf. Thompson, p. 69 (19).

44   self; for your opinions, I suppose, are very much his." Meno: "Yes."

This almost literal translation omits the puns contained in the first sentence and does not do justice to the special paratactic character of the second.

The literal assertion in the phrase: *Ou pany eimi mnêmôn*, I have not the best of memories, is, no doubt, a part of Socrates' ironic "code,"[26] as Alcibiades, for one, in the *Protagoras*[27] well knows. But in the texture (and sound) of the fuller phrase: *ou pany eimi mnêmôn, ô Menôn*, there seems to be embedded more than one pun and more than one pertinent connotation.

In the first place, we cannot help remembering that, according to Cornelius Nepos,[28] to Plutarch,[29] and to others,[30] *Mnêmôn* was the nickname of King Artaxerxes II. The phrase could, therefore, be also understood as saying: "I am not quite Artaxerxes, Meno." The reports about the subsequent events in Asia that have reached us can be taken to mean either that Meno, by command of Artaxerxes, was tortured a whole year and then put to death,[31] or that, on the contrary, Meno succeeded, with the help of Ariaeus and Tissaphernes, in beguiling Artaxerxes and did not at all suffer the fate of the other leaders of the Greek mercenaries. Depending on the version we tend to accept, the pun intimates: "I, Socrates, am not going to torture and to kill you, Meno" or "You, Meno, will not succeed in eluding me."

Such ironic implications, anticipating Meno's future, are, of course, beyond Meno's reach, but are understandable to us, the listeners or readers. And we should not disregard the possible further implication that Socrates might yet prove to be a more redoubtable foe of Meno than the Great King himself.

In the second place, the words ". . . *mnêmôn, ô Menôn*" form a curious jingle. Playing with names is a common pastime and, throughout the Platonic dialogues, names, characters and roles are playfully attuned to each other in all kinds of modes. The name "Meno," by itself, could be associated with the stem of *menein* ("to stay as before," "to stay put"—generally not in a pejorative sense) and this association might be mean-

26. Although not quite in the same way as the terms σμικρόν τι, ἴσως, οὐδέν.
27. 336 d 2–4 (cf. 334 c 8 – d 5).
28. *De regibus* 1, 3–4.
29. *Life of Artaxerxes*, 1.
30. See Pauly-Wissowa, *Real-Enz., s.v.* Artaxerxes.
31. Xenophon, *Anabasis* II, 6, 29, reports this only from hearsay.

ingful in the context of the dialogue. But the core of that jingle seems to be the combination of the letters *m* and *n*, the Indo-European stem of so many words related to our power of remembering and recollecting as in the words: *mnêmê, memini, mens,* mind.[32] We note that in the name "Meno" the sequence of those two letters is somewhat deranged.

As to the content and syntax of the second sentence,[33] what seems to be common to the two subjects, "he" and "you," is *not* common to both, and it is the particle *te* which carries this ambiguity: Gorgias might well *know what aretê is,* while Meno might merely *know what Gorgias said it is.* The difference seems crucial.

To "know" what somebody said about something, that is, to *remember* what was said, can, at best, produce an opinion about that something in the one who remembers. The parataxis of the second sentence opposes the possible *knowing* of Gorgias to the possible *opining* of Meno and, at the same time, tends to veil the difference between them. In the last sentence of Socrates' reply the difference seems to disappear completely, inasmuch as the sentence suggests the similarity of *opinions* held by both Gorgias and Meno. In Socrates' reply as a whole the problems that "knowing," "opining," and "remembering" pose as well as the problems of their mutual relationships are, at any rate, conspicuously present.

The question arises whether Socrates' suggestion, accepted by Meno himself, that Meno's opinions are very much those of Gorgias, provides us for the first time, or does not provide us at all, with an important insight into Meno's character. For most opinions of most of us—and not only those of Meno—are derived from, and identical with, opinions of "somebody else." The accumulation of such opinions is what is generally called "education."

Since Gorgias, in any case, is not present, says Socrates, it [71 d 4–8] is up to Meno himself to tell what human excellence is and to refute Socrates' assertion that he never met any one who knew what it was. And what a happy refutation that would

---

32. Cf. *Cratyl.* 437 b 2–4 combines μνήμη with μονή. (Cf. also the pun in Aeschylus, *Agamemnon* 154–55).

33. Cf. Ed. Schwyzer-A. Debrunner, *Griechische Grammatik* II, 1949, 631 ff.; 573 f. (in *Handbuch der Altertumswissenschaft,* 2. Abt., 1. Teil, 2. Bd.); H. W. Smyth, *A Greek Grammar for Colleges,* 1920, §§ 2168, 2974; J. D. Denniston. *The Greek Particles,* 2nd ed., pp. 511 ff.

be! For "if you turn out to be a knower, and [therefore also] Gorgias," it would appear that he, Socrates, had actually met at least two people, Gorgias and Meno, who knew! In the protasis of the hypothetical sentence he uses, Socrates shifts back from "opinions" to "knowledge" for both Meno and Gorgias.

4.

[71 e 1 – 72 a 5]   Meno proceeds to tell in what human excellence consists. He insists—four times (*ou chalepon, rhaidion, ou chalepon, ouk aporia eipein*) —that this telling does not present any difficulty. The sort of thing human excellence is depends, according to his statement, on the circumstances of the person in whom it is exhibited, that is on his sex, his age, his status in the human community, on the kind of action he is engaged in, on the goal he pursues, and so on. And Meno does not forget to add that lack of excellence manifests itself in equally diversified ways. He describes excellence more concretely in only two cases, that of the adult man in his activities as a citizen and that of the married woman in her position as head of the household. The other cases are apparently obvious enough not to need any further description. The descriptions given, however, throw some light on how Meno might understand "lack of excellence" (*kakia*), the opposite of *aretê*. A man who possesses *aretê*, a "good man" or an "excellent man," is a man, says Meno, who is skillful enough (*hikanos*) to manage public affairs in such a way as to benefit his friends and harm his enemies and to be careful not to suffer harm himself. (Meno omits to add: "but rather to benefit himself.") *Kakia*,[34] then, would characterize a man who lacks that skill; this lack would make him "incompetent," "defective," "bad." Similarly, "lack of excellence" in a woman would render her "inefficient" in her household duties and "defective" in her submission to her husband, make her a "poor" or "bad" woman. Let us reflect: this understanding is not peculiar to Meno. The meaning of "badness" (*kakia*), in common parlance, stretches indeed from "insufficiency" to "viciousness." And the ambiguity of that meaning was, no doubt, also pres-

---

34. Or μοχθηρία (cf., for example, *Phaedo* 93 b 8 – c 2), or πονηρία (cf., for example, *Theaet.* 176 b 4–5 and *Soph.* 228 b 8–9); cf. also *Apol.* 39 a – b. Πανουργία has a somewhat different status (cf. below p. 89 and p. 188, note 60).

ent in Meno's real or feigned surprise at Socrates' profession of ignorance in the matter of human excellence.

Meno's statement is meant to represent, if we remember what was said before, not only Meno's but also Gorgias' view.[35] It does not show much of Gorgias' eloquence[36] except for the studied facility with which it is uttered. The subject does not seem to require any special rhetorical effort. The view expressed here agrees with commonly accepted, if not always clearly stated, standards, and the terms in which it is expressed agree, in their ambiguity, with those used in common speech. What is said by Meno, and meant by Gorgias, "stands to reason."

5.

Socrates is not satisfied with Meno's statement because it [72 a 6 – c 5] does not answer the question he, Socrates, has raised. Socrates' question "what is *aretê?*" whatever else may be said about it, tends, in its "simplicity," to cut across all the unavoidable ambiguities of what is commonly accepted both in speech and in fact.[37] That makes the question itself rather dark for our common understanding and requires, for the sake of elucidation, a special rhetorical effort on Socrates' part.

It seems, says Socrates, that a huge piece of good luck has struck him, since, searching for *one aretê*, he has found a swarm of virtues. Where? In Meno's keeping. (Meno surrounded by Virtues!) The image of a "swarm" leads Socrates on. He proposes to clarify his question by repeating it with regard to bees: what precisely do we mean by "bee"? What is "bee"? Now, the way this auxiliary question is put to Meno is characterized by two rhetorical devices which seem to serve the same purpose. (1) Socrates, in phrasing the question *melittês peri ousias ho ti pot' esti,* introduces a word that has an unusual, a non-colloquial meaning; (2) he embodies within the question, in three hypothetical clauses, an imaginary exchange between him and Meno, patterned on the preceding exchange, and he continues in this hypothetical mode even after Meno has spoken his part.

1. *"Ousia,"* "beingness" or simply "being," has the flavor of a "technical" term, that is, of a term coined to signify aspects

---

35. Cf. Aristotle, *Polit.* I, 13, 1260 a 27 ff.
36. Cf. *Symp.* 198 c and 197 c – e.
37. Cf. Leo Strauss, *What is Political Philosophy?* 1959, p. 90.

of things which are usually not touched upon in common speech and which come into sight only after searching reflection and repeated investigation. The beingness of a bee is not the subject matter of ordinary discourse, where *ousia* has a simple and easily communicable meaning (with which the "technical" meaning is ultimately connected); searching reflection and repeated investigation, on the other hand, are the bases of any *techne,* any "discipline," any "science."

2. The device—not unusual with Socrates—of condensing an exchange into a series of hypothetical clauses deprives the conversation of its directness and removes it to a "methodical" (or "topical") level, again characteristic of a *techne,* and does this, it should be noted, independently of the cogency of the argument itself.

Bees, the argument runs, may differ from each other in color, size and other respects, but they do not differ in their being bees (*tôi melittas einai*). What, then, is that in virtue of which they are all the same (*hôi . . . taúton eisin hapasai*), namely "bee"? The direct and taunting question is put to Meno: "You could, couldn't you, give me an answer to that?" And Meno's reply is: "I could."

He could perhaps. But some doubt is permitted on this point. To tell what is common to all bees and, by the same token, what differentiates all bees from anything else, that is, to "define" what "bee" is, is not an easy task. Quite apart from the difficulty that "queens" and "drones" pose in this case,[38] such "defining" presupposes the agreed acceptance of a much larger frame within which the defining takes place—as all known classifications of living beings show—and ultimately perhaps agreement on the structure of the entire universe.[39] Does Socrates want us to understand the immensity of the problem by picking bees as an example?[40] The difficulty of defining is hardly lessened in the case of "human excellence." Meno, apparently misled by Socrates' taunting question about so "trivial" an example, is probably guilty of too great a rashness in letting Socrates have his way. *We* should be on our

---

38. Cf. *Rep.* VIII, 552 c, 554 b, d, 556 a, 559 c, d, 564 b, e, 565 c, 567 d (also IX, 573 a) and Aristotle, *Hist. animal.* V, 22, 553 b 7 ff.; IX, 40, 624 b 20 ff. (L. Robin, *Platon, Œuvres complètes* [Pléiade] I, 1289–90, note 6, suggests—in view of 72 b 5–6—that Plato may have had in mind *all* hymenoptera, which seems unlikely).

39. Echoes of activities in the Academy dealing with the problem of defining living beings, animals, and plants, reach us through Epicrates (Athenaeus II, 59 d–f) and the famous anecdote of Diogenes' mocking those activities (Diog. Laert. VI, 40). We can find, of course, some evidence of them in the *Sophist* and the *Statesman.*

40. Cf. *Phaedo* 82 b 6 and the irony of the context.

guard. And we should not overlook at least one considerable
difference between "bee" and "excellence": the latter has its
counterpart in "insufficiency" or "badness," but with the possible exception of a drone there is no counterpart to a bee.

Having thus disposed of the auxiliary question, as if it were [72 c 6 – d 3]
settled or could easily be settled, Socrates immediately draws
the consequence with regard to *aretê*. Even if there are many
different *aretai,* says Socrates, they all have a certain aspect,
one and the same, mind you, in virtue of which they are
what they are, namely *aretai* (*hen ge ti eidos taúton hapasai
echousi, di' ho eisin aretai*). To answer the question, "what
is human excellence?" and to make manifest what it is, one
should, I suppose, says Socrates, keep one's eye on what looks
like that "one and the same" in all the variety.

Socrates uses the word *eidos* to designate that "one and the
same." This word *eidos* reminds us, no less than it may have
reminded Plato's contemporaries, of that "much babbled-
about"[41] doctrine, the "doctrine of ideas," linked with Socrates' and Plato's names. We might do well, however, to reflect on the choice of that word—not only here, in the *Meno,*
but also in other Platonic dialogues—from a certain distance.

Words used in common speech do not always preserve their
commonly accepted meaning. This commonly accepted meaning itself ranges, more often than not, over a series of connected shadings and connotations. In the perspective of a
detached inquiry the meaning of a word usually loses its "natural" ambiguity, becomes more fixed, gains a definite significance determined by the scope of the attempted and sustained
investigation, which investigation may lead to the establish-
ment of a "science," a *technê.* The inquirer would then, of
necessity, turn into an "expert" who ought to be able to pass
his knowledge on to others, who ought to be able, in other
words, to become a "teacher." It is thus that words do indeed
become "technical" and transcend the habitual and familiar.
And yet, the "technical" use of words tends, in turn, to become accepted, to win a familiarity of its own and to merge,
somewhat hazily, with the colloquial use of those same words.[42]
This process goes on today as it went on in Plato's day. It
seems that Plato never loses sight of it: there is a constant
tendency on his part (with or without the help of sometimes

---

41. *Phaedo* 100 b 1–5: ἐκεῖνα τὰ πολυθρύλητα (cf. 76 d 7–9 and also
 Tim. 51 b 8 f.).
42. Cf., for instance, the use of εἶδος in *Rep.* III, 402 c – d, V, 476 a 5,
 477 c 4, X, 597 b 14 or in *Theaet.* 157 b/c.

legitimate and sometimes playfully fanciful etymologies) to compare the "technical" mode of speaking with the more colloquial one, to mirror one in the other, and, on weighty occasions, to derive from their interplay meanings not conveyed by either. This happens, for example, in the case of *eidos*.

In the present context, the word *eidos,* just as the word *ousia* which Socrates used a short while ago, has a definite "technical" character. We are aware of the fact, as Meno might well be, that the term is widely used with regard to information or knowledge gained in detached inquiries of all sorts, whatever its precise meaning in any given case may be.[43]

43. The technical use of the word "εἶδος" (and "ἰδέα") is apparent in the exposition of rhetorical, medical, and mathematical τέχναι as well as in Democritus. The colloquial use of the word shades into a technical one in Herodotus and Thucydides, less so in the former, more so in the latter. See all the evidence collected by A. E. Taylor in "The Words εἶδος, ἰδέα in Pre-Platonic Literature," *Varia Socratica* (1911) and—so far as the literature attributed to Hippocrates is concerned—put into proper perspective by C. M. Gillespie, "The Use of εἶδος and ἰδέα in Hippocrates," *The Classical Quarterly,* VI (1912), 179–203. The technical use of the word "εἶδος" in mathematics continues, hardly touched by the Platonic-Aristotelian tradition, later on, for example, in Euclid, *Elements* VI, 19, Porism; 25; *Data,* Def. 3, etc., in Apollonius I, 12–14; 21 (cf. Def. 11), in Nicomachus, in Diophantus, *Arithmetica,* ed. Tannery, p. 14, 25–27 and *passim.*
　　With reference to the colloquial use of the word, it is curious to observe Taylor's emphatic rejection (*op. cit.,* p. 183) of "the supposition that the εἶδος, ἰδέα of the Platonic philosophy have been derived from the use in which these words are mere verbals of ἰδεῖν." In support of this rejection Taylor quotes (pp. 182 f.) Aristotle's explanation of *Iliad* X, 316 (*Poetics* 1461 a 12–14) and Plato's *Protagoras* (352 a), where, in the main, facial "looks" are opposed to the "looks" of the entire body. In quoting these passages Taylor seems to imply that only a face can be called "ugly to look at." As if only Socrates' face and not precisely his whole "silenic" body was meant to be described as "ugly *looking*" in Alcibiades' panegyric (*Symp.* 215 b 4 f.) and in Meno's gibe (*Meno* 80 a 5)! (Cf. *Charm.* 154 d 4–5; 158 a 7 – b 1; also Gillespie, *op. cit.,* p. 181.) What somebody or something altogether "looks" like, that is what εἶδος and ἰδέα colloquially—and primarily —mean. Taylor himself says (p. 187) with reference to the meaning of ἰδέα in Thucydides II, 51: "This meaning [of symptoms of the disease regarded collectively] would come naturally from the literal one of 'look', 'appearance'." And it is this literal or rather familiar meaning from which Plato derives—by way of contrast, paradox, and pun—his understanding of the εἶδος as ἀειδές (cf. *Phaedo* 80 d, 79 a; *Gorg.* 493 b; also below p. 137, note 93.)
　　In *A Commentary to Plato's Timaeus,* 1928, p. 330, Taylor translates "ἕν γέ τι εἶδος ταὐτὸν . . . ἔχουσι. . . ." with "have a *something* in common." This, again, is not quite sufficient.
　　(Cf. also K. von Fritz, *Philosophie and sprachlicher Ausdruck bei Demokrit, Plato und Aristoteles,* 1938; P. Friedländer, *Plato* I, pp. 16 ff.)

The term is a "learned" one. It appears that Socrates is trying
at this point, above all, to make Meno adopt an inquiring attitude, to induce in him the mood of learning.[44] "You do
understand (*manthaneis*), or don't you, what I am saying?"
he asks. But Meno replies: "It seems to me that I understand;
however, I do not as yet grasp what is being asked as I wish
I should." A judicious answer! Still, it appears that Meno's effort to understand does not match Socrates' effort to be understood.

Socrates perseveres. He brings up a whole set of examples [72 d 4 – 73 a 5]
to make Meno understand. What about "health," "tallness,"
(bodily) "strength"? Does it seem that man's health and
woman's health, as far as health goes, differ? Whenever and
wherever there is "health," whoever the healthy one might
be, we face the same *eidos*—"health." Meno agrees. And does
not that hold for tallness and strength, too? If a woman be
strong, her strength will not differ "in kind" from the strength
of a man: "the woman will be strong with regard to the same
aspect (*tôi autôi eidei*), that is, with the same strength (*kai
têi autêi ischyï*)." Lest that assertion be misunderstood, Socrates adds with "technical" precision: by the words "with the
same [strength]" (*to têi autêi*) I mean: with regard to "being
strength" (*pros to ischys einai*), strength in man and strength
in woman are not at all different. Meno agrees.

These examples are somewhat closer to the phenomenon of
excellence than the example of the bee, inasmuch as all three,
health, tallness, strength, can be present in human beings to a
greater or lesser degree and reach down to their opposites,
sickness, shortness, weakness.

Turning back to *aretê*, Socrates wants Meno to apply to it
what has been gained by the consideration of the examples
just given. Will excellence be different in any way with regard to "being excellence," whether it be found in a child or
in an old man, in a woman or in a man, he asks. Meno's
reply is: "It seems to me somehow, Socrates, that this case is
no longer similar to those others."

We see that Socrates' methodical effort has been in vain.
Meno is unable to draw the inference suggested by the exam-

44. Something similar happens in the *Euthyphro*, where Euthyphro, the
"expert" in things divine, is asked by Socrates about the εἶδος, the
ἰδέα, the οὐσία of the ὅσιον (6 d – e, 11 a). Yet the dialogue as a
whole strongly suggests that the ὅσιον has no εἶδος, since it is—at
best—a μόριον τοῦ δικαίου (12 d).

ples presented to him. But, on the other hand, we should ask ourselves: is this inability altogether blindness? Is there not some justification for Meno's reluctance to follow Socrates at this point? Does not human excellence belong to an order different from that of strength and tallness and health? And if Meno is not very quick in crossing the eidetic bridge built for him by Socrates, at least he does not run the danger of joining the ranks of those "friends of ideas"[45] who, in their eagerness to embrace the doctrine, might miss its most decisive points.

6.

[73 a 6 – c 5] Socrates has to abandon his "methodical" line of attack. He goes back to Meno's own words, that is, to the level of the habitual and the familiar, the level of accepted standards and views. Let's see (*ti de?*), says Socrates, did you not say that man's excellence consists in managing the affairs of the city in the right way (*eu*) and woman's excellence in managing the household in the same way? (Meno had used the word *eu* only with regard to women.) And can the right way be achieved in either case without acting prudently and justly? There is no objection on Meno's part. The managing in either case, then, Socrates continues, must be done with justice and prudence. Necessarily so, says Meno. Both, then, woman and man, need justice and prudence, if they want to be *good* human beings, that is, human beings possessing *aretê*. So it appears, says Meno. Let's see (*ti de?*), Socrates continues, does not the same hold for child and old man, if they are to be called "good"? Meno agrees again. And after this quick run-down the quick conclusion follows: "All human beings are good in the same way" (*tôi autôi tropôi*). (For they become good by obtaining the same things—*tôn autôn . . . tychontes*—Socrates adds somewhat vaguely.) And they could not be good "in the same way" (*tôi autôi tropôi*) if theirs were not "the same *aretê*." No, indeed, says Meno.

Let us consider. What follows with some cogency from the premises in the preceding argument is that human beings are good if they are prudent and just, if they possess prudence and justice. But then they are good precisely not because they share in "the same *aretê*," but rather because they share in *two aretai*. It is in *that* sense of sharing in two virtues (at

45. *Soph.* 248 a 4.

least) that they are good "in the same way." (No wonder that Socrates was vague about their "obtaining the same things.") The phrase "in the same way" (*tôi autôi tropôi*), that Socrates uses twice, thus contrasts strikingly with the previous "technical" phrase "with regard to the same aspect" (*tôi autôi eidei*), which implied the strict oneness and sameness of the *eidos "aretê"* (72 c 7; d 8) and which was used only once.

While in the previous argument Meno was not willing to draw an at least plausible inference suggested by Socrates, he is now unable to see the contradiction in Socrates' conclusion. Is it because, in spite of his (and Gorgias') ability to enumerate different kinds of excellence that have little in common between them, he does not see any incompatibility in regarding excellence as being one and many (in this case: one and two) at the same time? Here again he may be right. Or is it simply because the reasoning Socrates has just presented has a familiar ring which does not tax Meno's thinking?

At any rate, what the intricate "technical" argument could not accomplish, the appeal to the habitually acceptable did. Meno seems to see Socrates' point now: he surmises that Socrates is seeking something which is one (*hen ti*) for all cases (*kata pantôn*), as he, Meno, himself will imply in a moment (73 d 1). The way is cleared for Socrates to put his original question before Meno again.

II

1.

[73 c 6 – e 2] Socrates takes up that question where it was left a while ago (71 d) and, under the assumption that one and the same excellence is present in all cases, challenges Meno: "Make an attempt (*peirô*) to tell, to recollect,[1] what Georgias says it is and you, too, following him (*kai sy met' ekeinou*) ."

There are three points of emphasis in this challenge: first, the renewed stress on Meno's merely *repeating* Gorgias' words; secondly, the necessity, therefore, to *recall* Gorgias' utterances on the subject; thirdly, a certain *effort* required from Meno to satisfy Socrates' curiosity.

Meno accepts Socrates' challenge. We witness his *first attempt* to give an adequate answer to the question understood by him now, it seems, in its "generality." This answer is:

"What else [is what I and Gorgias are saying that human excellence is] but the ability to rule over men?"

Immediately, Socrates raises objections. Before considering them, however, let us ponder Meno's statement.

To be able to rule, to "exert authority," to "lead"—is not such power recognized, at all times, as a sign, at least, of excellence, provided, of course, that power be genuine, that is not one derived from somebody else "behind the scenes"? Does not this criterion of excellence play a decisive role even in Plato's *Republic*? There, certainly, this very power of ruling (*dynamis politikê*) stems from a pursuit of a rather different nature (*philosophia*)[2] which nurtures, in men engaged in it, the desire *not* to rule.[3] But the true *ability* to rule is still what characterizes the "best." Meno's statement, as it stands, does not preclude this "Socratic" interpretation regardless of whether Meno would accept it or not. And we can also understand that Meno is not thinking of children, women, or very old men, let alone slaves, in making the statement. Its generality is a reasonably restricted one.

1. Cf. Stock's note to 73 c 7 (p. 9 of the Notes).
2. *Rep.* V, 473 d 3.
3. *Rep.* VII, 520 d 2 – e 4.

This last point is the first target of Socrates' objections. If
Meno's statement were true, then excellent children as well as
excellent slaves would be able to rule, to rule over their
parents or masters, and would a slave, however excellent, who
rules, still be slave? "I do not think so at all" (*ou pany moi
dokei . . .*),[4] says Meno. And Socrates reinforces that utterance by saying: "Indeed, it is not likely [that you do], my
excellent man" (*ou gar eikos, ô ariste*). (We should note this
somewhat ambiguous emphasis on Socrates' part, the significance of which is not yet quite apparent.) He then immediately turns to another, more serious criticism. "You say
'ability to rule'; shall we not add, right there, the words
'justly, not unjustly'?" Meno: "I do think so, indeed." What
else can one reply? Is not a just man universally praised? Is
not Justice praiseworthy under any circumstances? "For justice, Socrates, is excellence." Socrates: "Excellence, Meno, or
some excellence?" Meno: "What do you mean by that?"

We see now clearly that Meno has *not* grasped, although he
had seemed to, the difference between the various *aretai* and
aretê in its sameness and oneness that Socrates is asking about.
It is also clear that Socrates is going back on his own words
which, in the preceding argument, had blurred that distinction.

Socrates proceeds to clarify that distinction anew by [73 e 3 – 74 b 3]
choosing a new example, this time one which lends itself to a
colloquial as well as to various "technical" interpretations.
The example is *schêma*, "figure," used first of all in the colloquial sense of "closed surface of a visible thing," commonly
identified with the "shape" of that thing. Visible things are
shaped in innumerably different ways. Facing a more or less
"roundly" curved object, we may call its shape, its surface, its
schêma, – "roundishness" (*strongylotês* – 73 e 3 f., 74 b 5–7).
Asked what "roundishness" is, Socrates goes on, he would say:
a certain kind of shaped surface (*schêma ti*), not just shaped
surface (*ouch houtôs haplôs*[5] *hoti schêma*), for the good reason that there are other surfaces or shapes of things.

Meno is quick to take that up. You would be right in saying that, he hastens to remark, just as *I too* (*kai egô*) am
rightly saying that there is not only justice but that there
are other kinds of excellence, too. And Socrates, insisting:
"What are they, tell me! Just as *I too* (*kai egô*) could name

4. Cf. Thompson, p. 69 (19).
5. Cf. Thompson, p. 84 (21).

for you other surfaces as well, if you bid me do that, *you too*
(*kai sy*) do name for me other excellences."

There is some bantering in this exchange, centering about
the words *kai egô* and *kai sy*. (We are reminded of Socrates'
identifying himself ironically with his fellow citizens at the
beginning of the dialogue (71 b 1) and of the phrase *kai sy*
which Socrates has already used twice in speaking to Meno,
in the ambiguously paratactical sentence, 71 c 10, and in his
recent challenge, 73 c 7 f.)

Meno obliges: "Well then, I think courage is excellence
and [so is] soundness of mind and wisdom and loftiness and
a great many other excellences."

That is what Socrates, clearly, expected to hear. Who would
not, in answer to Socrates' challenge, give the same or a
similar list of acknowledged virtues? And Socrates can point
out that he and Meno, while looking for *one* excellence, have
once more discovered many, though not in the same way as
before. But the one which runs through them all, he says, they
are unable to find.

Meno admits readily that, while with regard to all the examples given by Socrates he could meet the latter's demand,
he is still unable to get hold of the one excellence that applies
to all cases of excellence in the way Socrates is looking for it.
Socrates, on his part, says (rather darkly): "No wonder"
(*eikotôs ge*). And he pledges to do all he can to bring Meno
and himself closer to the matter. In the meantime, however,
we observe that Meno's first attempt to come to grips with
human excellence in its "generality" has failed.

2.

[74 b 3 – e 10]   Socrates begins by pointing to the universality of the underlying problem. It is no less a problem than that of "defining"
which was already encountered in the case of the "bee,"[6]
and it is *this* problem that is going to be discussed now at
great length.

"You do understand (*manthaneis*), I suppose, that it is
the same way with everything," says Socrates. He goes back
to the example of "shaped surfaces." Again, he brings up an
hypothetical preliminary exchange between Meno and, this
time, somebody else, who may ask the question, "what is
'shaped surface'?" In so doing Socrates again gives "methodi-

6. P. 48.

cal" precision to the exchange he himself just had with Meno on the subject. The answer, " 'shaped surface' is roundishness," would provoke a further question, which would test that definition by turning it around (by "conversion"[7]) : "is 'roundishness' 'shaped surface' or *a* shaped surface?" and Meno's answer to that would certainly be: *a* shaped surface. Meno agrees. And Meno would give that answer, would he not, because there are other shapes or surfaces as well. Meno agrees. "And if the interrogator asked you, further on, which ones those were, you would tell him." Meno: "I would."

The pattern of this exchange is repeated in another condensed and partly indirect account, where color (*chrôma*) is substituted for *schêma*. The hypothetical sequence of questions and answers runs as follows: "What is color?" "White." "Is 'white' color or *a* color?" "A color." The last answer would be given because there are other colors as well. Meno agrees. And if the interrogator urged Meno to name other colors, Meno would name others, each of which is no less color than "white" is. Meno agrees.

Both accounts then merge into one, which takes the form of direct speech. The subject "color" is dropped, only the example "shaped surface" is under consideration. Socrates first refers to what he had said before (74 a 7–10), with regard to human excellence, about always ending up with many things instead of with the one they were looking for, but now he refuses to stop in resignation. Since *all* the many and differently shaped surfaces are called by *one name* (*heni tini . . . onomati*) the question *has* to be answered: What is that which is called by that one name, "*schêma*"? This question is put to Meno directly. Socrates is painstakingly precise[8] in seeking, and finding, Meno's agreement about various aspects of the problem at hand. That which is called "*schêma*" comprises (*katechei*) even surfaces "opposed" to each other (*enantia onta allêlois*), as roundly curved ones and straight ones are. (At this point, 74 d 8 – e 9, Socrates abandons the rather unusual term *hê strongylotês* in favor of the more common one *to strongylon*, "the [more or less] roundly curved," as opposed to *to euthy*, "the straight," without altering the meaning of what he is talking about.[9]) A curved sur-

---

7. ἀντιστροφή – Aristotle, *Prior Anal.* I, 3, 25 a 40; 45, 50 b 32.
8. Cf. *Phaedo* 102 d 3: συγγραφικῶς.
9. Cf. *Tim.* 73 d 4 and the context. (A. E. Taylor, *A Commentary on Plato's Timaeus*, p. 522, quotes the phrase στρογγύλα καὶ προμήκη διῃρεῖτο σχήματα but, quite meaningfully, substitutes for "σχήματα" – "εἴδη".)

face is no more (and no less) "shaped surface" than a straight surface, while it is not true that a curved one is no more curved than a straight one or a straight one no more straight than a curved one. (We should note that the opposition between "straight" and "curved" is not quite the same as that between *aretê* and *kakia,* or strength and weakness, but perhaps comparable to that between "bee" and "drone".)

[74 e 11 – 75 b 1]   Socrates grows more insistent in soliciting Meno's answer. The direct injunction, "make an attempt" (*peirô*) to give that answer, is used again (cf. 73 c 6). Socrates then refers back to the hypothetical questioner (mentioning "color" again) and, anticipating Meno's possible answer, "I just do not understand what you want, fellow, just do not know what you are saying," envisages the questioner's possible surprise and possible retort: "You do not understand that I am seeking what can be called 'the same about[10] all those surfaces' (*to epi pasi toutois taúton*)?" The new, and seemingly vague, phrasing of the question is supposed to help Meno, we must assume, in the effort he is being asked to make. "Or could you not, even on this understanding,[11] answer the question, if somebody were to ask you: what is the same about the roundly curved (surface) and the straight (surface) and about all the others, which you certainly call 'surfaces', [what is] the same about all of them?" (There is heavy emphasis on the word *epi,* which is repeated altogether four times.) The injunction follows again: "Make an attempt" (*peirô*) to answer, and Socrates adds: "so that [in making it] you may also go through an exercise for your answer regarding human excellence."

Meno's reaction to all this elaborate and insistent urging is indeed surprising. He bluntly, and rudely, refuses to go through the proposed exercise. "No! You, Socrates, give the answer," is his reply. This refusal is the more surprising since Meno *did* make an attempt to "define" what excellence was. Now he wants to be *told* what *schêma* is.

[75 b 2 – c 1]   There is a tinge of rebuke in Socrates' response, and a hint at Meno's being accustomed to, and spoiled by, the indulgences of his lovers, because he is still young and beautiful, as will be stated explicitly a little later on (76 b–c). "Do you want me to do you the favor?" he asks and, upon Meno's affirmative, and self-confident, answer, continues: "And you,

---

10. This translation of ἐπί will find its justification later.
11. Cf. Thompson, pp. 88 f. (7).

on your part, will you then be willing to tell me about ex- **59**
cellence?" Meno again utters assent. "Well then," concludes
Socrates, "the effort has to be made, for it will be worth
while." Meno approves.

Socrates' effort is introduced by him as follows: "So let us
make an attempt (*peirômetha*) to tell you what 'shaped surface' is. And consider whether you agree that it is what I am
going to say it is." This is what Socrates then says:

"Let us take 'shaped surface' clearly to be the only thing,
among all existing things, which always accompanies color."

And Socrates adds: "Does that suffice you? Or do you want
to look for it in some other way? I certainly should be well
content if you described excellence to me merely the way [I
just described 'shaped surface']."

Whatever Meno's response, we have to consider Socrates'
statement most attentively.

1. Its meaning is clear: wherever and whenever we see
color, either some patch or patches of it, or widely spread,
whether uniformly or in distinctly diversified patterns or in
ever changing nuances, we actually see *colored surfaces;* and,
conversely, we become aware of surfaces of whatever shape
only by seeing color. The phenomenon of "color" and the
phenomenon of "surface" are *co-extensive,* and we mean both,
when, in ordinary discourse, we speak of surfaces of things.
Socrates' statement describes in words something we all can
see, and does it with precision.

2. Socrates' query whether the way he "defines" *schêma*
suffices Meno leaves the possibility open that there might be
another way or other ways of "defining" it (*hikanôs—allôs
pôs—houtôs*). The "definition" offered by Socrates is, at all
events, commensurate in its precision only with the colloquial
meaning of *schêma.* It can stand, with regard to its universality, the test of "conversion," for it is also true that *chrôma* always accompanies *schêma.* But *schêma* and *chrôma* are not
"identified" in Socrates' statement.[12] Its universality consists
in the fact that *schêma* and *chrôma* are under all circumstances
mutually complementary: one cannot be without the other.
And it should perhaps be noted that our familiarity with both
of them does not seem quite evenly balanced: are we not more
familiar with "colors" than with "surfaces"? Moreover,

12. That was done according to Aristotle, *De sensu* 3, 439 a 30 f., by
the "Pythagoreans": τὸ γὰρ χρῶμα ἢ ἐν τῷ πέρατί ἐστιν ἢ πέρας
διὸ καὶ οἱ Πυθαγόρειοι τὴν ἐπιφάνειαν χροιὰν ἐκάλουν. Cf. *Phys.* IV.
3, 210 b 1–8.

chrôma has only *schêma* as a necessary "companion," while *schêma* seems to need "body" as another necessary complement.

3. Why did Socrates choose the examples of "color" and "surface," which then conjointly provide an example of a suitable "definition" to be used for the purpose of defining human excellence? Can we avoid being reminded again[13] of the "Socratic" dictum about excellence and knowledge? Is not Socrates hinting at the relation between those two when he declares that he would be well content to receive the same kind of information regarding "human excellence" that he gave regarding "shaped surface"? He would be satisfied, it seems, to hear from Meno that knowledge always *accompanies* excellence. And the exercise Meno is urged to make with regard to *schêma* would actually provide him with the *pattern* of the answer concerning *aretê*. The analogy might even cover the degree to which the two "complements" are familiar to us: are we not, on balance, slightly more familiar with "excellence" than with "knowledge" or think, at least, that we are? And has not knowledge perhaps other necessary "complements"?

4. We understand retrospectively that the exchange which preceded Socrates' statement (beginning with 74 b 3) led to it, and could conceivably have led Meno to a similar statement, in a carefully calculated way. We understand now (a) why "color" was introduced as a second, as it were, complementary, example immediately after the example of "surface." We also understand (b) the emphasis on the preposition *epi* used finally to formulate the relation between all the *various* surfaces and the *sameness* they all exhibit: this preposition hints at something conjoined or attached to, or linked with, or even directly seated on, all those surfaces; this cannot be said of either *dia* or *kata* used previously by Socrates and Meno respectively (74 a 9; 73 d 1, 74 b 1).[14]

[75 c 2–8] What is Meno's response? He says, with reference to Socrates' statement and accompanying questions: "But that is really naïve, Socrates!" And he explains what he means as follows: " 'Shaped surface,' you say, don't you, is what always accompanies color (*chroa*). All right. But now if somebody were to

13. Cf. p. 43.
14. Cf. Ed. Schwyzer-A. Debrunner, *op. cit.*, II, 465–68, and Ast, *Lexic. Platon.* I, 766–68. See also *Parm.* 131 b 9, 132 c 3; *Phaedo* 116 e 2; *Soph.* 240 a 5 and Aristotle, *De anima* II, 6, 418 a 29.

say that he did not know this thing, *chroa,* and that he was as perplexed about it as about *schêma,* what would you think about the answer you just gave?" Socrates: "That it was true, I should think."

We have to consider attentively what is involved in Meno's objection.

1. Echoing Socrates, Meno appeals to a hypothetical interlocutor. While the hypothetical questioner introduced by Socrates seems to be just another Socrates, it is not clear whether Meno's imaginary personage is just another Meno.

2. In what sense can anyone not "know" color? We are all familiar with colors and color, except those of us who are blind or color-blind. But it does not seem that Meno has that exception in mind. So far as he is concerned, he has already indicated[15] that he is acquainted with colors and he will have another opportunity, in the discussion which follows, to show that color cannot be "unknown" to him. Could the hypothetical personage Meno appeals to be totally unacquainted with colors? That does not seem likely either.

One might argue that Meno, in objecting to Socrates' definition, does not at all deny that virtually every one is familiar with colors and color; what he seems to demand now is rather a "general" statement concerning color, in the very sense in which Socrates demanded to be informed about what universally corresponds to the one name *schêma.*[16] But then Meno's demand would mean that he had failed to observe the peculiar kind of universality and convertibility in Socrates' definition of *schêma,* according to which *schêma* and *chrôma* are mutually complementary. Had he not missed that, could he have phrased his objection the way he did? Would he not rather have attacked the mode and pattern of Socrates' "definition" by declaring it to be insufficient? Socrates had given him the opportunity to do precisely that.[17] It is unlikely, therefore, that Meno is disturbed by the kind of generality or universality Socrates makes use of in his definition. Indeed, in all that was said by Meno up to this point he hardly showed himself familiar with the very character of a universal statement. Does he really understand what he is asking now?

3. In stating his objection Meno substitutes the word *chroa* for the word *chrôma.* Whatever Meno's reasons for making

15. P. 57.
16. Pp. 55 ff.
17. P. 59.

this substitution,[18] his use of the word *chroa* seems, ironically enough, to support Socrates' "definition" of *schêma* rather than his own objection to it. For *chroa* is directly related to *chrôs* and can mean, like *chroia*, both "skin" and "color of the skin."[19]

4. We might conjecture that Meno, in raising his objection, is relying on his remembrance of a well-known *technê* which prides itself on never using "unknown" terms, a *technê*, that is, which begins with something agreed upon as true (*alêthes ti homologoumenon*) and reaches, through agreed consequences, an indubitable result.[20] It seems, in other words, that Meno remembers at this point the procedure of "synthetic" mathematics (Geometry), of which the *Elements* of Euclid are a late example, and which serves—not only for Aristotle—as the model for any apodeictic discipline. (May he not have been trained in this kind of mathematics in Gorgias' school?) This conjecture is borne out by the fact that Socrates, in his reaction to Meno's objection, refers almost immediately to that geometrical *technê* and meets, in so doing, with Meno's understanding. It would follow that Meno's objection entails a special "technical" re-interpretation of the meaning of *schêma*.

5. Whatever weight we might attach to Meno's dissatisfaction with Socrates' statement, it is hard not to suspect Meno of deliberately delaying his playing the part he had agreed to play. Such behavior may well be called disputatious and one could accuse Meno of merely competing for some verbal victory without caring in the slightest about the matter under investigation. And could not Gorgias' schooling be held responsible for this attitude?[21]

18. See pp. 60 f.
19. Cf. p. 59, note 12.
20. Cf. Scholion to Euclid, *Elements* XIII, Prop. 1–5 (Heiberg-Menge IV, 364 f.) and Pappus VII (Hultsch II, 634, 11 ff.). See also T. L. Heath, *The Thirteen Books of Euclid's Elements*, 1926, I, 137 f. and III, 442.
21. Aristotle, *De sophist. elench.* 34, 183 b 36–38, reports: ". . . the training given by those who produce themselves in disputations for money was somewhat similar to the [pedagogical] practice of Gorgias (καὶ γὰρ τῶν περὶ τοὺς ἐριστικοὺς λόγους μισθαρνούντων ὁμοία τις ἦν ἡ παίδευσις τῇ Γοργίου πραγματείᾳ). See also *De sophist. elench.* 11, 171 b 22–26, and *Phaedo* 90 c, 91 a (φιλοσόφως—φιλονίκως), *Gorg.* 457 d 4–5, *Euthyd.* 278 b 2 ff., *Soph.* 225 b–c, 232 b ff. (Cf. Thompson, pp. 272 ff., Excursus V; A. E. Taylor, *Varius Socratica*, 1911, *The* δισσοὶ λόγοι, esp. pp. 106 f., 108–11, 115–21, 124–28; R. Robinson, *Plato's Earlier Dialectic*, 1941, pp. 88–92,—R. Hackforth, *Plato's Phaedo*, 1955, p. 108, note 1.)

It is the possibility of such an attitude on Meno's part that [75 c 8 – d 7]
Socrates is trying to remove before meeting Meno's objection
in Meno's own terms.

Having reasserted his stand in the matter of *schêma* and
claimed that he had stated the truth about it, Socrates declares that he refuses to consider Meno as one of those "wise
men" who are but "eristically" and "agonistically" disposed
and consequently refuses to throw at him the challenge: just
refute me. If people, he goes on, desire to discourse with one
another as friends, which he and Meno are at the present
moment (*nyni*), answers should be given in a gentler vein,
more appropriate to such friendly discoursing (*dialektikôte-
ron*). And the more appropriate way of conversing with
each other consists, one ought perhaps to assume (*isôs*), in giving not only answers which tell the truth but in giving them
also in terms which the interlocutor would concede (*proso-
mologêi*) that he knows. "Accordingly,[22] I too (*kai egô*) shall
make an attempt (*peirasomai*) to speak to you in this vein."

The attenuating little word *isôs* seems to indicate that Socrates is enunciating a *rule* which should govern any friendly
and, therefore, *serious* conversation, but that he is also warning against possible misunderstandings of the very meaning of
that rule. The rule demands "agreement" about terms. But
the term "agreement" (*homologia*) itself is susceptible of different interpretations. It may be the kind of agreement on
which Socrates bases his arguments whenever he appeals to
the habitually accepted and familiar.[23] There is also the need
for agreement on terms in any "technical" discourse: *homologia* governs the method of synthetic mathematics as well as
of any other apodeictic discipline. That is the kind of *homologia* Meno seems to have in mind in raising his objection in
the first place. But is it the same that Socrates is apparently
eager to achieve? Whatever the possible misunderstandings of
the term *homologia*, however, in subjecting himself to the
rule he enunciates, Socrates should be in a position to meet
Meno's criticism.

This now is how Socrates attempts to satisfy Meno by *not* [75 e 1 – 76 a 8]
introducing "unknown" terms.

22. Cf. Thompson, p. 91 (10).
23. Cf. pp. 52 f., also Xenophon, *Memorab.* IV, 6, 15.

While in all the previous discussion about *aretê* and *schêma* the problem was to find what corresponded to the *one name* used to designate a wide variety of phenomena, Socrates begins his attempt by bringing up a *variety of names* which designate one and the same thing. The names are: *teleutê* (end), *peras* (limit), *eschaton* (ultimate).

Their several colloquial meanings, in their ambiguity, shade into one another, although they could be distinguished with precision. Prodicus could probably have undertaken this distinguishing,[24] if he had not actually done so (as, later on, Aristotle, for one, certainly did[25]). But Socrates *narrows* the range of all those meanings down to one, that of "limit" (*peras*), noting that Prodicus might well object to this procedure. What emerges as a result of this narrowing down is implied in all those meanings as something simple in itself, not "multicolored" (*poikilon*), as Socrates chooses to express it in a punning reference to the previous argument, with regard both to the role "color" played in it and to the simple-mindedness of which he was accused by Meno.[26] But while this simple thing is "one and the same" (*tauton*) in all cases, one could not say, we ought to note, that it "comprises" (*katechei* – 74 d 8) them all.[27] It is not a "whole."

Meno is following Socrates at this point: "I think, I understand (*oimai manthanein*) what you are talking about."

Socrates then turns directly to the geometrical *technê* and asks Meno whether the name "surface" (*epipedon*) and also the name "solid" (*stereon*) mean something to him, whether they mean the very things that are dealt with, under those names, in (plane and solid) Geometry (*en geômetriais*).[28] Meno says that they do.

Socrates is now able to define *schêma* according to the prescription implied in Meno's objection. Meno has probably already grasped from all the preliminaries, Socrates intimates, what this definition will be. "With regard to every *schêma* indeed,[29] that in which the solid ends, that I say is *schêma*. Or,

24. As one concerned with the "correct use of words" (περὶ ὀνομάτων ὀρθότητος—*Euthyd.* 977 e 4). Cf. *Protag.* 337 a – c; 340 a – c.
25. *Phys.* II, 2, 194 a 30 ff.; *Met.* V, 16–17.
26. 75 c 2: εὐηθες. Cf. *Gorg.* 491 d 10 (also *Theaet.* 146 d 3–6).
27. It is, in Aristotle's terminology, the result of an "abstraction" (ἀφαίρεσις).
28. Cf. Euclid, *Elements* I, Def. 7 (and 5); XI, Def. 1. (For the plural γεωμετρίαι cf. *Rep.* VI, 510 c 2, 511 b 1, VII, 528 a – d, 533 b 7, 536 d 5.)
29. κατὰ γὰρ παντὸς σχήματος—Socrates uses κατά as Meno had done previously (cf. p. 60).

putting it more succinctly, I could state: *schema* is 'limit of
solid.' "

No response whatsoever from Meno. Instead he asks: "And
what do you say that color is, Socrates?"

Thus ends Socrates' attempt to meet Meno's objection in
Meno's own terms. We have to try to understand what has
actually taken place.

1. It is clear that Socrates, following Meno, has abandoned
the colloquial meaning of *schema* altogether. In the definition
he has just given, the word does not mean "closed surface of
a visible thing" but a geometrical entity, "figure," as defined,
for example, in Euclid[30]: "Figure is that which is contained
by any boundary or boundaries," where "boundary," in turn,
is defined[31] as the limit (*peras*) of something. *Schema*, in Socrates' second definition, is a "technical" word signifying a
"bounded surface area" akin to *epipedon* and to *epipha-
neia*.[32] Socrates' second statement is indeed a strictly geometrical definition.[33]

2. This shift in the meaning of *schema* is justifiable because
what is in question is not *schema* itself but the right way of
"defining," of coping adequately with something "universal,"
and finally of describing "human excellence" in *all* its manifestations. It seems, moreover, that Meno as well as we are
made to face a type of definition which, whatever its merits,
may be at variance with what that final task requires.

3. It was the introduction of "color" in Socrates' first statement that provoked Meno to raise his objection, since he
could claim that it meant the introduction of something "unknown." In Socrates' second statement "solid" plays a role
comparable to the one that "color" played in the first. Meno,
queried about that term, acknowledged that he was familiar
with it, and indeed he did not raise any objection to Socrates' second statement. We have to ask, however: in what
sense is "solid" "known" to Meno or to anyone else? The
geometrical meaning of *stereon* does not imply any solidity at
all.[34] There is hardly anything in the world less solid than a

30. *Elements* I, Def. 14: Σχῆμά ἐστι τὸ ὑπό τινος ἢ τινων ὅρων περιεχόμενον.
31. *Ibid.*, Def. 13: Ὅρος ἐστίν, ὅ τινός ἐστι πέρας (Πέρας is not defined in
    Euclid.)
32. Cf. *ibid.*, Def. 5, 6, and 7, XI, Def. 2, and Heath, *op. cit.*, I, 169
    (also A. E. Taylor, *A Commentary on Plato's Timaeus,* p. 362).
33. Cf. Euclid, *Elements* I, Def. 3, 6; XI, Def. 2.
34. Geometrical στερεά are not ἀντίτυπα—see Euclid, *Elements*, ed. Hei-
    berg, Vol. V, p. 593: Scholia in librum XI, ad Def. 1. Cf. the
    term "σχῆμα στερεόν" in Definitions 9, 10, 12, 13, 25–28 of Book XI
    of the *Elements*.

geometrical "solid." The familiarity with that geometrical term (and other "technical" terms of the same kind) is not based on any kind of direct perception, let alone of "knowledge," but simply on the *habit* of using such terms without real understanding. But is not this habit itself in keeping with the ways of the technicians themselves,[35] who proceed as if they knew (*hôs eidotes*) what the entities are which they start with, taking them as perfectly obvious suppositions (*hôs panti phanerai*), and end up—everybody agreeing on the terms (*homologoumenôs*) —with what they set out to investigate? And yet there is nothing obvious about those entities. They are necessary because without them the deductive process could neither begin nor go on. They thus indeed underlie as necessary suppositions, as *hypotheseis,* the path of deduction. But the terms which denote them and out of which their definitions are constructed neither indicate what they are nor reveal their peculiar mode of being. A *technê* of a very different kind seems required to accomplish that.

Comparing Socrates' procedure which led to his first statement with the procedure which led to the second, we become aware of a sort of inverse ratio between the degree of familiarity with which we face the object to be defined and the amount of preparation required for the defining itself: the preliminaries in the case of colored surfaces, which are quite familiar to us, are as long and elaborate as the preliminaries in the case of "geometrical figure," an entity the familiarity of which is either non-existent or illusory, are short and condensed.

We may conclude that Meno is far better acquainted with "color" than with geometrical "solid." That he does not object to Socrates' second statement seems to be due to his, Meno's, familiarity with the *technê* of Geometry (which we should note) and to his matter-of-course acceptance of anything related to it. This attitude is by no means unique. The dialogue, as it proceeds, may tell us still more about Meno's relation to "solidity." And we should certainly not ignore the connection between the strictly geometrical relation of *schêma* to *stereon* and the "complementary" link which seems to bind "shaped surface" to "solid body."

4. Since Meno does not object to Socrates' geometrical definition, he, tacitly at least, acknowledges that Socrates has done his part (cf. 75 b). That he goes back to an abandoned issue

35. *Rep.* VI, 510 ff. and VII, 533 b ff.

and asks Socrates to tell him about "color" at this point, is not only in keeping with his habit of expecting to be *told* about things, but is also a clear indication that he is definitely trying to postpone, and possibly to avoid, taking his turn in answering the question about *aretê*. We need not merely suspect him of that any longer, as we have done before[36]: his purpose is now comically and pitifully evident.

4.

Socrates takes Meno gently and playfully to task, although he uses strong words. He calls him outrageous (*hybristês*) and reproaches him for continually ordering an old man to give answers, while not willing himself to use his power of recollection so as to be able to tell what Gorgias said that human excellence was. (The stress is on the participle *anamnêstheis*.[37]) And after Meno has promised again to tell Socrates about *aretê* as soon as Socrates has told him about *chrôma*, mention is made, this time explicitly,[38] of the fact that the beautiful Meno still has lovers who spoil him and whom he is apparently used to tyrannizing, judging from his peremptory tone. It may also not have escaped Meno, says Socrates, that he, Socrates, cannot resist beautiful youths. "So I will indulge you and answer." And Meno insists that he proceed. [76 a 9 – 77 a 2]

The hope of continuing the conversation rests now on Socrates' ability to satisfy Meno in such a way as not to permit him to evade an answer again. We shall have to watch how Socrates goes about that task, to find out what he considers the most promising way of eliciting Meno's contribution. It cannot be any longer, we know now, a matter of reasoned discourse.

Socrates first inquires whether Meno wishes him to answer in Gorgias' manner which Meno would follow best. "I do wish that, how should I not?" is Meno's reply. Socrates then asks whether it is not true that both, Gorgias and Meno, following Empedocles, hold that certain "effluences" of things (*tôn ontôn*) find their way into our bodies through "passages" (*poroi*) of appropriate size. Meno confirms this. "And further," Socrates asks, " 'sight' means something to you, doesn't it?" "Yes," says Meno, thereby confirming incidentally that

36. P. 62.
37. Cf. 73 c 7 and p. 21, note 54.
38. Cf. p. 58.

color cannot be "unknown" to him.[39] From this, says Socrates with comical solemnity—evoking, by way of introduction into what is to be revealed now, the Aristophanic shade of Pindar —Meno may infer the answer he is seeking, to wit: "Color is an effluence of bounded surfaces (*aporroê schêmatôn*), [an effluence] commensurate with, and perceptible to, sight."[40]

We notice (a) that Socrates now says *chroa*, instead of *chrôma*, as Meno, probably following Empedocles,[41] had already done before (75 c 5), and (b) that Socrates uses (with or without Empedocles' authority) the phrase *aporroê schêmatôn*.[42] This latter phrase is significant because it implies the actual *identity* of color and bounded surface, which Socrates, as we have seen,[43] did not assert. According to the coarser

39. Cf. p. 61.
40. It is pretty clear that Socrates, in quoting Pindar's words "perceive what I tell you" (ξύνες ὅ τοι λέγω) (see fr. 105, Schroeder), does not refer to whatever might have been Pindar's meaning, but to Aristophanes' *Birds*, 945 (cf. Thompson, p. 96; Bekker's edition of Aristophanes, 1829, Vol. II, 253 and Vol. IV, 195, notes to v. 941 and v. 945). In the *Birds*, the "nimble servant of the Muses" (v. 909), in using these words, implies that the jerkin (σπολάς), a garment made of *skins* of animals, which he has just received from Peisthetaerus, requires a more dignified "complement," namely a tunic (χιτών): ἀκλεὴς δ' ἔβα σπολάς ἄνευ χιτῶνος (v. 944). Here, in the dialogue, Meno asks Socrates, who has just offered him a definition of "σχῆμα," to supplement it with a definition of "color." Socrates turns Aristophanes' joke around: he, as the giver, hints at his providing a fancy "complement" to his geometrical definition of σχῆμα. In the *Birds*, Peisthetaerus despoils the priest of his tunic (as well as of his jerkin) to satisfy the poet (as far as one can infer from the context, it is the priest who, in all likelihood, is the victim in this case); in the dialogue, Socrates takes from the priestly Empedocles words that are going to please Meno.

Pindar's phrase may well have become, through Aristophanes, something of a proverbial expression (cf. *Phaedr.* 236 d 2), but here, in the *Meno,* it has been put, it seems, to a more pointed use.
41. Theophrastus, in his account of Empedocles' views (*De sensu* I, 7 = Diels-Kranz, 7th ed., I, 31, A 86, p. 301) uses the word χρῶμα. But there is no reason why he should have retained Empedocles' terminology.
42. All codices agree on the version σχημάτων. One codex has a marginal note which suggests χρημάτων instead. Diels-Kranz, 7th ed., II, 82, B 4, p. 283 (cf. Diels, 3rd ed., 1912, II, 246) apparently favor χρημάτων because it is "perhaps the genuine Gorgian" version, as if that, even if it were provable, could have any bearing on what Plato wrote. (Cf. R. S. Bluck, *Plato's Meno,* 1961, p. 252.)

Alexander Aphrod., *Comment. on Aristotle's De sensu,* p. 24 (Wendland) reports: ταύτης τῆς δόξης καὶ Πλάτων μνημονεύει ὡς οὔσης Ἐμπεδοκλέους ἐν Μένωνι, καὶ ὁρίζεται κατὰ τὴν δόξαν τὴν ἐκείνου τὸ χ ρ ῶ μ α ἀπορροὴν σ ω μ ά τ ω ν ὄψει σύμμετρον καὶ αἰσθητήν. It is clear that Alexander does not quote the Platonic text "literally." He may have in view *Tim.* 67 c 6 – 7.
43. P. 59.

view expressed here, the tiny portions of surfaces (or "films") that penetrate into our eyes *are* portions of color.[44]

We may assume that Meno himself does not notice this implication at all. In any event, he does not raise any objection whatsoever to what Socrates has just said. On the contrary, he praises Socrates' "answer" highly. And we learn from Socrates' reaction to this praise both why Meno is so pleased and why Socrates chose that particular way of pleasing him. My answer, he says, "was perhaps phrased according to what is habitual with you" (*Isôs gar soi kata synêtheian eirêtai*). We are reminded of the emphasis Socrates put, in the beginning of the dialogue, on Gorgias' inculcating certain habits in his pupils.[45] Are we not made to observe, here again, the fruits of Gorgias' pedagogy?

It appears indeed that Meno is perfectly content to hear all over again something he had heard before, to hear from somebody else what is already recorded in his memory. He is pleased to have the words of others serve as an echo, even as not too reliable an echo, of his own verbal memories which he seems to cherish. A little later on, taunted by Socrates to prolong his stay in Athens so that he could be initiated into the mysteries, Meno retorts: "But I should stay, Socrates, if you would tell many things of that sort (*polla toiauta*)."

In his eagerness to flatter his memory, as it were, Meno does not appear to mind or even to understand the comprehensive emptiness of the "Empedoclean" statement as formulated by Socrates. It is Socrates himself who "deflates" its meaning completely, thereby vindicating his mocking reference to Pindar's phrase. For in addition to learning from that statement what color is, says Socrates, it will be easy for Meno to understand that he could use it as well to state what sound, odor, and many other things of the same kind are. (All that Meno would have to do for this purpose is to substitute corresponding terms for the term "sight" in the body of the "answer."). "Quite so," says Meno.[46] And Socrates goes one step further to explain Meno's exaggerated liking of that exuberant

---

44. The question is, of course, not whether Socrates (or Plato) reproduces faithfully or distorts Empedocles' view, but what means are being used here to impress Meno so as to let us see Meno's "nature." According to Aristotle, *De sensu*, 437 b 23 – 438 a 5, Empedocles' views about "color" and "sight" are, at any rate, ambiguous.

45. Cf. p. 41.

46. Meno is too rash: it is not easy to understand "sound," for example, as an ἀπορροὴ σχημάτων (or, for that matter, χρημάτων).

statement: "The answer is indeed in the tragic vein,[47] Meno, and that's why it pleases you more than that about surface." "Yes," says Meno. "No," says Socrates, addressing Meno with pronounced and "tragic" formality, "I, for my part, am convinced, son of Alexidemus, that the other one (*ekeinê*) was the better answer." Can we have any doubts as to which "other one" Socrates means, the geometrical—narrow—one which was given in Meno's own terms, or the first—sober—one which, correlating "surface" and "color," hinted at a possibly satisfactory answer about "human excellence"?[48]

47. Thompson, p. 97, quotes Heindorf's note to *Cratyl.* 414 c (see Bekker's edition of Plato's works, Vol. IV, London, 1826, p. 267), in which the phrase τραγῳδεῖν τὰ ὀνόματα is explicated to mean: σεμνότερα καὶ θαυμαστότερα ποιεῖν. This meaning is implied, according to Heindorf, in *Cratyl.* 418 d, *Rep.* III, 413 b and *Meno* 76 e (the passage we are concerned with now). Heindorf also invokes the authority of Guillaume Budé.

This is what Budé (*Commentarii linguae graecae*, Coloniae, 1530, p. 440, or Paris, 1548, p. 845) has to say with reference to Theophrastus, *Hist. plantarum*, IX, 8, 5: "Verum ἐπιτραγῳδεῖν . . . significat tragice aliquid narrare, hoc est, cum amplificatione et commiseratione. Sed ponitur pro admirationem ciere, vel *ita narrare ut in admirationem evadere rem velimus*. . . ." (Cf. also Plutarch, *Life of Artaxerxes*, 18, 7.)

It seems that Edmonde Grimal in her interpretation of the passage in question (*Revue des études grecques*, LV, 1942) has not sufficiently taken this traditional understanding into account. Nor has she considered the relation which "color" has to real and to pretended ἀρετή.

48. Cf. R. G. Hoerber, "Plato's Meno," *Phronesis*, 5 (1960), 94 – 97.

III

1.

It is not possible for Meno now to withhold his promised answer about excellence any longer. Socrates presses the point. He first assures Meno that he, Socrates, would not, for his own and Meno's sake (cf. 75 b 6), relent in his endeavor to tell "things of that sort" (which assurance we should note), although he is not certain whether he could tell "many" of them. (It might not be easy, after all, to cope with the richness of Meno's memory.) Meno is then urged once more to make an attempt (*peirô*) to fulfill his promise and to tell Socrates what human excellence "in an over-all way" (*kata holou*) is. He is warned not to "break it up" again by producing many pieces of it instead of keeping it "whole and sound" (*holên kai hygiê*). And he is referred to the model patterns (*paradeigmata*) of "definitions" which Socrates offered him—the sober one, the narrow one, and the "tragic," if empty, one.

Thereupon Meno makes his *second attempt* to state what human excellence in its "generality" is. But he does not take into account any of the patterns presented to him. This is what he says: "Well now, it seems to me, Socrates, that human excellence is, as the poet says, 'both to take delight in high things and to master them.' And I, too (*kai egô*), say that this is excellence: longing for (*epithymounta*) the high things, to be able to get hold of them."

It is as if Meno, without any effort, lets his memory speak for him again. This time it is a poet, not Gorgias, whom he quotes. We cannot help gaining the impression that the remembered opinion of somebody else *always* "accompanies" what Meno thinks. This appears to be his "habit," summarized in the formula "*kai egô.*" Has not this habit been especially nurtured by Gorgias? As Aristotle reports in the treatise *On Sophistical Refutations,* Gorgias' pedagogical practice was somewhat similar to that of the professional "debaters."[1] The

1. See p. 62, note 21.

masters of this pseudo-art made their pupils, as Aristotle further reports,[2] "learn by heart" (*ekmanthanein*) various kinds of speeches or else questions aimed at leading to the refutation of the opponent, on the assumption that, most of the time, the respective arguments would follow the examples committed to memory. Meno, too, seems to have had extensive practice in "memorizing." But, in his case, the capacity of retaining in memory the material offered for absorption appears exceptionally high.

We had occasion to wonder whether the similarity of Meno's and Gorgias' opinions, suggested by Socrates and confirmed by Meno,[3] pointed to an important trait of Meno's character. We see now that this similarity points indeed to a peculiar condition which is Meno's own: his thinking is *always* "colored" by what other people say and by what has some standing in the eyes of the world. If this condition is to a large degree the general condition of men, it seems to characterize Meno in his very being. He seems to be nothing but his "memory."

It has frequently appeared plausible to liken our "memories" to persistent "imprints," or "marks," or "pictures," "on" something in us that we call our "memory,"[4] whatever structure and way of "functioning" we assign to it. This memory of ours is, at any rate, inseparable from its "contents," just as the surface of a visible body is inconceivable without its coloring. And just as the surface colors provide the visible "skin" or "envelope" of the body, so do our memories form the horizon within which we live. If it be true that Meno's very being is nothing but his memory, he himself would be very much like the bounded surface of a written sheet. And the marks on that sheet would represent not only the opinions of particular men but also, and even more so, the all-pervasive and habitually accepted opinions of mankind.

We cannot be certain, at this juncture, whether the impression we have thus gained gives us a sufficiently solid basis not

---

2. *Sophist. elench.* 34, 183 b 38 – 184 a 1: λόγους γὰρ οἱ μὲν ῥητορικοὺς οἱ δὲ ἐρωτητικοὺς ἐδίδοσαν ἐ κ μ α ν θ ά ν ε ι ν, εἰς οὓς πλειστάκις ἐμπίπτειν ᾠήθησαν ἑκάτεροι τοὺς ἀλλήλων λόγους.

Cf. also *Protag.* 325 e 5 and "ἐξεπιστάμενος"—*Phaedr.* 228 b 4. This "memorizing" is not necessarily only "by rote": *Ion* 530 b 10 ff.: . . . τὴν τούτου [sc. Ὁμήρου] διάνοιαν ἐκμανθάνειν, μὴ μόνον τὰ ἔπη. The irony of the sentence, however, can be inferred from 534 b 7 – 535 a 10. This kind of παίδευσις is, of course, not out of line with the traditional unsophisticated παιδεία practiced through centuries.

3. Cf. pp. 44, 45.

4. Cf. pp. 109 f., 161.

only for describing an important trait in Meno's character but
also for deciding "who" he is. We are reminded of the jingle
in Socrates little speech concerning his own "poor memory."[5]
That jingle, so far as Meno's name was concerned, seemed to
hint at some possible "derangement" of Meno's memory. A
great deal may depend on our gaining insight into the nature
of this "derangement."

Socrates' questions and criticism, related to Meno's second
attempt to "define" human excellence, focus, at any rate, on
the habitually accepted opinions hidden in the latter's statement. Once before[6] the appeal to such opinions had helped
the conversation along.

As in the case of Meno's first attempt, the statement he has
just made is perfectly meaningful. To set oneself high goals
and to be able to reach them, is this not the most telling
manifestation of human excellence? What could be called into
question are the noble goals, "the high things" (*ta kala*) that
Meno has in mind. We can expect Socrates to raise this question.

2.

Socrates does this in a twofold way by taking up first the   [77 b 6 – 78 b 2]
subordinate clause in Meno's statement ("longing for the high
things") and then its main clause ("to be able to get hold of
them"). It is one thing, however, to find out what noble
goals Meno is thinking of, and another to discover what guides
his choice. It is the second, and clearly more important, aspect of the problem which is considered first.

Socrates and Meno agree quickly on equating one who
longs for the high things (*ta kala*) with one who desires
"good things" (*agatha*), although this seems to reduce
Meno's terms to a more "trivial" level. Does Meno imply
then, Socrates asks, that some people long for "the good
things" (*tagatha*) while other people long for "the bad
things" (*ta kaka*)? "Do not all men, my best of men, seem
to you to desire (*epithymein*) the good things?" "No," says
Meno. And in what follows, Meno is made to say that some
people do long for bad things and do so with full cognizance
of the badness of those things, while other people just mistake
bad things for good ones.

Surely, whenever we desire something, we understand it, to

5. Cf. pp. 43, 44 f.
6. Pp. 52–53.

the extent that it is desirable, to be a "good thing." Meno's claim, on the other hand, that a desired thing may be "bad" in spite of its being desired is rooted in the commonly accepted view that the goodness or the badness of things cannot simply depend on their being desirable or not desirable. And this view, in turn, is based on the common awareness of the whimsical and shifting nature of most of our desires. On what grounds, then, do we attribute "goodness" or "badness" to things?

Socrates makes Meno agree that, if a man longs for something, we understand him to desire that that something become *his*. ("What else?" says Meno.[7]) But, the argument goes on, does he who desires bad things, that is, desires the possession of them, hold that such possession will do him good (*ôphelein*) or does he know that the presence of bad things in or about him will harm him? Meno: "There are some who hold that the bad things will do them good (*ôphelein*) —there are others who know that they will be harmful." Socrates: "Do you really think that those people know the bad things to be bad, who hold that the bad things will do them good (*ôphelein*)?" Meno: "No, that I do not believe."

Why does Meno not believe that? Is it not because it is commonly and plausibly held that what benefits us (*ôphelei*), that is, "does us good," cannot be bad? And is not this view, again, based on the common understanding that the goodness or badness of things depends on the *effect* the appropriation of those things has on us?

It follows from Meno's admission, at any rate, according to Socrates, that all people who desire bad things are either mistaken or ignorant: they think that the bad things in question are good inasmuch as they "do them good." Meno is not unwilling to draw that conclusion. The possibility that some people might want bad things so as to be harmed by them is apparently not taken as something worthy of consideration by either Socrates or Meno. This will be confirmed by what follows.

One could assume that Socrates thus has made his point, to wit, that no man really desires what is "bad." The only pertinent distinction that can be made, it seems, with regard to what people pursue, is that some desire truly good things and others things that merely appear to them to be good. But, if it is not possible, as agreed, that bad things should benefit us,

7. This exchange curiously mirrors the exchange between Diotima and Socrates *Symp.* 204 d 4–7.

the possibility of bad things merely appearing to be good
makes the "benefit" itself doubtful. We might be mistaken
about the beneficial effect, too: the "benefit" might be a merely
apparent one, we might actually be harmed without realizing
it. The argument has to go on. The—possibly only apparent—
effects things have on us do not provide a sufficiently reliable
ground for our attributing "goodness" or "badness" to those
things. And, therefore, the validity of the Socratic dictum that
no one desires bad things is not yet sufficiently established.

Let's see, says Socrates, those who desire bad things, as you
say (*hôs phês sy*), that is, are neither mistaken about their badness nor ignorant about their effect on us, do know, do they
not, that they will be harmed by them. Necessarily so, says
Meno. Following this up, Socrates makes Meno agree that those
who are thus harmed must consider themselves miserable
(*athlioi*). And then there is a curious further step, an "addition," in the argument: Socrates suggests, and Meno agrees
again, that the "miserable ones" are "unhappy" (*kakodaimones*). Whereupon Socrates asks: "Now, is there anyone who
is willing (*bouletai*) to be miserable and unhappy, Meno?"
"I do not think so, Socrates," says Meno.

While we could entertain doubts as to the beneficial effect
merely apparently good things have on us, it is not possible to
be uncertain about our feeling miserable, whenever this occurs. Moreover, it is the firmly held and virtually unassailable
opinion of mankind that nobody is *willing* to be miserable,
regardless of his transient desires and the real or imagined
benefits he might derive from the fulfillment of those desires.
That is why Socrates can so easily shift from the word
epithymein (which means "desiring," without necessarily
implying any reflection about it) to the word *boulesthai*
(which implies consideration and deliberate choice).[8] And,
since it is the bad things which bring us misery, he can conclude now rather firmly: "Nobody, therefore, Meno, wills
(*bouletai*) the bad things."

Socrates adds, echoing the poet's words in reverse, as it
were: "For what else is to be miserable but 'both to long for
the low things and to bring them upon oneself'" (*ti gar
allo estin athlion einai ê epithymein te tôn kakôn kai
ktasthai?*).

8. The difference in meaning between ἐπιθυμεῖν and βούλεσθαι is not always conspicuously clear, but it is not weak enough to escape Prodicus'
attention (*Protag.* 340 a 8 f.). In the passage of the *Meno* under
consideration Socrates exploits both the difference and the similarity
between the two. (cf. *Charm.* 167 e 1–6.)

Meno cannot help succumbing to the apparent force of the argument and accepts its results. He does not suspect Socrates of tampering with the meaning of his, Meno's, statement by substituting *boulesthai* for *epithymein* in the subordinate clause. And yet it is only this substitution which seems to permit Socrates to ignore altogether the possibility of differentiating between men according to the intensity with which they long for the good things. Meno assents to Socrates' conclusion that "nobody wills the bad things" (*oudeis bouletai ta kaka*) and repeats this conclusion in Socrates' own words. Like anyone else, Meno does not want to feel "miserable." We understand that this is not only the basis of his acceptance of Socrates' dictum but also the ultimate reason which guides his choice of the "high things."

Can *we* accept Socrates' conclusion? The argument has led from the desirability of things and the beneficial effect their possession may have on us—both insufficient criteria for our judging those things to be "good"—to the misery which bad things produce in us. But could not "good" things make us feel "miserable" too? This possibility alone seems to invalidate the cogency of the argument.[9] Moreover, can we overlook the fact that Socrates, to convince Meno, uses the device of shifting from the "positive" side of things to the "negative" one, from being benefited to being harmed and made "miserable"? And why does Socrates, in making that shift, find it necessary to characterize the "miserable ones" (*athlioi*) still further as *kakodaimones*? It is true, the mythical "overtones" of the word *kakodaimones* conjure up the vision of people possessed by superhuman malevolent powers. And the reduction of those overtones to simpler human connotations still leaves us with the picture of unfortunate people dragged down by "bad things" so that the word provides a direct link between "misery" and the "badness" of things which bring "misery" about. But even so, the addition of the term *kakodaimones* does not add anything to the force of the argument itself, since *athlios* and *kakodaimôn* are essentially synonymous. Why then this seemingly superfluous "addition"?[10]

There is no necessary connection between our *feeling* "mis-

9. In Xenophon, *Memorab.* I, 6, 3, Antiphon is quoted as having called Socrates a κακοδαιμονίας διδάσκαλος because he was a living example of how not to care about a comfortable life.

10. The term κακοδαίμων occurs rarely (and κακοδαιμονία never) in Plato. In the *Republic*, in the story about the corpses, Leontius addresses his eyes by using this word (440 a 3). In the *Symposium*, the word is applied—rather ambiguously—to Apollodorus (173 d 1).

erable" and our *understanding* what "misery" truly is. The common interpretations of "misery" based on the certainty of the feeling of misery may well be misguided. Ought not our understanding of what misery or unhappiness is depend rather decisively on the understanding of their "opposite," on the understanding of *happiness*?[11] The advantage of the word *kakodaimôn* (or *kakodaimonia*) over many other words which denote the same or a similar human condition is precisely this: that it reminds us, by its very sound and structure, of its "opposite," of *eudaimonia*, of happiness. It seems as if the sudden introduction of the *kakodaimones* at the very end of Socrates' argument is meant to invite us (over Meno's head, as it were) to turn our attention to *eudaimonia*, not only for an understanding of "misery" but also for a final decision about things "good" and "bad."

Everything would have to be considered anew. For *eudaimonia*, "good fortune" or "happiness," then as now, has a range of meanings which covers all the goals, all the "high" or "good" things which men pursue at all times: health, and wealth, and beauty, and prosperity, and pleasures of various kinds, and fame, and power, and communion with others, and insight.[12] We would have to decide about the "rightness," or the right order, of those goals. Most of the time we shy away from this all-important task.[13] Can the dialogue help us to begin tackling it?

3.

Meno's acceptance of Socrates' conclusion makes the subordinate clause of his own statement look irrelevant to the purpose of defining human excellence. Since striving for the good things appears to be common to all men and does not, therefore, make one man different from, and better than, any other, Meno's statement reduces itself, Socrates intimates, to the assertion that the better the man the more able will he be to get hold of the good things. Accordingly, Socrates modifies the main clause of Meno's statement, with Meno's full approval, as follows: "Human excellence is the ability to get hold of the good things."

Meno, we observe, does not go back on the identification of the "high things" with the "good things."

[78 b 3 – d 3]

11. See especially *Symp.* 204 e 5 – 205 a 3.
12. Cf. Aristotle, *Nic. Eth.* I, 4, 1095 a 20–26.
13. Cf. *Gorg.* 472 c 6 – d 1; also 470 d 5 – e 11; *Apol.* 36 d 5 – e 1.

The truth of Meno's statement, in the version proposed by Socrates and endorsed by Meno, is to be tested now. But even before the testing begins Socrates remarks: "You might well be right indeed" (*isôs gar an eu legois*). We understand Socrates to mean that the decision as to whether Meno's statement is true or not will depend on what things or sort of things Meno considers "high" or "good."

Socrates' questioning and Meno's answers bring out[14] that Meno's list of "good things" contains health and wealth, the acquisition of gold and silver, as well as of honors and offices in the state. Upon Socrates' asking him whether he would list other "good things" besides, Meno replies without hesitation: "No, I mean everything of this sort."[15] It is in securing those listed things for himself that Meno feels apparently safe from "misery." And not to leave any possible doubt about that, Socrates says (with some sarcasm, to be sure, and also imitating somewhat the manner in which Meno had introduced his question about "color") : "All right, so getting hold of gold and silver, that is human excellence according to Meno, the hereditary friend of the Great King." In saying that, Socrates substitutes "gold and silver" for "the good things" in the statement under consideration, but omits mention of "health" and "honors and offices," these goods being presumably understood by Meno as mere means to the main end, to wit, the acquisition of wealth. We also note that Meno is now credited with an understanding of human excellence as consisting in the actual getting of gold and silver, not in the ability (*dynamis*) to do so. The mention of Meno's relation to the Persian dynasty, furthermore, seems to point to an important—potential or actual—source of his revenue.

And now comes Socrates' attack which takes the form of an "addition."

[78 d 3 – 79 a 2]   Should not something (*ti*) be added "to this getting-in" of the goods (*toutôi tôi porôi*), Socrates asks, say, the words "according to what is just in the eyes of men and the gods" (*to dikaiôs kai hosiôs*)? "Or does that make no difference to you? And, even though someone might get those things unjustly, would you speak [in such a case] of excellence all the same?"

Meno denies this. He is perfectly willing to make the "addi-

---

14. Whether we adopt Sehrwald's reading or not.
15. Cf. Thompson, p. 106 (25).

tion" suggested by Socrates and sanctioned by the common opinion of mankind, just as he immediately consented to the same "addition" after his first attempt to "define" human excellence (see 73 d 7–8; cf. 73 a 6 ff.). No wonder, his memory registers habitually accepted opinions only too well. No doubt, "unjust" acquisition of wealth is considered the opposite of excellence, is considered to be viciousness (*kakia*).

Socrates exploits that point fully. It seems, therefore, says he, that some such addition "to this getting-in" (*toutôi tôi porôi*) is indeed required, the addition of "justice," *or* of "moderation," *or* of "piety," "*or* of some other part of excellence" (*ê allo ti morion aretês*). For otherwise, all the acquisitiveness in the world, although it will provide us with goods, will not be "excellence." And Meno—of all people, Meno—echoes: "How indeed could there be excellence without those?"

It follows, and Meno accepts the consequence, that to avoid getting gold and silver, either for oneself or for somebody else, whenever the getting itself would involve injustice, is a sign of human excellence. In other words, to be able to stay poor is, under certain circumstances, a sign of human excellence. And, therefore, success in getting (*ho poros*) the goods mentioned by Meno would no more constitute human excellence than success in not getting (*he aporia*) them. In either case, human excellence will obtain if what is done is done "with justice" (*meta dikaiosynês*), and viciousness will obtain if it is done "without anything of this sort" (*aneu pantôn tôn toioutôn*). Meno: "It seems to me that it must be as you say."

We have to note (a) that Socrates is playing with the word *porizesthai* by punning on the Empedoclean *poroi* and the influx effected through them and also by using the word *aporia*, full of weighty connotations, to signify the opposite of *poros*, that is, poverty, need, want;[16] (b) that, more generally, the language Socrates uses in discussing the (modified) main clause of Meno's statement is indeed far from precise, "technically" or otherwise,[17] reflecting the appeal to habitually accepted opinions.

More important still, we note, is the result of this brief and not very precise exchange: taken at its face value, Meno's acceptance of Socrates "addition" means that Meno repudiates

---

16. Cf. Thompson, p. 107 (44) and Bluck, p. 263.
17. Notably in the case of αὐτά (78 d 6) and of ἐκπορίζουσα (78 e 2), both words directly connected in the text with ἀρετή (cf. Stock's Notes, p. 15, and Bluck, pp. 262, 263).

his own statement. Not the ability to get hold of the goods he listed makes for excellence, but rather the presence of what has been labeled by Socrates as "parts of excellence" and is commonly attributed to, and distributed among, good or excellent men.

It is not this repudiation, however, that Socrates is mainly concerned with. For if he were, the refutation of Meno's second attempt to "define" human excellence could stop right here and now. Yet Socrates continues the argument. Why?

We might conjecture that, at this point, Socrates takes Meno's obvious inconsistency as expressing a basic, if usually hidden, haziness in the generally accepted views about human excellence. It is this haziness that seems to be Socrates' main target now. And this conjecture both supports and is supported by the impression we previously gained: Meno's utterances are but an echo of what is commonly opined, said and proclaimed, his memory being a faithful register or reprint of widely accepted views, which he can reproduce at the slightest prodding. Continuing the argument with Meno thus may well mean embarking on an argument about what is habitually and generally taken for granted in the matter of human excellence.

The lever for this argument has been carefully built and prepared. In the discussion of Meno's first attempt to "define" human excellence, the "oneness" of that excellence was emphasized throughout. Socrates' warning, immediately preceding Meno's second attempt, to speak about *aretê* "in an overall way" (*kata holou* – 77 a 6), not to break it up (77 a 7–8) and to keep it "whole and sound" (*holên kai hygiê* – 77 a 9), introduced a new theme, only once alluded to in the previous discussion (*katechei* – 74 d 8), that of the *"wholeness"* of excellence. In the discussion of Meno's second attempt the correlative term *morion aretês* ("part of excellence") makes its appearance (78 e 1) [18] and is repeated with ever increasing frequency over and over again (79 a 3; b 2; b 5; b 6; b 9 f.; c 5; c 8; [d 7]), while the warning not to break human excellence into fragments (79 a 9–10; c 2–3) as well as the references to its "wholeness" (79 b 7; c 1; d 7) are again taken up. It is this opposition of "whole" and "parts" which is finally used to confound Meno once more and with him, this time, a hazy, if persistent and widely spread, opinion among men, an opinion not confined to any particular time or particular country.

18. Cf. *Protag.* 329 c ff.; *Symp.* 184 c 6; *Laws* 696 b, 791 c—Thompson, p. 107 (38).

Meno is reminded that just a while ago[19] he was asked not   [79 a 3 – c 3]
to break up excellence, not "to coin it into small money" (*mê
katagnynai mêde kermatizein*), and was also offered model
patterns (*paradeigmata*) for the answer he had promised to
give about excellence, and now "you tell me that human excellence is the ability to get hold of the good things 'with
justice,' and that again, you say, is 'a part of human excellence.' " Isn't that sheer mockery? And Socrates goes on explaining[20] why this sort of answer, especially because of the
appended "addition" (which he himself proposed), will not do.

The answer amounts to saying that human excellence consists in doing whatever one does with a "part" of that excellence. Meno had been asked to say what the *whole* of human
excellence was (cf. 77 a). What Meno is saying now, however, presupposes that an answer to that question has already been given and that Socrates ought to consider the
whole of human excellence as something known to him. But
far from telling what this "whole" is, all that Meno has done
is to break it into "parts," as if he were changing a big piece
of money into small coins. Let us not forget, however: these
"parts" are acknowledged not only by Meno but also by most
of us to represent some excellence.[21] We characterize men who
show that they possess some of those "parts" (justice, or wise
moderation, or courage, or piety, or modesty, for example) as
good or excellent men. And yet we are uncertain about the
common source, the common character, or a "common de-
nominator" which may permit us to use these common
words. We also doubt whether that commonness indicates any
"wholeness."

Meno's second attempt to "define" human excellence, an at-   [79 c 3 – e 4]
tempt already repudiated by him,[22] is thus made to appear to
have floundered as the first had done: now as then a multiplicity has been reached where something "one and whole"
was expected to be found. We remember: the pattern was set
from the very beginning, when Meno presented Socrates with

19. Cf. p. 71.
20. Van Heusde's reading of 79 b 7 can be challenged: cf. *Cratyl.* 398
    a, *Gorg.* 497 d – see Buttmann's note in Bekker's edition of Plato's
    works, IV, 29, Thompson, p. 241 (18), Bluck, pp. 264 f. Hirschig's
    reading of 78 d 7 seems plausible.
21. P. 56.
22. Pp. 79 f.

a "swarm" of virtues. In this respect, too, Meno—not without Socrates' help—indulges in repeating himself.

The new failure gives Socrates the opportunity to speak to Meno in this vein: It seems to me, Meno, my friend (*ô phile Menôn*), you ought to face again and anew (*palin ex archês* – 79 c 3; *palin* – c 7) the same old question, what is human excellence (*ti estin aretê*)? For it is odd to say that acting "with justice," that is, with a part of human excellence, constitutes human excellence. "Do you think that one knows what human excellence is in part when one does not know what it itself [the whole of it] is?" Meno says that he does not think so.

Socrates reminds Meno that, when they were considering the question of *schêma*, the attempt was made to give an answer in terms of things still sought, that is, still "unknown," and not yet agreed upon (*dia tôn eti zêtoumenôn kai mêpô hômologêmenôn*). "We rejected this kind of answer, didn't we?" says Socrates, an obvious misrepresentation of what had happened then. Meno's memory seems to fail him: he does not make any attempt to correct the record. On the contrary, he says: "And rightly indeed, Socrates, did we reject it [that kind of answer]." *We* shall have to put the record straight.

Shielded by Meno's acquiescence, Socrates, winding up this phase of the discussion, exhorts Meno to avoid falling into the same trap. While the *whole* of human excellence is still being sought (*eti zêtoumenês aretês holês ho ti estin*), he should not venture to reveal to anyone what it is by referring to its "parts," nor should he use such a device in any other case. Socrates repeats, Meno ought to face once more (*palin*) the question: "In all that you say, what do you imply that human excellence is?" And to ascertain Meno's (and our) reaction to this kind of criticism, Socrates adds: "Or do I seem to you to say nothing?" Meno: "It seems to me that what you say is right." Let us consider whether it is.

5.

1. It was Meno who objected to Socrates' introducing something "unknown" into the "definition" of *schêma*. Socrates stuck to his statement and maintained its truth. In accordance with a rule that should be observed in a serious and friendly conversation, Socrates was willing, however, to provide Meno with a "definition" that suited the latter's wishes. This definition was patterned on the procedure of "synthetic" mathe-

matics which avoids "unknown" terms, but it was by no means
certain that this procedure and the kind of *homologia* demanded and realized in it were suited to the task at hand.
In no sense did Socrates agree with Meno on rejecting as
totally unsuitable answers containing "unknown terms."[23]

2. Whatever the merits of the "synthetically" apodeictic
procedure, the relation of "whole" and "parts" hardly enters
into it. The "synthetic" deduction or construction usually
proceeds from the "simpler" to the "more complex" and, if it
ever reaches a "whole," it does so by building it up out of
"known" elements, which cannot be considered to be "parts"
before the whole is built.

3. The language Socrates uses in exhorting Meno to
avoid answering in terms "of things still sought and not yet
agreed upon" (79 d 3; 6) has nevertheless a familiar "mathematical" ring, hinting at a mathematical procedure which is
not "synthetic." *To zêtoumenon* and *to homologoumenon* are
indeed terms used to describe the "analytical" method in
mathematics. They correspond to the modern terms: the "unknown" and the "given." The definition of mathematical analysis, formulated in antiquity, can be paraphrased as follows:
analysis is the method by which what is sought, *to zêtoumenon*
(the "unknown"), is taken as something agreed upon, as an
homologoumenon (as if it were "given"), and then followed
up through necessary consecutive steps until something previously agreed upon as true (something "given") is reached.[24]
It is also the method of setting up an "equation," a method
named by Vieta (in 1591) —in agreement with the terminology
of Greek mathematicians—the "analytical art" and considered in the sixteenth and seventeenth centuries, in accordance with an ancient tradition, as constituting the Mathesis
universalis, the "universal science."[25] All mathematics today
is an outgrowth of this tradition. As far as geometrical considerations are concerned, there is enough evidence for the use
of this method in ancient times, even in Plato's own time.[26]

23. Cf. pp. 62–66.
24. Cf. p. 62, note 20.
25. Cf. Jacob Klein, "Die griechische Logistik und die Entstehung der
   Algebra," *Quellen und Studien zur Geschichte der Mathematik,
   Astronomic und Physik*, Abt. B, Bd. 3, Heft 2, 1936, §11, §12, B.
26. Cf. Th. L. Heath, *The Thirteen Books of Euclid's Elements* I, 137
   ff., also *A History of Greek Mathematics* I, 168.
      As to the use of "analysis" in matters "arithmetical," Thymaridas'
   ἐπάνθημα could be cited as an example. This is done by Nesselmann,
   Die Algebra der Griechen, 1842, pp. 232 ff., by P. Tannery, *Pour
   l'histoire de la science hellène*, 2nd ed., 1930, pp. 396–99, also

4. Ancient writers[27] have credited Plato himself, somewhat vaguely, with introducing—through Leodamas of Thasos—the analytical method into mathematics. It is unlikely that they are right. But it is possible to understand what in Plato's work gave rise to that claim. In a Platonic dialogue, and the *Meno* is no exception, that which is being investigated, the *zêtoumenon* (be it excellence, piety, courage, prudence, or justice), is considered from the point of view of various and varying opinions, genuinely or tentatively or perfunctorily held by those who participate in the conversation. To hold an opinion about that which is under consideration means to take—or, at worst, to pretend to take—the *zêtoumenon*, the "unknown," as if it were "known." To test an opinion means to follow it up through necessary consequences until a patent absurdity (a "contradiction") or something incontrovertibly true comes into sight. Depending on whether the former or the latter happens, the opinion is either refuted or vindicated. To vindicate (or verify) an opinion means to transform a *zêtoumenon* into an *homologoumenon,* into something one has to agree to, to transform the hitherto "unknown" into a truth now indeed "known."[28] However seldom, if ever, such vindicating occurs in a Platonic dialogue, the "dialectical" process, which is "analytical" in its very conception and structure, tends toward that end.

It might be useful to remind ourselves of what Socrates has to say about this dialectical or analytical procedure in the *Theaetetus*. The young mathematician Theaetetus has been trying hard, for quite a while, to answer Socrates' question, "What is knowledge (*epistêmê*)?" In the midst of the discussion (196 d ff.) Socrates suddenly proposes to "behave shamefully" (*anaischyntein*) by trying to describe "knowing." Why should that be "shameful," Theaetetus asks. Socrates retorts by asking: Does it not seem shameless (*anaides*) to make pronouncements about "knowing," not knowing what "knowl-

---

Mémoires scientifiques I, 106–10, by M. Cantor, *Vorlesungen über Geschichte der Mathematik*, 3rd ed., 1906, I, 158 f., by Heath, *A History of Greek Mathematics*, 1921, I, 94 ff., by P.-H. Michel, *De Pythagore à Euclide, Contribution à l'histoire des mathématiques préeuclidiennes*, 1950, pp. 283–86. Cf. however Diels-Kranz, 7th ed., I, 447.

27. Proclus in *Eucl.* (Friedlein), p. 211, 19–22, and Diogenes Laertius III, 24. The latter refers to Favorinus' Παντοδαπὴ ἱστορία (cf. v. Wilamowitz-Moellendorf, Letter to E. Maas in *Philologische Untersuchungen* 3, (1880), 142–64; H. Cherniss, "Plato as Mathematician," *Rev. of Metaph.* IV, 3 (1951), 395, 418).

28. Cf. Aristotle, *Nic. Eth.* III, 3, 1112 b 20–24.

edge" is. And he adds this remark: "Actually, Theaetetus, we have been infected all along with an impurity in conversing (*mê katharôs dialegesthai*)," referring to the fact that, in their discussion, they had been using phrases like "we know," "we do not know," "we are ignorant," "we understand" innumerable times (and again so at that very moment), as if they could communicate with each other in these phrases while ignorant about "knowledge." "But in what manner will you converse, Socrates, if you abstain from using those phrases?" asks Theaetetus. And Socrates—for once, it seems, lifting his ironic mask—responds: "In no manner, being just the man I am" (197 a 1). If he were one of those disputatious persons (*antilogikos*),[29] he continues, he certainly would not permit any reference to what is still "unknown." Being plain and simple-minded men (*phauloi*), Socrates and Theaetetus decide to proceed with their "impure" discussion.

We conclude that, according to Socrates, a serious and friendly conversation cannot avoid referring to things not yet "known," provided there is agreement on the point of ignorance.

5. The question arises whether the consideration of "wholes" and their "parts" has any place within a procedure which deals with opinions "analytically." It seems that it does. Generally, any opinion on any subject can be understood to catch some "partially" true aspect of the subject under investigation. This means that, however mistaken each of us may be about that subject as a "whole," we are talking together about "the same thing" or, at least, are making an effort to talk about "the same thing." (That is why conversing among ourselves, or, as we say, "exchanging opinions," *is* possible and *can* be fruitful.) But that, in turn, indicates a common, if usually hidden, ground along which the conversation proceeds and where the "whole" is really "located." This "back-ground" is the *zêtoumenon* and its continuing presence manifests itself in our ability to opine, that is, to cloak what remains "unknown" with the guise of the "known." The dialectical-analytical process thus tends indeed through "parts" toward a "whole." That is why it is not at all impossible to talk about "properties" of something of which we do not know what it is.[30]

29. See L. Campbell's note to the passage in *The Theaetetus of Plato*, 2nd ed., 1883, p. 197. – Cf. L. Campbell, *The Sophistes and Politicus of Plato*, 1867, pp. XI–XII, LIV, also Thompson p. 280, and above p. 62, note 21. Cf. esp. *Theaet.* 232 e 2–5.
30. Cf. p. 42.

6. There are subjects, on the other hand, which, independently of the opinions we have about them, seem to be "divided" in themselves and thus present a peculiar difficulty. It might be helpful to consider a passage in the *Sophist* which is not unrelated to this difficulty as well as to the problem Socrates and Meno are directly concerned with.

Knowledge, it is said in the *Sophist* (257 c 7 – d 3), although one would suppose that it is "one" (*mia*) in itself, appears to be "fractioned" (*phainetai katakekermatisthai*), and each of its separate "parts" has a name of its own. That is why we speak of the many "arts" and "sciences." This peculiarity of knowledge makes it "similar" to one of the ultimate "beginnings" (*archai*) of all being (and one of the main themes of the *Sophist*), to "The Other" (*tháteron*), the "oneness" of which is nothing but its being divided throughout into "parts" (258 d 7 – e 3), as its very name indicates, for an "other" is always an "other of an other" (*heteron heterou*).[31] It is this *archê* on which the difference between any one thing and any other thing depends and from which all duality and plurality stem; it makes the multiplicity of things and ultimately, therefore, a "world" possible. The meaning of "oneness" in the case of "The Other," as in the case of "knowledge," is thus difficult to grasp. We might well ask: Is "The Other" at all "one"? Is knowledge "one"? And is each of them a "whole"? And do not these rather extravagant questions apply also to "human excellence," considering the Socratic dictum linking it with "knowledge"?[32] Did not this extravagant aspect of the search for the *one aretê* prompt Socrates to say a while ago "no wonder" in reply to Meno's admission that he could not find it?[33]

The extravagance of these questions and the peculiar way of arriving at them justify the stand taken by Meno as to the multiple aspect of excellence at the beginning of the dialogue, a stand to which Meno, with Socrates' help, reverts all the time, as they justify Gorgias and the opinion commonly and generally held in this matter. The question about the *whole* of human excellence is not within the scope of ordinary discourse, be it colloquial or even, in the usual meaning of the word, "technical." In this sense, Socrates, in saying what he last said, is indeed saying "nothing." Contrasted with the common opinion about human excellence, Socrates' insistence on

31. See, for example, *Parm.* 164 c 1 f.
32. Cf. pp. 43 and 60.
33. Cf. p. 56.

the aspect of its "wholeness" (here, in the *Meno,* as well as in other dialogues) seems to demand less an answer than a wondering reflection as to what underlies our ordinary speaking and thinking on that subject, seems to demand a pause, a turning away from the habitually accepted to its hidden "background," as a precondition for looking at the "wholeness" of things.[34] In this sense, Socrates, in saying what he last said, is saying "everything."[35]

As to Meno himself, asking him to disregard the familiar "parts" of human excellence in his attempt to reveal the "whole" of it, under the pretense that those parts are "unknown" as long as the whole is not known, means asking him to abandon the ground on which he stands. From what we have learned about Meno so far, we can hardly expect him to comply with this radical demand; nor can we expect him to see through Socrates' misleading rejection of the use of the "unknown." Still, Meno's reassertion of the rightness of that rejection permits Socrates to pursue his questioning for our, if perhaps not for Meno's, benefit.

34. Cf. *Rep.* VI, 486 a.
35. Cf. Leo Strauss, *What is Political Philosophy?* 1959, pp. 38 f.; also *Natural Right and History,* 1953, pp. 122 f.

IV

1.

[79 e 5 – 80 c 6] This time, Socrates' question is more direct and more blunt. "Then answer again and anew (*palin ex archês*): What do both of you, you and your friend, say that human excellence is?" We understand that, were Meno to answer now, it would indeed mean an entirely new undertaking on his part. His memory would be of no help to him. But no new answer is forthcoming: there is no third attempt on Meno's part to cope with the problem of excellence. Meno has had enough of this "game." He has enough of being constantly on the defensive. He evidently decides to "regain the initiative" and to do that by using a rather common device: he is going to attack Socrates himself.

Even before he had conversed with Socrates, says Meno, he had been hearing that all Socrates was wont to do was to put himself in a state of perplexity (*aporein*) and to make others feel perplexed, too; that is what he, Meno, is experiencing now—finding himself full of perplexity (*aporia*), a victim apparently of Socrates' "magic" jugglery. According to Gorgias' (and *not only* Gorgias') standards, which Meno has made his own[1] this is an undignified, nay, ridiculous position to be in. Since it has come to that—the crowd about Meno is watching—he, Meno, is going to reciprocate and poke fun at Socrates, too.

There appears very definitely to exist, says Meno, the greatest similarity, "in looks and otherwise," between Socrates and that well-known seafish, the torpedo: whoever comes close to it and touches it is benumbed by it, and Socrates seems to have had a similar effect on him, Meno. His soul and his mouth, says Meno, have become numb, truly numb, so that he is unable to find and to give the answer which ought to be on the tip of his tongue, since, in the past, he has spoken so often, and so well, he thought, about human excellence—and to so many people. And now he cannot even (*oude*) say what it

1. Cf. p. 41.

is, all in all (cf. 71 a 6, b 3, 5) .[2] (We note: Meno obviously
thinks that that is *the least* he should be able to say. Considering his surprise at Socrates' inability to state what human excellence, all in all, is,[3] Meno must indeed feel humiliated and
ashamed to see himself in a position no better than that of
Socrates.) Meno is angry and he utters something that
amounts to a threat: Socrates is well advised not to go abroad,
for if he indulged in this kind of practice in a foreign city, he
would probably be arrested as a juggler, a "magician" (*goês*) .
There is an ominous ring about this remark, if we think of
the association—mentioned later in the dialogue—between
Meno and Anytus, one of the men who brought Socrates to
trial.[4]

This is Socrates' answer to Meno's gibe: Clever rogue (*panourgos*) that you are, Meno, you almost beguiled me. Now,
how so? asks the (probably) surprised Meno. Socrates: "I perceive the reason why you drew an image of me." Meno:
"Why do you think I did?" Socrates: "That I might reciprocate in drawing one of you. This I do know of all beautiful
youths, that they are delighted when images are made of them,
for theirs is the gain: the images of beautiful youths are beautiful also, aren't they? *But I shall not reciprocate by drawing
an image of you.*"

Let us try to understand what this exchange means in the
context of the dialogue.

As once before,[5] in the case of *kai egô* and *kai sy*, there is
some bantering going on here, this time about "reciprocity."
And the scales are, as they were then, highly uneven. Meno
takes "revenge" for the ridicule he thinks Socrates has in-
flicted upon him by mocking Socrates in the image of the
numb-fish. He also calls Socrates a *goês*. This is a term used
often enough in Platonic dialogues,[6] and perhaps also in contemporary polite conversation, to describe a "crafty" one, a
"sophist." Socrates counters by calling Meno, jokingly, to be
sure, a *panourgos* (and underscores this appellation a little
later on – 81 e 6) .[7] This again is a term peculiarly well suited
to characterize a "sophist," perhaps more so than any other,
for "to know all things" (*panta epistasthai*) [8] and "to know

2. Cf. pp. 40 f.
3. Cf. p. 41.
4. Cf. Thompson, p. 111 (21).
5. Cf. p. 56.
6. *Symp.* 203 d 8; *Rep. X*, 598 d 3; *Soph.* 235 a 8; *Statesman* 291 c 3.
7. Cf. Aristotle, *Nic. Eth.* VI, 12, 1144 a 23–28.
8. *Soph.* 233 a 3 (cf. 239 c 6: πανούργως).

how to make and to do all things without exception by a single art" (*poiein kai dran miai technêi synapanta epistasthai pragmata*) [9] is the ultimate claim either explicitly made[10] or tacitly implied in the "profession" of a sophist. But this mutual "name calling" has no parallel in a mutual "image drawing." When, according to Socrates himself, it seems to be Socrates' turn to present an image of Meno, he refuses to play the game.[11] Why?

Is it not, because there is no need for any image? Meno's soul, in Meno's lifetime, will presumably be stripped "naked" by Socrates[12]: Meno will be shown as what he *is*, for all to see. The stripping has already gone pretty far. Socrates' emphatic refusal to draw an image of Meno prepares us, we suspect, for the final stage of Meno's "undressing." And in that sense there is full, if still uneven, reciprocity in the exchange of threats: what is at stake though, whatever Meno might think, is not Socrates' life, nor Meno's for that matter, but for both of them their *aretê*, their excellence. And there is no telling what a faithful image of Meno, the "beautiful," might look like.

[80 c 6 – e 5] Socrates questions the faithfulness of the torpedo image, because it is not clear whether the fish, while benumbing those who touch it, is or is not benumbed itself. As for himself, says Socrates, he shares the perplexity he plunges others into. It is his own state of perplexity, above all, which makes him convey that state to others. If the fish, says Socrates, is subject to torpor too, then he, Socrates, indeed resembles it; otherwise, he does not. Whereupon he tries to appease Meno and to return to the main question again: "So now, as to human excellence, I do not know what it is, while you perhaps knew it indeed in the past, before you touched me, but now [having touched me] you are, no doubt, like one who does not know. Be that as it may, I want to consider, with you, what human excellence is and to search for it, in common with you."

9. *Soph.* 233 d 9–10 (cf. *Rep.* X, 598 c 7 – d 5; *Theaet.* 177 a 7–8; *Euthyd.* 300 d 7–8).
10. Cf. *Hipp. min.* 368 b 2 – e 2, where—in addition to reckoning, geometry, and astronomy—the various arts in which Hippias is supposed to be exceedingly competent are listed; among them τὸ μνημονικὸν τέχνημα (d 6–7 – cf. 369 a 7) is particularly stressed.
11. Cf. *Rep.* VI, 487 e 6 ff. (see Thompson, p. 112).
12. Cf. *Charm.* 154 d – e; *Laches* 187 e – 188 a: *Theaet.* 162 b 3; 169 a 6 – b 4; *Gorg.* 523 c – e; 524 d; also *Rep.* VI, 487 e 6 and below p. 190, note 71.

It is at this point that Meno raises a crucial objection. Judging from Socrates' (amplifying as well as simplifying) recapitulation of it,[13] it belongs to the arsenal of well-known themes and arguments stored up in Meno's memory, as we might have expected.

How can you search for something, says Meno, of which you know nothing at all? What sort of thing of all the things you do not know will you set as the goal of your search? And even if you were lucky enough to hit at its very center, how could you know that it is the thing you did not know?

Socrates: "Yes, I do understand what sort of thing you want to say, Meno." And, with reference to Meno's sea fishing expedition that had just yielded the torpedo, Socrates continues: "Look how eristic[14] this argument you are landing (*katageis*[15]) is! [It says] namely that it is not given to man to search [for anything], neither for what he knows nor for what he does not know: he certainly would not search for what he knows, for he knows it and there is no need then for any search; nor would he search for what he does not know, for he would not know what to search for."

We cannot help observing that, whatever the effect of the torpedo, *this argument* must definitely produce torpor and numbness in those who accept its validity, for they would not make the vain attempt to improve their understanding, no matter what the subject might be, would not make any move in this direction and would "stay put,"[16] contentedly and unashamedly slothful (*argoi* – 86 b 9). It will be Meno's privilege then, if he puts this argument to use to benumb other people as well as himself.

There are other observations to be made on this occasion.

1. While Socrates, in restating the argument with great precision, speaks of those who "know" as well as of those who do "not know," Meno does not mention the "knowers" at all.

2. Meno's attack has brought up a theme that has not been explicitly touched upon in the conversation so far, the theme of "searching" (*zêtein*) and "learning" (*manthanein*). We do remember, however, a certain stress on the word *manthanein* (with its double meaning of "understanding" and "learn-

---

13. Especially from the way the word "τοῦτον" (80 e 2) is emphasized. See also *Euthyd.* 275 d 2 ff. (cf. Thompson, pp. 113 f.).

14. Cf. p. 62, note 21.

15. Cf. Homer, *Odyssey* XIX, 186, where Odysseus reports to his wife, lovingly and lyingly, how the force of the wind landed him (κατήγαγεν) in Crete.

16. Cf. p. 44.

ing"[17]) (72 d 1, 2; 74 b 3; 75 e 6), the ambiguous use of the term *zêtoumenon*[18] and the strong emphasis, mostly in connection with the effort Meno was invited to make, on the word *peiran* (73 c 6; 75 a 1, 8; b 8; d 7; 77 a 5). Meno, as we have seen, was conspicuously reluctant to make the effort Socrates requested of him. It seems that his behavior throughout the conversation was in agreement with the consequence that flows from the argument he has just presented.

3. On its own merits, the argument does not lack persuasiveness, aside from a flaw. It presupposes a field of "holes," as it were, each "hole" representing something "unknown" and without any link to any other "hole." According to this view, anything "unknown" is separated and isolated from everything else. This view ignores the way the "unknown" generally presents itself *as* an "unknown," circumscribed by questions that arise "naturally" whenever we become aware of some inconsistency or of a lack of connection between the "known" pieces of our experience. It is true, our familiarity with these "pieces" tends to obscure their intrinsic incompleteness as well as their mutual relationship. An attempt to refute the argument directly would inevitably confront us again with the problem of the "whole" and its "parts," not to mention the problems of "knowing" and "not knowing," of "question" and "answer," and of the structure of a world in which questioning and answering are possible at all. The argument goes to the roots of things.

[81 a 1 – b 3]   Meno has confidence in its strength. "Don't you think, this is a beautiful argument, Socrates?" he asks, almost triumphantly, as it seems. "No," says Socrates. Meno: "Can you tell me why?" "Yes," says Socrates. And he begins with considerable solemnity: "For I have heard men as well as women with an expert knowledge of the highest things (*ta theia pragmata*) . . . ."

Socrates does not finish the sentence. He pauses.

In Platonic dialogues there are many instances of Socrates' interrupting his speech. As a rule, such interruptions occur when Socrates is about to say something of rather crucial importance, when he comes near touching the truth. On such occasions he acts as if he were "looking at something within

17. Cf. *Euthyd.* 277 e 5 – 278 a 7; Aristotle, *Sophist. Elench.* 4, 165 b 32–34.
18. Cf. pp. 82–84.

himself" (*pros heauton ti skepsamenos*),[19] as he also sometimes
does, according to the testimony of Aristodemus and Alcibiades in the *Symposium,* when not engaged in discussions. At
those times he remains standing,[20] lost in search, impervious
to anything about him, reflecting (*synnoêsas*), that is, "turning his gaze back into himself."[21] These periods of intense
reflection may last a whole night.[22] But however intense and
prolonged, they do not seem to differ in kind from what happens to Socrates for short stretches of time while conversing
with others. We are witnessing such a short period of an "inward" gaze right now, and we cannot help wondering what
this pause portends and signifies.

The beginning, then, of Socrates' sentence ("For I have
heard men as well as women with expert knowledge of the
highest things . . .") is followed by a moment, at least, of
silence. Into this silence Meno, rather impatiently, injects himself with the words: "Say what?" "Something true, as far as I
can see, and noble," is Socrates' most gentle rebuke. But
Meno, stirred up, keeps on: "What is it and who are the
speakers?" Socrates' measured reply does not provide Meno
with any specific information about the latter point. It says
no more than that the speakers are (a) priests and priestesses
of a certain kind, to wit, those who have made it their business
to be able to give a reasoned account (*logon didonai*) of the
sacred things they have the care of, and (b) many poets, again
of a certain kind—Pindar is among them—those, that is, who
combine their skill in the use of words with the capacity to
reach up to the highest, the divine, levels. What is being
stressed by Socrates in either case is that both a certain close-
ness to the highest order of things (*to theion*) and an ability
to speak (*legein*), not babble, about it are indispensable in
dealing with the difficult matter at hand. Then, finally, Socrates turns to *what* these people say, not without warning
Meno: "But consider whether they seem to you to speak the
truth."

It is clear that there is quite a divergence in aim and interest between Meno and Socrates at this point. While Socrates is concerned about the argument brought into the dis-

19. *Phaedo* 95 e 7. Cf. *Phaedr.* 277 d 4 – 6.
20. *Symp.* 175 a 7–9; 220 c 3–5.
21. *Symp.* 174 d 5: . . . τὸν οὖν Σωκράτη ἑαυτῷ πως προσέχοντα τὸν
νοῦν . . . . (Cf. *Charm.* 160 d 5–6 and e 2–3).
22. *Symp.* 220 c, d.

cussion by Meno, about the right way of settling the question raised in it and the truth of the matter itself, Meno, aroused by Socrates' solemnity, seems to sense an opportunity to add something "new" to the treasures of his vast storehouse, his memory. He is, therefore, interested no less in the names of the authors than in the content of what promises to be a memorable piece of wisdom Socrates is about to divulge.

We understand that this divergence between Socrates and Meno was foreshadowed in the syntax of the sentence which invited Meno to report what he and Gorgias thought about human excellence and which alluded to the discrepancy between knowing something and knowing what somebody else has said about that something.[23] We should note that Socrates, too, is now preparing himself to report what he has *heard* other people say.

2.

[81 b 3 – d 4]   This, then, is the story Socrates has to tell, as he claims, from hearsay, and which he attributes to a select, if, on the whole, anonymous, group of people. And we should not forget that this story is meant to counterbalance Meno's argument about the impossibility of learning.

The soul of man is deathless. Sometimes it ends its sojourn in this world of ours—we call this "dying"—and sometimes it comes back into it—we call this "being born"—but it never perishes. . . . Since it is deathless and has been born into this world of ours many times and since it has thus been seeing (*eôrakyia*) the things of this world and the things of the nether world, has been seeing *all* things, there is nothing that it has not learned, nothing, therefore, it does not know (*memathêken*). No wonder, then, that, when in this world, it is able to recollect (*anamnêsthênai*) what it already knew before about excellence and other things; for all that has come into being (*physis hapasa*) is connected in kinship and, since the soul has learned and, therefore, knows (*memathêkyias*) all things, a man, if he only recollects or, as we say, "learns" one single thing, is perfectly capable of coming up with (capable of recollecting) all the others, provided that man has courage and does not grow tired of searching.

The train of thought just reproduced is interrupted[24] in Socrates' account by a contention related to the main theme

23. Cf. p. 45.
24. Cf. Thompson, p. 120 (30); Bluck, p. 277.

not directly, but as an important corollary: because of the soul's deathless nature and its only temporary sojourn in our world (*dia tauta*) one ought to live one's life here in a manner most pleasing to divinity (*hôs hosiôtata*). It is this corollary which is supported by a quotation from Pindar, while the main theme receives support from Pindar's verses only by implication. These verses, which occupy the middle position in Socrates' account, speak of souls that have paid the penalty for an ancient wrong and, thus purified, are sent by Persephone, after a period of time ("in the ninth year"), back from Hades to the light of our sun; it is from these souls that illustrious kings and men of lightning-like strength and of surpassing wisdom arise, whom mankind then calls heroes without blemish for all time to come.

Pindar's verses sing the excellence of certain men. And we see that in Socrates' account of what he heard other people say the song of excellence is "enveloped" by the theme of learning.

The connection apparently implied between the soul's deathless nature and human excellence on this earth is that, unless the soul were deathless, Persephone would not be able to accept the penalty for certain crimes and could not release the perpetrators of those crimes from the bonds of Hades. This nexus remains somewhat obscure.

The theme of learning is not presented here in an argument. It is taken up in a story, a myth. We should look more closely at its characteristic features.

1. As in any myth, a temporal sequence of actions and events is described,[25] in terms taken from our common experience but not always left commensurate with it. The soul, although not subject to death, is yet subject to change. Not only does it change its abode at certain intervals of time—it has been learning for quite a while in the past. It is implied that that process of "learning" has come to an end: the verb is used twice in the perfect tense. The soul, therefore, knows. But the use of the perfect tense is not without ambiguity: if the assertion that the soul has been "learning" at some time past were to be taken literally, Meno's crucial objection could be fully applied to the initial "learning" of the undying soul itself.

2. This "learning," however, is characterized as "seeing." Since part of the time, at least, the soul is presumably without

25. Cf. *Rep.* III, 392 c 6 – d 4.

a body and, therefore, lacks the organs of sense, what it has "seen" is not all visible and the meaning of seeing itself cannot be the familiar one.

3. A most important passage in Socrates' account is the statement, almost casually made, that *"all* that has come into being is connected in kinship" (*tês physeôs hapasês syngenous ousês*), because without this assumption the entire account would not hold together. By virtue of this assumption everything, every bit the soul recollects can be understood as a "part" of a *"whole"* and can be traced back to a common origin. The word *physis* is attuned to the assumption of kinship, of a common ancestry (the *syngeneia*) of *all* that is. This assumption makes the world a "whole."

4. The learning or seeing embraces all, not necessarily visible, things. At a certain time the soul must have been filled with *complete* knowledge. We commonly associate, however darkly and hazily, the word "soul" with phenomena of life, with living—and, therefore, dying—beings, with "animate" beings. Here the soul seems to acquire a somewhat different status, considering that it is outside the grip of death and is, furthermore, the ultimate recipient of *knowledge*. The mythical account of "learning" seems to imply a meaning of "soul" which differs from the commonly accepted one: "soul" appears to be linked to all-comprehensive knowledge as well as to the aspect of the world as a "whole." It is presumably this *all*-comprehending character of the "soul" and its relation to the whole in its wholeness that make it possible to assign the content of the myth to the highest or divine levels. For "things divine" (*ta theia pragmata*) are the "highest" because they are all-comprehensive.

5. Our ability to recollect forgotten things, whenever we are rather mysteriously aware of their being forgotten, and to do this deliberately, actively, "with an effort," depends on our power to "look *into* ourselves." We reminisce best when we close our eyes. The myth emphasizes this aspect of our recollecting and learning power: the accumulated "knowledge" is "inside," is "within" the soul.

6. Courage and tireless searching on the part of the "learner" are mentioned in a conditional clause at the very end of Socrates' account. But we are left wondering whence the courage to undertake the search might come and how one could expect to sustain the tireless effort for that search. And yet, as Socrates will make clear in a moment and repeat emphatically later on, the emphasis on that courage and that

tireless effort is more relevant to him than anything else in
the story we have just heard him telling.

The next sentence, "For searching and learning, one has to [81 d 4 – 82 b 8]
conclude, are altogether recollection" (*to gar zêtein ara kai to
manthanein anamnêsis holon estin*), seems to indicate as
much the story's own conclusion as the inference Socrates himself is drawing from it. It is perhaps significant that the boundary between the story Socrates claims to tell "from hearsay"
and his own contribution to, or interpretation of, it is not
easily discernible. But it is certainly Socrates who, in what
immediately follows, insists on opposing to the argument
about the impossibility of learning, championed by Meno,
the main lesson to be derived from the myth of recollection.
That argument, he says, should not be listened to because it
would make us slothful and can be sweet music only to the
ears of the weak, while the story he has just told makes us
active and eager to engage in searching. Trusting in its truth,
Socrates prods Meno once more, he is prepared to search for
the answer to the question, "What is human excellence?" in
common with Meno.

"Yes," says Meno, who is evidently preoccupied with what
he has heard. He seems particularly interested in the allega-
tion that, properly speaking, there is no "learning." Is not
the assertion that what is called learning is but "recollection"
(*anamnêsis*) an echo of his own experience, his own "memorizing"?[26] What about that? Could not Socrates teach him
(*didaxai*) that this is so?

Clearly, Meno does not realize that his request contradicts
itself: he wants to learn that one does not learn.

We might feel inclined to teach Meno a lesson by telling
him about this contradiction. But would not this telling make
us similarly assailable? All of us are indeed likely to commit
the same error. Socrates is not willing to follow this pattern.
Instead of pointing his finger at Meno's fallacy, he imputes to
Meno the intention to involve him, Socrates, in a fatal contradiction. For Socrates' story implies that there is no such
thing as "teaching" (*didachê*), if teaching is conceived as an
activity that "pours" knowledge into the pupil: if learning
consists in "recollecting," the pupil can find knowledge not in
the words uttered by somebody else, but only in what he finds
within himself. And in attributing to Meno that clever intention, Socrates again throws the epithet *panourgos* at Meno,

26. Cf. p. 72, note 2.

reminding Meno, and us, that he had already done so a short while ago.

Meno candidly swears that nothing was farther from his mind and, by explaining why he said what he said, puts his own seal on Socrates' previous characterization of his ways as well as on the impression we have gained of him.[27] "I spoke from habit," are his words. Indeed, he always wants to be "told." In this case, he wants to be shown more reliably that learning is what Socrates says it is—which seems quite reasonable and legitimate—and he asks Socrates to undertake this showing,[28] if the latter knows of any way in which that can be done. "It isn't easy, though," is Socrates' reaction to Meno's plea. (We cannot help comparing this cautious attitude of Socrates with the self-assurance displayed by Meno when, in the beginning of the dialogue, he made his speech about human excellence.[29] And the very fact that this comparison forces itself on us reminds us that what is at stake, in the present exchange about learning as well as in the "showing" which follows it, is still human excellence.) Nevertheless, Socrates continues, he is willing to make an attempt to satisfy Meno, for Meno's sake. He is going to "exhibit"—to Meno, to the crowd about him and to us—that "learning is recollecting": he will not talk "about" it, for that would serve no good purpose, would be "teaching" in the sense rejected by him; he will make manifest what he means by presenting a case of actual "recollecting." It will be an *epideixis*.

Socrates invites Meno to call forward one of the many attendants who surround him, anyone he wishes, so that Socrates may perform the exhibition on him (*en toutôi*). Meno obliges. A young slave steps forward. Socrates makes sure that he and the boy speak the same language.[30] And, before addressing the boy, Socrates asks Meno to pay close attention (*proseche . . . ton noun*) to what is going to happen so as to be able to judge whether the boy is recollecting by himself or is learning from Socrates. Meno says that he will. So shall we.

The stage is set for the "exhibition."

---

27. Cf. pp. 41, 58, 69, 71.
28. Meno uses the word "ἐνδείξασθαι" which, *in the present context* and in agreement with Socrates' (though not Meno's) view, could well be translated by "immonstration." (Cf. Ast, *Lexic. Platon.*, vv. ἐνδείκνυμι and ἔνδειξις, also A. E. Taylor, *A Commentary on Plato's Timaeus*, p. 317.) See *Statesman* 277 d 1–2.
29. See p. 46.
30. Cf. *Charm.* 159 a 6–7.

Let us not forget that the more important *epideixis* is the one in which Meno himself is the main participant. The most "telling" part of this *epideixis* began with Meno's raising the question about the possibility or impossibility of learning. It now seems to approach a climactic point.

We have to realize that the dialogue, at this stage, will proceed on three levels simultaneously, the first two of which are "imitations." There will be (a) a conversation between Socrates and the young slave, in which the latter is supposed to "learn" something and to show, by the manner in which he does it, that his learning is nothing but recollection. There is (b) Meno (with his crowd about him) who is urged to watch that conversation in order to learn (that is, to "recollect") that "learning is recollecting." And finally (c) we, the readers or listeners, have to watch Meno's and the slave's performances, presented to us as imitations of actions, in order to learn (that is, to "recollect") *our* lesson about human excellence.

Although all three levels interlock, we shall try, in what follows, to separate them one from another as far as possible.

4.

The young slave has to find the answer to a question which, [82 b 9 – 85 b 7] in "technical" terms, can be formulated as follows: given the length of the side of a square, how long is the side of the square the area of which is double the area of the given square? Since the boy had never previously had any instruction in matters geometrical, as we might guess and as will be stated explicitly later (85 d 13 – e 6), "technical" language is reduced to a minimum and "orthodox" (synthetic) geometrical methods are not used at all in the conversation between him and Socrates. Moreover, as *we* know from the very beginning and as Meno presumably has heard before,[31] the given side and the side sought are "incommensurable magnitudes,"[32] and an answer in terms of the length of the given side is "impossible."[33] At best, this side can only be drawn or "shown." And Socrates will hint at this situation at every decisive turn of the search.

The process of finding the answer stretches through three

31. Cf. pp. 62, 64.
32. Cf. Euclid, *Elements* X, Def. 1.
33. If post-Cartesian notations and notions are barred.

stages apart from being interrupted twice by exchanges between Socrates and Meno which belong to the *epideixis* we are more urgently concerned with. These three stages parallel closely the three stages through which Socrates and Meno had been going—and have not yet finished going—in their discussion of human excellence considered in its "generality."

Stage 1 (82 b 9 – e 3). Socrates draws four lines enclosing a certain "space" (*chôrion*) in the dust (Fig. 1) and asks the boy whether he is familiar with the kind of "space" called "square space" (*tetragônon chôrion*).[34] The boy says he is. Socrates also draws the lines "through the middle" which make it easy to assign the length of two feet to the sides of that square. It is quickly ascertained that the space in question contains four ("square") feet. The question is: how long is the side of an area which is similarly shaped but twice as big, or, more "technically," what is the side of the double square?

Fig. 1

It is interesting to compare the phrase Socrates uses to exhort the boy to give his *first* answer to that question with the phrase Socrates used to exhort Meno before the latter's first attempt. Socrates had then said (73 c 6–7): make an attempt to tell—to recollect . . . ; he says now (82 d 8): make an attempt to tell me. The word "recollect" is omitted now. In Meno's case, it was Gorgias' saying that was to be recollected. In the boy's case, any "recollecting" to be done would be of something the boy himself already "knows" or, speaking mythically, of something the soul "in" him "knew before." There is no point in exhorting the boy to "recollect"—he would not understand what he is being asked to do—he is just to do it.

Nor can the boy see that the word *pêlikos* (82 d 8) Socrates uses, in this first exhortation, with regard to the line in question hints at the non-numerical character of the expected answer.[35] In its "technical" meaning, the word *pêlikos* refers mostly to continuous magnitudes (not to discrete units the assemblage of which form a "number" and which we "count" whenever we assign a "number" to something) and implies, therefore, possible "incommensurability."[36]

We observe, finally, that before the boy has had a chance

---

34. The term τετράγωνος is both "technical" (cf. Euclid, *Elements* I, Def. 22) and easily understandable, but χωρίον—like πέρας (cf. p. 65, note 31)—is of a more colloquial nature. In Euclid χωρίον is used (cf. *Elements* X, Def. 2) but not defined.

35. Cf. ἀπὸ ποίας γραμμῆς – 83 c 3–4; e 11 f.; 85 b 1–2 and ὁποία – 82 e 5.

36. Cf. Euclid, *Elements* V, Def. 3.

to answer Socrates rephrases the question in such a way as to make the boy's answer almost inevitable: "The side of this space here [pointing to Fig. 1] is two feet long. What will be that of the other space which is double?" Boy: "Obviously (*délon dé . . . hoti . . .*[37]) double that length, Socrates."

Stage 2 (82 e 14 – 83 e 2). The boy is quickly refuted. Socrates draws (Fig. 2) four lines, each twice as long as each line in the previous drawing and, by a series of questions, lets the boy see that the resulting "square space" is *four* times the previous one, while only a double one was wanted. This second figure also helps Socrates to prepare the way for the boy's second attempt. The preparation culminates in Socrates' asking: "Will not [the double space] result from a line longer than that one [pointing to a side in Fig. 1] and shorter than this one [pointing to a side in Fig. 2]?"[38] and in his drawing the conclusion, in form of a question, that the side of the double space must be longer than the one of two feet and shorter than the one of four feet. The boy assents.

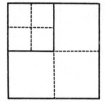

Fig. 2

Then Socrates again exhorts the boy to provide the answer to the problem posed (83 e 1). As in the exhortation preceding Meno's second attempt (77 a 5), *peirô* is again used; also, the word *pêlikos*, the full meaning of which escapes the boy, reappears. Again, almost inevitably comes the boy's *second* answer: the length of the side of the double space will be "three feet."

Stage 3 (83 e 2 – 84 a 2; 84 d 3 – 85 b 7). The boy's second answer is easily refuted by the drawing of a new figure (Fig. 3), in which each side of the given square is extended to the length of three feet. The resulting "square space" will be, as the questioning brings out, one of nine ("square") feet, not one of eight, as required. "Three feet," therefore, cannot be the precise length of the line in question.

Without further "preparation" Socrates exhorts the boy for the third time to give the answer they are after: "Make an attempt (*peirô*) to tell us [that answer] precisely (*akribôs*). And if you don't want to count [so as to indicate the *number* of feet] (*arithmein*), just *show* (*deixon*) from what line [the double square will result]." We see that once more, and this time as clearly as he can under the circumstances, Socrates points to the incommensurability of the line given and the line sought.

Fig. 3

37. Cf. Thompson, p. 131 (36); Bluck, p. 296.
38. The words "τοσαύτης" (83 c 8) and "τοσησδί" (d 1) point to the fact that the length of these lines is *countable*.

The boy's emphatic reaction to that exhortation is that he really does not know. His *aporia* is evident.

To help the boy out of this perplexity, Socrates goes back to his first drawing and completes it (Fig. 4) so as to have, as in Fig. 2, a square space of sixteen ("square") feet. The drawing of the new figure is done by Socrates while he continues his questioning and makes sure that the boy "understands" (*manthaneis?* – 84 d 4) and remembers what was said before (*ê ou memnêsai?* – 84 e 3). And it is Socrates again who finally draws the diagonals inside the four squares (each equal to the given one) that constitute the new figure. Each diagonal cuts each of the small squares in half and all four diagonals are equal in length, as the boy can see (or thinks that he can see). Socrates invites the boy to consider the space contained by these diagonals and asks: "How large is this space?" (*pêlikon*[39] *ti esti touto to chôrion?*) The boy has no answer: he cannot follow Socrates at this point. All he says is: "I do not understand" (*ou manthanô*). Through a series of questions it becomes clear that that space (four halves of the small squares) is precisely (*akribôs*) the double of the given square. The solution of the problem is at hand. "From what line [does the double square result]?" asks Socrates. And the boy, pointing to a diagonal, says: "From this one." With considerable gravity Socrates puts a seal on this conclusion: "If 'diagonal' be the name of such a line [as the "experts" call it], then, as you, Meno's slave, say, the double space results from the diagonal." The boy has the last word: "Very definitely so, Socrates!"

The straight question-answer pattern in all this exchange between Socrates and the young slave is interrupted only once by a seemingly marginal "pedagogical" remark on Socrates' part. Replying to one of Socrates' suggestive questions, the boy says (83 d 1): "Yes, it seems to me that this is so" (*Emoige dokei houtô*). Whereupon Socrates: "Excellent! What seems to you [to be true] (*to . . . soi dokoun*), just that keep answering!"[40] It is the boy's *own* opinions that Socrates wants to hear. But does not Socrates "manipulate" those opinions throughout in a rather transparent way?

We have to consider this question as well as the entire "exhibition" of the young slave carefully, before turning back to the main *epideixis* involving Meno himself.

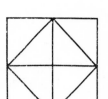

Fig. 4

39. Cf. Euclid, *Elements* X, Def. 2–4, and above p. 100.
40. Cf. Thompson, p. 236 (4); Bluck, p. 300.

1. In almost half of all the questions and answers nothing but the boy's most elementary counting and reckoning skill is being taxed. Only slightly fewer in number are the questions and answers dealing with purely "geometrical" properties of the figures drawn, but, however plausible and even correct the answers may be, they lack technical precision and reliability. Only a few of Socrates' questions, in fact only the one immediately following his first exhortation and those immediately preceding his second exhortation, are calculated to elicit patently false answers from the boy. But these few are indeed decisive for the "exhibition." Furthermore, the direction that the inquiry takes is completely determined by the order of the questions that Socrates asks. Finally, it is Socrates who draws all the figures and, above all, the diagonals on which the solution of the problem entirely depends.

It can, therefore, be justly said that Socrates puts the answers into the boy's "mouth." Does he put them in the boy's "mind"?

2. All questions Socrates asks, except the main one, permit only three types of answer: (a) "yes," (b) "no," (c) the result of some counting or reckoning. Accordingly, the boy's replies are either straight in the affirmative (most of the time, in fact), or straight (and even emphatically – 83 b 7) in the negative, or simply arithmetical. There are only three deviations from this pattern, all related directly to the main question: (a) the boy's emphatic assertion of ignorance ("I do not know" – 84 a 2), (b) his initial helplessness with regard to the square formed by the four diagonals ("I do not understand" – 85 a 4 f.), (c) his pointing to the diagonal (85 b 2). The "arithmetical" answers are all correct, except for the two brought about by Socrates' "suggestive" questions. The questions leading to the refutation of these two false answers require no change in the pattern of the answers. To decide, then, whether Socrates puts the answers "into the boy's mind," or, in other words, whether he "manipulates" the boy's opinions, means to gauge the significance of the boy's "yes" and "no."

3. Disregarding for a moment the possibility of our being perplexed, what makes us choose the answer "yes" or the answer "no" in the case of a question that confronts us with nothing but this alternative? Do we actually have a choice in

this matter? We do, but this choice is not between the "yes" and the "no," but between two possible ways of arriving at the answer.

We may make our answer depend on something not related to what the question is about, as, for instance, on our desire to please or to harm other people, on the urge to satisfy our vanity, on the pursuit of some cherished plans, or simply, and most frequently, on what we have heard other people say, persuasively or even casually. And this way may be chosen, whether the question concerns itself with what *happened* to us or around us in the past up to the present moment or with our *thoughts* on any possible subject.

On the other hand, we may make our answer depend uniquely on the matter that the question is concerned with. If the question is about *events* involving us in some manner, we would try to give, as we say, a "truthful" account of them, regardless of the subsequent effects this accounting may have. If the question asks what we *think* about a given subject, we would try to find and to state what seems *necessarily* inherent in, or connected with, that subject. It is this kind of question that both the slave and Meno have to answer.[41]

But how can we possibly find the necessity inherent in, or connected with, a given subject matter except through and in our thinking (*dianoeisthai*) about it? The choice we have, so far as our answering is concerned, is thus the choice of submitting or of not submitting ourselves to the necessity revealed by our thinking. It is the only necessity that it is in our power to submit or not to submit to.

This second way of answering demands from us, therefore, that—while looking for the right answer—we look "*into* ourselves," if our thinking can be said to take place "inside" of us. (We never quite abandon this manner of speaking.) Have we not been witnessing such an inward gaze in the pause which preceded Socrates' reporting the story of "recollection"?

Regardless of the mistakes we are even then bound to make, this "looking into ourselves" can make us understand, can make us *learn*, that what the question puts before us is *necessarily* true or *necessarily* untrue and can compel us, consequently, to answer "yes" or "no," as the case may be.

4. The two ways of answering are two ways of arriving at an "opinion" (*doxa*). We may confirm or deny the "proposi-

41. Cf. *Charm.* 165 b 5 ff.

tion" contained in the question, and thereby utter an opinion, for "extraneous" reasons, especially by "repeating" what other people say, as we do most of the time. Or we may assent to, or reject, that "proposition" by drawing the assent or the denial from ourselves. Such assent to, or rejection of, a proposition such *phasis* or *apophasis*,[42] constitutes an opinion of a different kind. It cannot be "induced" or "manipulated" because its source is not "outside" the person who holds it. It is the completion of our own thinking (*dianoias apoteleutêsis*[43]) on a given subject.

5. Has the boy followed the first or the second way? Did he answer somewhat haphazardly or perhaps with the purpose of pleasing Socrates? Or did we not rather have the opportunity to observe that *what* the boy (either falsely or correctly) assented to or rejected came from nobody else but Socrates, but that the *assent* and the *rejection* came from nobody but the *boy himself?* His "yes" and his "no" indicated what *he* held to be true or untrue: they represented *his* opinions no less than the arithmetical answers represented the results of *his* counting and reckoning.

We had the opportunity to observe this inasmuch as we, within ourselves, kept confirming, or disapproving of, the boy's answers and opinions. Socrates' marginal pedagogical remark[44] can indeed be understood as aimed no less at Meno and at us than as aimed at the boy. Had not Meno as well as we, the readers and listeners, been warned from the outset[45] to play close attention to the coming exchange?

6. Socrates' questions solicit and elicit—in this episode of the young slave no more than elsewhere—both false and correct answers. Indeed, Socrates' maieutic art, as we infer from what he says in the *Theaetetus* (150 b ff.; 210 b ff.), is more likely to make young men deliver "nonsense" (151 c 7) and "wind-eggs" (151 e 6; 210 b 9) than to make them deliver something "genuine and true" (150 c 3). But to submit oneself to refutation without getting angry and feeling disgraced is the first and indispensable step in the process of "giving birth" to something true, that is to say, in the process of learning. Facing the figures drawn before him on the dusty

---

42. *Soph.* 263 e 12 (cf. Aristotle, *Nic. Eth.* VI, 9, 1142 b 13–14).
43. *Soph.* 264 b 1. How this tentative or relative stage of completion is reached in our thinking—conditioned, as it usually is, by sense perceptions and opinions already firmly held—is vividly described in *Philebus* 38 b 12 – 39 c 6.
44. P. 102.
45. P. 98.

surface of the earth and listening to Socrates' provocative
questions, the young slave twice succumbs to a kind of superficial plausibility not unlike the one which characterizes the
"familiar" notions irrevocably commited to, and marked on,
Meno's memory.[46] Having been refuted, the boy reaches the
stage of complete perplexity without feeling disgraced and
ridiculed, and the subsequent questions of Socrates help him
to "see" the truth about the lines drawn by his "teacher,"
help him, in other words, to submit *himself* to reasons compelling him to accept that truth. A great deal, then, must
depend not only on the quality of the teacher but also on
the quality of the learner.

Socrates' role in this exchange of questions and answers is
to provide the condition under which the boy's learning can
take place. The "teacher" is not primarily *responsible* (*aitios*)
for the pupil's learning; this responsibility is the pupil's own.
But *without* the "teacher's" lead the pupil would not have
the opportunity to assume that responsibility. The crucial distinction made in the *Phaedo*[47] is directly applicable to the
pupil-teacher relationship: "One thing is what is truly *responsible* [for something], another thing is that without which
what is responsible could not possibly become [effectively]
responsible" (*allo men ti esti to aition tôi onti, allo de ekeino
aneu hou to aition ouk an pot' eiê aition*). To be unable to
make that distinction is a sign of "profound sluggishness" in
speaking and thinking (*pollê . . . kai makra rhathymia . . .
tou logou*[48]). If there be "teaching" and "learning," their
relationship could not be simply a "causal" one. Teaching
does not consist in speaking and insisting, learning not in
listening and repeating. The contrary view—it need hardly be
said that this is also Meno's view—is the prevailing one at
all times and not easy to correct.

But even though the teacher cannot "produce" knowledge
in the learner, cannot "pour" or "put" knowledge into the
learner's soul,[49] cannot be the "cause" of his learning, the
importance of the teacher in the process of learning matches
the importance of the learner's inner constitution. And in
providing the "necessary condition" for learning the teacher's role need not be confined to questioning. Other potent
teaching devices might "beget" in the soul of the learner not

46. Cf. pp. 47, 52 f., 55, 56, 61 f., 69–72.
47. 99 b 2–4.
48. *Ibid.*, 99 b 1–2.
49. Cf. *Symp.* 175 d; *Rep.* VII, 518 b/c (and above p. 97).

only an eagerness to learn, but also the desire to *act* in a certain way and thus to alter the conduct of his life.[50]

7. It is perhaps not unimportant to note that the boy learns *two* lessons at once, one implying the other: (a) that the space enclosed within the four diagonal lines *is* the double square, and (b) *what* the side of the square is.

8. So far as the conversation between Socrates and the young slave is concerned, Socrates certainly does not share the latter's perplexity, and yet Meno's torpedo image, in spite of what Socrates himself has said about it, could well be applied in this case, if only to the first two stages of the exhibition. In its last stage, however, Socrates, far from "be-numbing" his pupil, helps him to find his way out of the perplexity. Throughout the exhibition, Socrates seems to know all about the "double square," and it is this knowledge of his which enables him to play his role as a teacher. We are not certain, though, whether this situation will still pre-vail when, in his conversation with Meno, the problem of "human excellence" will be taken up again.

---

50. Cf. the τέχνη τῆς περιαγωγῆς – *Rep.* VII, 518 d 3 ff.

V

DIGRESSION:

ΑΝΑΜΝΗΣΙΣ AND ΜΝΗΜΗ

The exhibition thus presents a case of "teaching and learning" and makes us see both of them in their proper perspective: it makes us aware of the common misunderstanding
of them. That much we have indeed learned from witnessing
the event. The exhibition was designed, however, to clarify
the meaning of the myth told or retold by Socrates. No doubt
the myth lacked clarity and even persuasiveness. Meno was
perfectly justified in asking to be instructed about its content.
The exhibition was meant to show—to Meno and to us—that,
properly speaking, there is no learning—and no teaching
either—and that what goes under the name of "learning"
ought to be called "recollecting." Can *we* assent to that change
of names? Before we give or withhold our assent we have to
examine carefully not only what the term *anamnesis* by itself
implies but also, and above all, why this term, whenever it is
being related in Platonic dialogues to "learning," seems inseparably tied to a mythical frame. *Anamnesis* in that sense
is explicitly elaborated on in the *Meno* and the *Phaedo*, less
explicitly in the *Phaedrus*; it is lightly touched upon in the
Philebus, while its mention is avoided in the *Symposium*, the
Theaetetus and also the *Republic*, although the theme of
learning is certainly present in these latter dialogues.[1] We
shall have to consider what is said, and not said, in all these

---

1. The words ἀνάμνησις and ἀναμιμνήσκεσθαι occur, of course, often
enough in Platonic dialogues without any reference to the theme of
learning.

dialogues about recollecting, learning, and forgetting, even at
the risk of isolating these themes from the dramatic context in
which they appear.

1. ARISTOTLE'S TREATISE ON MEMORY AND RECOLLECTION

It might not be inappropriate to begin with an outline of
Aristotle's short treatise which has come down to us under the
title Περὶ μνήμης καὶ ἀναμνήσεως (449 b 3 – 453 b 11). This
treatise takes up the theme of recollection in a completely
non-mythical context, as a "topical" subject dealt with in certain other books (ἐν τοῖς ἐπιχειρηματικοῖς λόγοις – 451 a 19 f.[2]).
The same topic seems to underlie the composition of the
Meno. Aristotle's treatise could, in fact, be interpreted as a
sober commentary on the "abstracted" content of the dialogue,
as a transposition of the action presented there into a medium
free of any mythical encumbrance as well as of its dramatic
or mimetic counterpart. Conversely, in the light of that treatise, we can see how a topical subject provides the material
and texture for the construction of the mimetic action embodied in a Platonic dialogue.[3]

The treatise distinguishes sharply between μνημονεύειν and
ἀναμιμνήσκεσθαι (449 b 4–9). The first chapter deals with the
phenomenon of memory (μνήμη καὶ τὸ μνημονεύειν), the second with the activity of recollecting (ἀναμιμνήσκεσθαι).

Memories are about what happened in the *past*. Thus we
remember *that* and *what* we thought, learned, grasped immediately, heard and saw *in the past*. To remember is not
to have a sense perception or a notion of something "right
now," but to have or to experience these as having been had
or experienced in the past. Memories are time-laden. And because of their necessary connection with time, memories, although conceivably bearing on things severed from time, can
only be had by us as beings endowed with the power of sensing.
To remember something means to possess a more or less per-

---

2. Cf. *Top.* VIII, 11, 162 a 16, and Diog. Laert. V, 23, 24.
3. J. Freudenthal, "Zur Kritik und Exegese von Aristoteles' π ε ρ ὶ τ ῶ ν
κ ο ι ν ῶ ν σ ώ μ α τ ο ς κ α ὶ ψ υ χ ῆ ς ἔ ρ γ ω ν (*parva naturalia*), II,
zu de memoria," *Rheinisches Museum für Philologie*, Neue Folge, Bd.
24 (1869), pp. 403–4, clearly recognizes the similarity: "So stimmt
denn auch Ar. oft fast wörtlich mit Pl. überein". . . . "Um so
weniger darf man also in den ersten Worten [of the second chapter of
Aristotle's treatise] eine Polemik gegen Platon erblicken, wie sie manche
Commentatoren gewittert haben." Unfortunately, Freudenthal does
not do justice to Plato's treatment of ἀνάμνησις.

sistent image of that something as it happened or appeared in the past, comparable to a picture (ζωγράφημα – 450 a 32) or an imprint (τύπος) made by a seal ring (cf. 450 a 32 and b 16). In the terminology of the sixth and seventh books of the *Republic*[4] the faculty of remembering thus presents a special case of εἰκασία. Although Aristotle does not use that term, he devotes about a quarter of the chapter to the description and discussion of what is meant by it (450 b 12 ff.). To have a memory of something is tantamount to perceiving the "imprint"—a φάντασμα—as an *image* (ὡς εἰκών) of that which is no longer present (451 a 15). Some animals also seem to possess this ability (450 a 15–16).

On the other hand, to recollect something (τὸ ἀναμιμνήσκεσθαι or ἡ ἀνάμνησις) does not at all mean to have something "in one's memory"; nor does it mean to reacquire (ἀνάληψις) the same memory of that something, nor even to acquire (λῆψις) such a memory at all (451 a 20–21). "When one is [actively] learning (μάθῃ) or passively experiencing (πάθῃ) [something] for the first time one is neither reacquiring a memory [of that something], for there was none before, nor is one acquiring one initially; but when the [firm] possession (ἕξις) [of what is being learned] or[5] the [full] experience is achieved, then there is memory: memory does not arise while the experience is going on" (451 a 21–25). It takes time for memory to "materialize" and it is seldom in our power to have something "in our memory" or, as we say, to remember. To be able to retain something "in memory" easily, to have a "good memory," is usually not given to people who are quick and good at learning as well as at recollecting, but to the slow ones (449 b 7–8; 453 a 4–5),[6] provided they are not *too* slow (450 b 8). "On the other hand, when one is [deliberately] recapturing (ἀναλαμβάνῃ) some knowledge or sense perception of anything else *formerly had*, the [firm] possession of which we called memory, then [the action of] recollecting takes place and this is what recollecting any of those [things mentioned] means. Remembering, on its part, supervenes and memory ensues" (451 b 2–6).

The action of recollection is, in most cases, an active search (ζήτησίς τις) (451 b 22–23; 30 f.; 452 a 7 f.; 22–24; *453 a 15; 22*), and Aristotle indicates the rules which govern it or should govern it to make it most successful. In this connection

4. 511 e 1 f.; 534 a.
5. Cf. Freudenthal, *op. cit.*, p. 404.
6. Cf. *Theaet.* 194 e 3–4.

he distinguishes two types of sequences which occur in the
process of recollection, one of which is due to *necessity* (ἐξ ἀνάγκης), the other to *habit* (ἔθει) (451 b 11–14). Because of the concatenation or consequential "association" of the "motions" involved, it is possible for recollection to occur even without active search (451 b 23 ff.). Aristotle explicitly mentions that mathematical subjects (τὰ μαθήματα), because of the ordered sequence (τάξις τις) which leads to their being grasped, are especially fitted for being recollected and remembered (εὐμνημόνευτα) (452 a 3–4⁷).

It is noteworthy that, throughout the chapter, the main example of what can be recovered is "knowledge" (ἐπιστήμη). Special care is taken to restrict the reacquisition of knowledge to the action of recollection and to make it clear that knowing is not the business of memory. An object of knowledge can be an object of memory only indirectly, "accidentally" (κατὰ συμβεβηκός), inasmuch as that object may happen to be remembered *as* an object "known" (cf. 451 a 28–31). In this sense it is indeed possible for us (οὐθὲν κωλύει) to remember what we once knew. Special care is taken, too, *not* to identify learning and recollecting. Even learning or rediscovering something for the second time, i.e., re-acquiring "lost" knowledge, need not mean recollecting (451 b 7–9), because the action of recollection is characterized by the accompanying awareness that what is being recollected, including something previously "known," has been *forgotten*, while such awareness is lacking in the case of learning.[8] That is why one can recollect "by oneself" (δι' αὑτοῦ), while learning proceeds "through somebody else" (δι' ἄλλου), i.e., requires a teacher (452 a 4–8). Whatever may ultimately make our *learning* possible, an additional internal source (ἐνούσης πλείονος ἀρχῆς ἢ ἐξ ἧς μανθάνουσιν – 451 b 9 f.) is required for our being able to recollect. This source seems to be no other than the mysterious awareness of having *forgotten* what we knew in the past.

We infer from this exposition: (1) it is the *past* status of the objects of recollection *as well as* of memory which makes *anamnesis* appear akin to *mneme;* (2) that is why so often the terms "recollection," "reminiscence," "remembrance," "memory," are used synonymously albeit imprecisely;[9] (3) the

---

7. Cf. *Phaedo* 73 a/b.
8. Cf. G. R. T. Ross's edition of Aristotle's *De sensu and De memoria* (1906), p. 263, note to 451 b 7.
9. Cf. Freudenthal, *op. cit.*, p. 402.

faculty of *eikasia* seems to play a role in both *anamnesis* and *mneme;* (4) and most importantly, the phenomenon of "recollecting" cannot be considered without taking into account its "opposite," the phenomenon of "forgetting," while the phenomenon of "having something in one's memory" does not have "forgetfulness" as its "opposite": we either have or do not have memories, we either keep them or lose them, but we lose them without being aware of our losing them, without being aware of our forgetting. To become aware of our having forgotten something means to begin recollecting.[10]

The question arises: can Socrates—or Plato—be unaware of the distinction between "recollecting" and "learning"? Needless to say this distinction is not an invention of Aristotle but rather one that offers itself to any one reflecting on the phenomena of "recollection" and "learning." Does Socrates—or Plato—simply deny that there is a difference between them? Or does Socrates—or Plato—change the meaning of *anamnesis?* Or is something else involved in the identification of "recollection" and "learning" as well as in the correlated identification of "forgetfulness" and "ignorance"?

To be able to deal with all these questions we shall have to consider: (a) the meaning of εἰκασία in books VI and VII of the *Republic;* (b) an extension of that meaning implied in the *Republic;* (c) the relations between εἰκασία, διάνοια, and ἀνάμνησις in the *Phaedo;* (d) the theme of ἀνάμνησις and μνήμη in the *Phaedrus* and the *Philebus;* (e) the avoidance of the ἀνάμνησις thesis in other dialogues and the stress on μνήμη in the *Theaetetus;* (f) the significance of the mythical frame which surrounds the recollection thesis.

2. THE MEANING OF εἰκασία

The term εἰκασία is used, in the sixth book of the *Republic* (511 e 2), to describe one of the possible "states of the soul" (παθήματα ἐν τῇ ψυχῇ – 511 d 7). This πάθημα is made to correspond to a section of an imaginary line which Socrates offers for Glaucon's consideration. Later, in the seventh book (534 a), the term is assigned directly to that section of the line itself.

10. Cf. *Hist. anim.* I, 1, 488 b 25–26: "Memory as well as receptivity to teaching is common to many beings, but nothing except man is able to recollect" (καὶ μνήμης καὶ διδαχῆς πολλὰ κοινωνεῖ, ἀναμιμνῄσκεσθαι δὲ οὐδὲν ἄλλο δύναται πλὴν ἄνθρωπος).

There are only *two* main segments of the line (509 d 6 f.):
one corresponding to the domain of the intelligible (τὸ νοητόν
or τὸ νοούμενον) under the leadership of the Good, the other
to the domain of the visible (τὸ ὁρατόν or τὸ ὁρώμενον) under
the leadership of the Sun. We are at home in the realm of
the visible, but we do have access to the realm of the intelligible. The two segments of the line are unequal in size.[11]
Glaucon is invited to reproduce the ratio that these two segments have to each other twice by subdividing each of them
into two subsections. Thus, within the domain of the intelligible two ways of being engaged in thought are to be
distinguished, while the domain of the visible is to be understood to comprise two kinds of visible objects to which two
different "states of the soul" correspond.

Socrates deals first (509 e – 510 a) with the latter sub-
division beginning with the "last" or "lowest"[12] subsection.
To it belong all natural "images" (εἰκόνες),[13] all shadows, everything that might appear on surfaces of liquids or on surfaces
of compact, smooth, and shining bodies, and so on. The other
subsection of the visible domain encompasses all those objects
which the objects of the last subsection resemble (ἔοικεν – 510
a 5). That is to say it encompasses all the "originals" the
images of which constitute the objects of the last section—
encompasses all the "originals" which the objects of the last
section "image" or mirror. The latter objects *depend,* therefore, for their appearing as images before our eyes on all the
primary visible objects around us, such as animals and plants
and man-made things. This relation of dependency determines the degree of clarity (σαφήνεια) and lack of clarity
(ἀσάφεια) with which we perceive the two kinds of objects
within the visible domain: image and original (τὸ ὁμοιωθέν—
τὸ ᾧ ὡμοιώθη) are related to each other in the same way in
which what is merely conjectural or "imagined" or opined
(τὸ δοξαστόν) is related to what is actually cognized (τὸ
γνωστόν).[14] The relation of *dependency* between "image" and
"original" determines the degree of genuineness, the degree of

11. The context makes the version ἄν, ἴσα (509 d 6) in one of the codices
    improbable.
12. Cf. τῷ ἀνωτάτω—τῷ τελευταίῳ (511 d 8, e 2).
13. They are called later on (532 c 1) φαντάσματα θεῖα.
14. These terms take up the distinction made in book V, 476 d 5 ff.,
    especially 478 a 10 ff., and anticipate what is said later in book VII,
    534 a 3–8, about the two main segments of the line.
    There is an ironic ambiguity in the term τὸ δοξαστόν itself: it may
    also mean "what is held in honor" (cf. δεδοξασμένοις – 511 a 8).

"truth" (ἀλήθεια) in each of them. The relation between their respective shares in truth is mirrored in the ratio between the sizes of the two subsections, the very same ratio that obtains between the two main segments of the line.

Now, the two subsections of the visible domain also correspond to the two ways in which the two kinds of visible objects affect us.

Our relation to all the animate and inanimate things around us is one of unfathomable familiarity. Even things and surroundings with which we happen to be, as we say, "unfamiliar," have an index of familiarity on them that does not make it too difficult for us to deal with them, to respond to them. We are indeed "at home" among all the familiar and unfamiliar things and faces of the visible world. Our basic attitude towards them is one of unquestionable trust (πίστις) which extends far beyond any distrust or suspicion we might feel on occasion. Overwhelmingly, we trust that all the familiar features of the visible world are here to stay, that things are as we see them. The usual and the unusual, the expected and the unexpected, routine and novelty, are labels put on things and events within the frame of our all-embracing, all-familiar common experience.

The second kind of visible object, the various "images" of visible objects of the first kind, are no less familiar[15] to us, but they affect us in a peculiar way. Although, on occasion, we might not differentiate between them and the primary visible objects, we do not, as a rule, confuse an "image" with an "original." On the contrary, we are able to see, and do see, images *as images*. It is this πάθημα of the soul, this faculty[16] of ours, to see an image *as an image* that Socrates calls εἰκασία.

There is the temptation to overlook the crucial importance of εἰκασία in Socrates' account because it is assigned to the lowest section of the line.[17] We are warned by Socrates that his account leaves quite a few things unsaid (509 c 5–11; cf. also 534 a 5–8). But this much is clear from his description of the divided line: the pattern of εἰκασία on the lowest level anticipates similar patterns on higher levels of the line. Is not, indeed, the ability to exert the faculty of εἰκασία a prerogative

15. No less δοξαστά (cf. 534 a 1–2; 6–7).
16. The meaning of "faculty" or "power" (δύναμις) is explained in 477 c–d.
17. H. J. Paton ("Plato's Theory of Ε Ι Κ Α Σ Ι Α," in *Proceedings of the Aristotelian Society* [1922], pp. 69 – 104) sees the importance of εἰκασία but it can hardly be said that he treats the subject adequately.

of human beings? Although some animals may possess the faculty of that special kind of εἰκασία which is intimately connected with their ability to remember,[18] no animal, so far as we can observe, is capable of seeing an outward image *as* an image.

The "state of the soul" called εἰκασία necessarily presupposes the other one which consists in our responding to the familiar visible things around us with trust. For we see "through" an image, as it were, its trustworthy original. Seeing an image as an image is a kind of "double seeing." Our response to an image cannot help reproducing the very mode of being of what we call "image" (εἰκών) : "image" is uniquely that which *is not* what it *is*.[19]

Thus, while πίστις can be had without εἰκασία, εἰκασία cannot come into play without πίστις. The prisoners in the cave, described in Book VII of the *Republic*, do not manifest any εἰκασία before they are able to turn their heads. Εἰκασία has a doubleness which πίστις has not. The subsection which corresponds to the εἰκόνες and to εἰκασία cannot be taken by itself: it is characterized by its *dependency* on, and its *relation* to, the subsection which corresponds to the primary visible objects and to our trust in them.

3. THE DIANOETIC EXTENSION OF εἰκασία

The two subsections of the domain of the intelligible correspond to two possible ways of our being engaged in thought. To one of them, the lower one, Socrates assigns the name of διάνοια, "thinking," to the other, the name of νόησις, "intellection" (511 d 8 f.), which later, in Book VII (533 e 8), is changed to ἐπιστήμη, "knowledge,"[20] while νόησις is then (534 a 2) referred to the entire segment of the intelligible. Again, Socrates takes up the lower section first. Before considering what he says let us turn to a later passage (523 a – 525 a) in which the "natural" functioning of our thinking, the primary and "simple" business of our διάνοια, is carefully described. This business consists in comparing, that is, in separating *and* relating.

a) The texture of our common experience in which we implicitly trust is woven out of a variety of perceptions. If we

18. See p. 110 and p. 112, note 10.
19. Cf. *Soph.* 240 b 12 – c 2 (also *Rep.* V, 477 a–b, 478 e and context).
20. More precisely: ἡ τοῦ διαλέγεσθαι ἐπιστήμη (511 c 5) ; cf. ἡ διαλεκτικὴ ἐπιστήμη (*Soph.* 253 d 2 ff.).

try to look at them in their nascent state, as it were, we can follow Socrates' exposition.

There are perceptions of visible things, says Socrates, which give us enough clarity about the things perceived (the perception of single fingers, for example) so that most of us do not feel compelled to raise any question about them (in particular, not to raise the question, *"what is* finger?"); there are other perceptions which must seem at first perplexing and confusing (a finger appears both big and small, thick and thin, hard and soft) because "opposite" qualities (τἀναντία) have been somehow "mixed up" (συγκεχυμένα) in them—as our reflecting about this "mix-up" *at once,* and with little effort on our part, informs us. Indeed, the very fact that we feel perplexed about such perceptions manifests the presence of διάνοια "in" them. For to apprehend "opposition" or "contradiction" is within the province of διάνοια, not of the senses. In such perplexing cases we cannot help weighing *in our thinking* what our sensing presents to us so as to be able to gain more clarity about it: we summon our slumbering thinking to come to the rescue and to survey what we perceive. This surveying removes the confusion, the contradiction or obstacle (ἐναντίωμα) arising in our perceptions, by *distinguishing* the *relations* in which a finger stands with regard (πρός) to its neighbor. A finger may be big in relation to its left neighbor and small in relation to its right neighbor. Or, as we read in the *Phaedo* (102 b–c), Simmias is tall not by virtue of being Simmias but by virtue of being *taller than* Socrates; and again Simmias is short not in virtue of being Simmias but in virtue of being *shorter than* Phaedo. Simmias is tall and short in different respects.[21]

In distinguishing those respects, our thinking, our διάνοια, both discriminates between and relates the things under consideration. In the case of a finger, the διάνοια has, first of all, to explore whether its being both big and small means that we are facing something which is "one" or whether it means that we are, for example, facing something which is "two." The conclusion is inescapable that "big" and "small" are, each of them, *one,* but are together *two* (ἐν ἑκάτερον, ἀμφότερα δὲ δύο[22]). Our sense of sight, by itself, without the help of our διάνοια,

---

21. Cf. *Theaet.* 154 c 1 – 155 c 5; 186 b 2–10; *Statesman* 283 d 11 – e 2.
22. 524 b 10. Cf. *Theaet.* 185 b 2; *Hipp. Maj.* 301 d 5 – 302 b 3. (Cf. also *Theaet.* 203 d 4 – 10; *Rep.* 475 e 9 – 476 a 8; 479 a 5 – b 8; 602 d 6 – 603 a 9; *Phaedo* 97 a 2–5; *Parmen.* 143 c 1 – d 5; *Soph.* 243 d 8 – e 2; 250 a – d.)

seems unable to make this distinction. Our thinking activity,
which Socrates at this point (524 c 7) calls by its generic
name – νόησις, fulfills the task. It can do this because its basic
function consists indeed in discriminating *and* relating, that
is to say, in *counting or numbering*. For in the act of counting
we both separate and combine the things we count. It can be
rightly said, therefore, that the act of counting (λογισμός) underlies *any* act of our διάνοια. Moreover, whenever we are engaged in counting, we substitute—as a matter of course, even
if we are not aware of what we are doing—for the varied and
always "unequal" visible things to be counted "pure" invisible
units (μονάδες) which in no way differ from each other and
which constitute the only *proper* medium of counting.[23]

Continued reflection on that act of counting leads to the es-
tablishment of τέχναι which supply us with a *precise* knowledge of all things numerable insofar as they are numerable
and of their properties as well as their mutual relations which
are rooted in their numerability. These τέχναι are Arithmetic
and Logistic. They give us the knowledge of numbers and of
the relations between them, whatever the things numbered
might be.[24]

Having been engaged in removing the confusion and contradiction inherent in some of our perceptions by separating
and relating the things perceived and having thus distinguished the different, and "opposite," relations in which one
and the same thing may stand to other things, especially with
regard to their size, our διάνοια proceeds still further in dealing with those relations themselves, the "bigger than . . ."
and the "smaller than . . .," the "taller than . . ." and the
"shorter than. . . ." It faces the problem of measuring. And
it solves this problem by discovering a medium in which those
relations acquire a *precise* meaning. That medium belongs to
another τέχνη, that of Geometry. It is here, then, among geometrical entities, that strict equality, for example, can be
found when certain conditions are fulfilled.

b) We now turn back to what Socrates has to say about the
lower subsection of the domain of the intelligible (510 b –
511 b).

"Technicians" who deal with numbers and geometrical entities, while looking at visible things, be they natural things
or man-made models or diagrams, use these visible things as
if they were "images" (ὡς εἰκόσι – 510 b 4; e 3; 511 a 6), that

23. Cf. *Phileb.* 56 d – e.
24. Cf. Jacob Klein, *op. cit.* Bd. 3, Heft 1, 1934, §§ 3 – 7.

is, they transform them *in thought* into "images" of those invisible objects, numbers and geometrical entities, which are usually called "mathematicals" (μαθήματα) because their structure can be precisely investigated, understood, learned and, therefore, also easily remembered.[25]

To begin thinking means—in any conceivable case and for any conceivable purpose—to begin searching for some clarity about the matter we are dealing with. Since visible things, as far as they are perceived, may lack clarity (σαφήνεια) and our response to them lacks precision (ἀκρίβεια), our thinking is bound to search for objects which would not suffer from lack of clarity and would lend themselves to being more precisely apprehended. Our thinking discovers, in its acts of thinking, such objects to be *its very own*. They are "objects of thought," "intelligible objects," νοητά. It is these intelligible objects, with their more truthful clarity, that cast light on the obscurity of visible things, an obscurity which the rays of the Sun cannot remove. They present themselves, in their clarity, as models or originals of the visible things. The process of *clarification*, achieved in discriminating between and relating visible things, is the proper, ordinary, and "natural" business of thinking. In it and through it we have constant access to the domain of the intelligible. Our daily speech bears witness to that.

Out of such ordinary, matter-of-course thinking activity grow all the disciplines, all the arts and sciences, in which the "natural" ways of our διάνοια acquire the character of artful and "methodical" procedures. This is particularly true of the τέχναι which deal with numerical and geometrical entities and relations. The methods of those basic (and kindred) disciplines can well serve as paradigms of what our διάνοια always practices, quite independently of, and prior to, its scientific, "technical" performance. That is why in the passage of the *Republic* under consideration those disciplines are singled out to describe the way in which our διάνοια operates, although the range of its activity by far transcends the limits of those disciplines.

In our thinking, then, be it "technical" or "natural," all the things and properties of the visible world with which we deal are taken to "resemble" (ἔοικε – 510 d 7) the invisible, yet

---

25. We have to note that the term μάθημα is studiously avoided in this passage, while it was used previously (504 d ff.) with regard to the "Good" and is used extensively later on (521 c ff.) in the outline of the education of the guardians.

more precise, objects of thought. It is clearly Socrates' contention that our διάνοια makes us interpret those things and properties *as images* of *invisible* νοητά. The best evidence for this contention is precisely the paradigmatic way in which arithmeticians and geometricians use pebbles and visible diagrams or models for their demonstrations, while they do not have, and do not want us to have, those visible figures and bodies "in mind" (διανοούμενοι). The proper objects of their reasoning are "pure" objects of thought, the "odd" and the "even," the "square" and other "figures," the "diagonal," the "three kinds of angles," and so on, of which the visible diagrams or models are but artful "images" (510 d 5 – 511 a 2).

Thus it appears that in our thinking we exercise a kind of εἰκασία which is different from the one we exercise in the domain of visible things and *their* images. This new kind of εἰκασία could be rightly called *dianoetic eikasia*. Let us not overlook that later, in the seventh book (534 a 1–2), the domain of εἰκασία *and* that of πίστις are *together* called the domain of "opinion" (δόξα), which domain thus corresponds to the *entire* segment of the visible. Now, according to what has been said in the fifth book (477 a – b; 478 e), the object of "opinion" (τὸ δοξαστόν) lies "between" what *is* and what *is not,* partaking of both and thus exhibiting the character of what we call "image."[26] Our διάνοια, therefore, cannot help interpreting *all* that is visible as having the character of an "image." Its work indeed appears to be based on *dianoetic eikasia.*

c) This work of our διάνοια is intended to remedy the insufficiency of our perceptions. It is, therefore, of necessity turned towards the visible things. Its field is coextensive with the territory of the visible world.[27] To accomplish its task of

---

26. See p. 115.
27. The geometrical proof, in the Greek manner, is as follows:

Let there be given a line subdivided into four sections.

Let these sections be designated by the letters A, B, C, D respectively.

Let the division be made according to the prescription:

$(A + B) : (C + D) :: A : B :: C : D.$

From $(A + B) : (C + D) :: C : D$ follows *alternando* (Euclid V, 16)

(1) $(A + B) : C :: (C + D) : D.$

From $A : B :: C : D$ follows *componendo* (Euclid V, 18)

(2) $(A + B) : B :: (C + D) : D.$

Therefore (Euclid V, 11)

(3) $(A + B) : C :: (A + B) : B$

and consequently (Euclid V, 9)

(4) $C = B.$

clarification, our διάνοια, according to Socrates' account, is compelled (ἀναγκάζεται – 510 b 5; cf. 511 a 4, c 7) to use (χρῆσθαι – 511 a 4) the intelligible objects, the "originals" of visible things, as "foundations" or "sup–positions" (ὑποθέσεις – 510 b 5, c 3, 6; 511 a 3), and to do that in a way not quite suited to the nature of foundations or "sup–positions": the διάνοια, instead of ascending from the foundations upwards (τῶν ὑποθέσεων ἀνωτέρω ἐκβαίνειν – 511 a 5 f.), towards its "source" (ἐπ' ἀρχήν), moves downwards, towards the final result (ἐπὶ τελευτήν – 510 b 6), that is to say, towards the visible things.

Not surprisingly,[28] Plato is playing with the meaning of the term ὑπόθεσις. There are accepted "technical" usages of this term, especially apparent from the treatise on *Ancient Medicine* (I, XIII, XV), attributed to Hippocrates, from "analytical" mathematical procedures, alluded to later in the *Meno*,[29] from the discussion in the *Parmenides* and also from its frequent, and varied, occurence in Aristotle.[30] Whatever the range of the "technical" meanings of ὑπόθεσις, they all imply something *without* which something else cannot be or cannot be conceived. As against that which depends, for its being or its being conceived, on a foundation or "supposition" (not necessarily a merely conjectural one), the foundation takes *precedence*. The nature of this precedence is in question.

In the passage under consideration Socrates puts an ambiguous emphasis on the preposition (and prefix) ὑπό vying with the preposition (and prefix) ἀπό. The foundation *under*lies that of which it is the foundation. Our διάνοια, in discriminating between and relating visible things, is indeed perpetually engaged in the business of providing *"sup-positions"* or foundations (ὑποτίθεσθαι) for what has to be clarified, is perpetually engaged in the business of *understanding*. The *dianoetic eikasia* it exercises consists in understanding visible things in terms of their intelligible foundations. It is thus that our διάνοια makes the visible things *depend* on intelligible "originals." But to make this dependency manifest, the various τέχναι must show that the wanted clarity about visible things can be *deduced from* the suppositions (ἐξ ὑποθέσεων – 510 b 5). That is to say, the τέχναι are out to prove or to "demonstrate" (ἀ π ο δεικνύναι) that the properties of the visi-

28. Cf. pp. 49 f.
29. Cf. pp. 83 and 207.
30. Cf. the account of ὑπόθεσις and ὑποτίθεσθαι (mostly in their colloquial use) given by R. Robinson, *Plato's Earlier Dialectic*, pp. 97–117.

ble world do indeed *follow* from something intelligible belonging to a "higher" level.[31] This has always been the endeavor of whatever arts and sciences of the visible world have
come into existence. The strict deductive procedures in ancient mathematics are a purified, and immensely fascinating,
version of that endeavor, inasmuch as here the final result
(τελευτή) reached in the conclusion of an ἀπόδειξις belongs itself to the domain of the intelligible.[32] That is why the mathematical disciplines—in their purity—are indispensable for the
education of the guardians of the city. But the "downward"
motion of a mathematical ἀπόδειξις still repeats the pattern of
all "technical" as well as of all "natural" thinking.

The "downward" path of the various τέχναι, and especially
of the mathematical ones, tends thus, of necessity, to transform
(511 b 5; c 7) the "suppositions," the ὑ π ο θέσεις, into "sources"
(ἀρχαί). Yet these sources, the intelligible entities from which
the διάνοια derives its "demonstrations," are themselves in want
of greater clarity.

The technicians proceed in their deductions as if such clarity
has been secured because of the agreement about the terms
or names which denote those suppositions. In the *Sophist*
(218 c 4–5), the Stranger, whose home is neither Athens nor
the visible world, has this to say about "agreement": "It is always necessary, with regard to everything, to have come to an
agreement about the thing itself through arguments rather
than about the mere name without argument" (δεῖ δὲ ἀεὶ
παντὸς πέρι τὸ πρᾶγμα αὐτὸ μᾶλλον διὰ λόγων ἢ τοὔνομα μόνον
συνωμολογῆσθαι χωρὶς λόγου). A technical ὁμολογία—with regard to entities "defined" in Geometry, for example—is not an
agreement about "things themselves."[33] Socrates, in the *Republic* (533 b 6 – d 7), is quite explicit on that point. The
various τέχναι, following the ordinary path and the usual concern of our διάνοια, remain turned toward the mire of that
"jumbled jungle" (βόρβορος βαρβαρικός τις) which the visible
world around us presents;[34] they are, therefore, by themselves,
not capable of dealing with the obscurity of their own "beginnings"; they are not sufficiently awake to give a reasonable

31. It is not unimportant to observe that the terms ἀπόδειξις and
ἀποδεικνύναι are *not* used in this passage.
32. Cf. 533 b 3–7.
33. Cf. pp. 63 and 66. (Cf. also in *Rep.* V, 454 a 6–7, the opposition
between "κατ᾽ εἴδη" and "κατ᾽ αὐτὸ τὸ ὄνομα" and in *Euthyd.* 278 b
5–7 the opposition between "τὰ πράγματα πῇ ἔχει" and "ἡ τῶν ὀνομάτων
διαφορά".)
34. Cf. *Phaedo* 69 c 5–7.

account (λόγον διδόναι) of their own sources. And thus, in Socrates' view, they do not deserve the name of "knowledges" (ἐπιστῆμαι) which we so often, from sheer habit, bestow upon them.

The kind of clarity they can reach is somewhere between the manifest clarity of knowledge and the pretended clarity of a mere opinion (533 d 5–6; 511 d 4–5). This limited clarity is the result of the peculiarly limited activity of our natural and technical διάνοια, an activity which consists in making the vast and diffuse jungle of the visible world depend on a plurality of more "precise" νοητά, an activity, however, which is not able to give an intelligible account of those νοητά themselves. In this, the clarity and precision attainable by our διάνοια is comparable to the clarity and precision sometimes achieved in our *dreams,* in which perhaps a somewhat similar activity of "supposition" takes place, followed by an ultimate identification of "image" and "original."[35] The power to clarify fully the suppositions of our διάνοια may not be given to mortal men.[36] But if an attempt is to be made—and the very activity of our thinking invites us to make it—it can be made only by *reversing the direction of our search,* by turning our attention away from the visible things towards the source or sources from which our διάνοια derives its clarifying function.[37]

d) This attempt—amounting, in Glaucon's appraisal, to a long and difficult task (συχνὸν ἔργον – 511 c 3 f.) —is made to correspond to the uppermost subsection of the divided line (511 b 3 – c 2). Here our διάνοια, our faculty of thinking, tackles the intelligible without any recourse to the visible and without transforming its "suppositions" into "sources": the suppositions from which, on the lower level, the ἀποδείξεις take off on their downward motion, are here truly suppositions (τῷ ὄντι ὑποθέσεις), bases, as it were, *on* which the διάνοια steps to rebound upwards (οἷον ἐπιβάσεις τε καὶ ὁρμαί[38]), so as to try

35. Cf. 476 c 5–8.
36. Cf. *Phaedo* 107 b 1: ἡ ἀνθρωπίνη ἀσθένεια, and the context (cf. pp. 146 f.).
37. It is pertinent to quote Aristotle (*Nic. Eth.* I, 4, 1095 a 30–33) in this connection: "Let us not fail to observe the difference between arguments which proceed *from* the beginnings and those which lead *towards* them. Rightly indeed did Plato, too, [presented with an argument] raise this question and inquire whether the way leads *from* the beginnings or *towards* the beginnings. . . ." (μὴ λανθανέτω δ' ἡμᾶς ὅτι διαφέρουσιν οἱ ἀπὸ τῶν ἀρχῶν λόγοι καὶ οἱ ἐπὶ τὰς ἀρχάς. εὖ γὰρ καὶ ὁ Πλάτων ἠπόρει τοῦτο καὶ ἐζήτει, πότερον ἀπὸ τῶν ἀρχῶν ἢ ἐπὶ τὰς ἀρχάς ἐστιν ἡ ὁδός . . . .)
38. Cf. 532 a 7: ὁρμᾶν.

to reach, step by step (ἐξ ὑποθέσεως ἰοῦσα – 510 b 7) the truly
"First." The "First" is self-sufficient in itself: it does not depend on a "higher" source nor is it in need of any "support"; it is in every sense "supposition-free" (ἀρχὴ ἀνυπόθετος –
510 b 7; τὸ ἀνυπόθετον – 511 b 6); it is the all-embracing
"whole" as such (ἡ τοῦ παντὸς ἀρχή[39] – 511 b 7).

The task set for the διάνοια in this section is indeed enor-
mous, far more so than Glaucon seems to realize. It taxes to
the utmost our power of discoursing, our "dialectical" power
(ἡ τοῦ διαλέγεσθαι δύναμις[40] – 511 b 4; 532 d 8; 533 a 8), that is,
the skill to consider in close argument, in question and answer,[41] what presents itself as having genuine being and intelligibility (511 c 5 f.; cf. 533 a 3: αὐτὸ τὸ ἀληθές), without any
"illustrations" from the domain of the visible (510 b 7–9; 511
c 1). But even here, on the highest level of its activity, on its
"dialectical march" (διαλεκτικὴ πορεία –532 b 4[42]), the διάνοια
must proceed from supposition to supposition, by distinguishing between, and relating, the intelligible objects it is dealing
with, by separating them into "parts" if they are susceptible of
being thus separated, and by collecting them into "wholes" if
they are susceptible of being thus collected. It is in such
διαιρέσεις and συναγωγαί that the dialectical art indeed consists.[43] And, therefore, this art demands not only motions
upwards, from multiplicity toward higher and more comprehensive unity, but also motions downwards, from unity toward lower and more dispersed multiplicity, down to the
"last" intelligible objects (511 b 7 – c 2).

The difference between the two subsections of the intelligible, then, does not simply lie in the directions which the
διάνοια takes. The difference is rather again—and this time de-
fying our common experience—one between "original" and
"image." The counting and numbering, to which, on the
lower level, the natural activity of our διάνοια with regard to
the visible aspects (τὰ ὁρώμενα εἴδη – 510 d 5) of our familiar
and trusted world can be reduced, can also be understood as

39. "τοῦ παντός" seems to be both an objective genitive and a genitive of
   content, the latter more than the former – cf. ἡ τοῦ ἀγαθοῦ ἰδέα (508
   e 3) – "the beginning of the whole" and "the beginning which is the
   whole."
40. Cf. p. 114, note 16.
41. Cf. *Cratyl.* 390 c 10-12.
42. As so often in the *Republic,* Socrates, in talking to Glaucon, uses
   terms with military connotations.
43. Cf. *Phaedr.* 266 b 3 – c 1; *Soph.* 253 c 6 – e 7; *Statesman* 285 a
   7 – b 6.

"imitating" the "dialectical" dividing and collecting which the διάνοια undertakes on the higher level. The objects, on that higher level, are collections or assemblages of intelligible units; these units, however, are not "indifferent" mathematical μονάδες which can be counted and indifferently "thrown together" (συμβληταί[44]), but are both invisible and *uncountable* εἴδη (511 c 1–2).[45] Those assemblages of εἴδη constitute the domain of the intelligible. Their noetic "shadows" are the pure numbers scrutinized and dealt with in the τέχναι of Arithmetic and Logistic, which τέχναι not only provide the foundation for all other disciplines but also reflect the activity of our natural διάνοια in its most basic mode.

This means that in the segment of the intelligible, too, the lower subsection is characterized by its dependency on, and its relation to, the higher one. Even the precision that may reign in the lower seems but a "shadow" of the precision to be secured in the higher.[46] Thus, indeed, as Socrates says (534 a 4–5), comparing the analogous subsections of the two main segments, dialectical νόησις (or ἐπιστήμη) is to πίστις as natural and technical διάνοια is to εἰκασία. In its surge upwards the faculty of *dianoetic eikasia*, which our natural διάνοια exercises with regard to the visible world, is changed into the power of dialectical insight.[47] This change is a radical one, involving a total turnabout, a total conversion (περιαγωγή – 518 c 8–9, d 4; 521 c 6; μεταστροφή – 518 d 5; 525 c 5; 532 b 7) of the entire soul (σὺν ὅλῃ τῇ ψυχῇ – 518 c 8). It marks the beginning of a new life, a life of φιλοσοφία (cf. 521 c 6–8; 527 b 10), tolerable only to a few (494 a 4–7). Φιλοσοφία is perpetually, and inevitably, in conflict with the tendency of our natural and technical διάνοια to be turned toward the familiar visible world and to be immersed in it. Still, let us not fail to observe that the dialectical journey *resumes* the *initial* impulse of the διάνοια to which we owe our admittance to the domain of the intelligible. The various τέχναι enhanced by their expertness tend to

44. See Aristotle, *Met.* XIII, 7, 1081 a 5–7.
45. Cf. Jacob Klein, *op. cit.*, § 7 C.
46. Cf. *Statesman* 284 d 1–2 and the context.
47. Since (p. 119, note 27) C = B, the inequality in length of the "intelligible" and "visible" subsections depends only on the sizes of A and D.
    If, then,
    A : B : : B : D or A : C : : C : D,
    A : D is in the *duplicate ratio* of either A : B or C : D (Euclid V, Def. 9). This expresses in mathematical terms the relation of the power of "dialectic" to the power of εἰκασία.

thwart that impulse. A great effort is needed to reactivate it.
And this effort could not be undertaken but for an intense
desire to embark upon, and to stay on, the new path.

In looking at the divided line, whether it be drawn in the
dust or just "imagined," Socrates and Glaucon themselves
show, by their very action of conversing and reasoning about
it, the twofold possibility open to our διάνοια.

First, there is the line that Glaucon is invited to consider
(509 d 6–8) in connection with what had just been said by
Socrates and understood by Glaucon. This line is drawn and
divided up expertly as if skilled mathematicians had been
putting down "suppositions" so as to be able to derive from
them certain conclusions.[48] But this is not what Socrates
wants Glaucon—and us—to do.

For, secondly, the intelligible geometrical features of the
line serve Socrates as bases, as "suppositions" in the strict
sense (τῷ ὄντι ὑποθέσεις), for leading Glaucon—and us—to an
understanding of the difference between the intelligible and
the visible and of the different levels within each of them. The
use made of the geometrical model by Socrates is wholly un-
geometrical.

Immediately afterwards (μετὰ ταῦτα δή . . . –514 a 1) the
pseudo-geometry is dispensed with and a strange "image"
(εἰκών– 515 a 4; 517 a 8) of a cave is presented to Glaucon and
to us in words. This "image" gives us an opportunity to exercise our fundamental power of εἰκασία (cf. ἀπείκασον – 514 a 1),
so as to enable us to refer the "imagined" cave back to a
"real" one. But at the same time our faculty of *dianoetic
eikasia* makes us understand that this "real" cave images our
natural and civic life within the familiar world around us.

We note that Socrates takes us, in the story of the cave as
well as in that of the divided line, on a predominantly *ascending* path (ἀνάβασις – 515 e 7; 517 b 4; ἄνοδος – 517 b 5;
ἐπάνοδος – 521 c 7).

4. Ἀνάμνησις, εἰκασία, AND διάνοια IN THE *Phaedo*

There is some justification for isolating the consideration
of the divided line from that of the rest of the *Republic*.
There is hardly any for treating certain parts of the *Phaedo*
while ignoring the whole of the dialogue.

48. As was done, for example, p. 119, note 27, and p. 124, note 47.

The least we can do is to keep in mind that the Socratic dialogue, entitled *Phaedo,* is from beginning to end a mythological mime.[49] The central event presented in it is not the death of Socrates. What is shown to us is the struggle between Fear of Death, the old and true Minotaurus, and Socrates, the new and true Theseus. We would not know about that event and its outcome but for Phaedo's telling the story to Echecrates and his friends. The thread of Phaedo's account retraces all the labyrinthine λόγοι which lead to the rebirth of Socrates.

Phaedo tells the story in Phlius, a city linked to the name of Pythagoras and to names of his followers.[50] Echecrates is one of them. Philolaos, with whom the young Thebans, Cebes and Simmias, have been personally connected,[51] is known as a "Pythagorean." Doctrines attributed to Pythagorean teaching keep reappearing throughout the dialogue.[52] The very use of

49. Cf. p. 18.

Schleiermacher, in the Introduction to his translation of the *Phaedo* (*op. cit.,* II, 3, p. 9), says: ". . . probably every one notices that no other dialogue—least of all the earliest ones, the *Phaedrus* and the *Protagoras*—fuses the mimic element with its subject-matter and unites both as much as the *Phaedo* does; nowhere else, therefore, was that element more justified in manifesting itself in its full splendor" (. . . sieht wol Jeder, dass das mimische auch in keinem anderen Gespräche, am wenigsten in den frühesten, dem Phaidros und dem Protagoras, so ganz in den Gegenstand verwachsen und inning mit ihm eines ist als hier [im Phaidon], und es also auch nirgends ein grösseres Recht hatte, sich in vollem Glanze zu zeigen).

Friedländer, *Platon* II, *Die platonischen Schriften,* 1930, p. 321, quotes Schleiermacher's statement and says: "In this dialogue [the Phaedo] it is even less permissible than anywhere else to separate the Event from the Theorem (if we may use this word in this context), taking the Event as the frame and the Theorem as the picture."

Robin, in the Notice to his translation of the *Phaedo, Platon, Œuvres complètes,* Coll. d. Univ. de France, 1934, pp. XXI-XXII, mentions—referring to Aristotle's *Poetics,* Fragment 61 (cf. p. 3, note 1), and *Rhet.* 1417 a 18 – 21—the "genre littéraire auquel appartient le dialogue philosophique" and characterizes the *Phaedo* as a "mime," but ends up by saying: ". . . what we have to study in the *Phaedo* is above all Plato's thought" (ce que nous avons à étudier dans le Phédon, c'est avant tout la pensée de Platon).

50. Diogenes Laertius I (Prooem.), 12; VIII, 46; Iamblichus, *De vita Pythagorica,* 267 (Diels-Kranz, 7th ed., I, 53, 2, p. 443, or 58, A, pp. 447–48).

51. 61 d 6 – e 9.

52. Above all that of rebirth, παλιγγενεσία (70 c – 72 d; 80 d – 84 b; 112 e 7 – 113 a 5). Cf. Servius, *In Vergilii carmina commentarii* (Thilo-Hagen), *ad Aen.* III, 68 (Liddell-Scott, *s.v.* μετεμψύχωσις) and Xenophanes in Diog. Laert. VIII, 36 (Diels-Kranz, 7th ed., I, 21 B, 7, p. 131, cf. also Empedocles, I, 31 B, 129, pp. 363–64). Furthermore, the doctrines of initiation and "purification," κάθαρσις (67 a,

the term φιλοσοφία points back to Pythagoras—and to Phlius;[53]
and Phaedo's report conveys, above anything else, the image
of a "philosophical" communion among friends gathered at a
place peculiarly suited to such an occasion: the jail in Athens,
where Socrates is going to die. It is here that the "Pythagorean
mode of life" (ὁ Πυθαγόρειος τρόπος τοῦ βίου) [54] is conjured up
for a short stretch of time to mark a moment of supreme
significance.

Some of the λόγοι in the dialogue take up the theme of
"recollection."

a) It is first brought up by Cebes (72 e 3) who refers,
cautiously, to a customary saying of Socrates himself: ". . .
according to that very same saying, Socrates, if it be true,
which you are wont to repeat so often, that namely our learning is nothing but recollection" (κατ' ἐκεῖνόν γε τὸν λόγον, ὦ
Σώκρατες, εἰ ἀληθής ἐστιν, ὃν σὺ εἴωθας θαμὰ λέγειν, ὅτι ἡμῖν ἡ
μάθησις οὐκ ἄλλο τι ἢ ἀνάμνησις τυγχάνει οὖσα—72 e 3–6). Simmias intervenes. He claims not to remember how this assertion—and its corollary about the undying nature of the soul—
can be "demonstrated" (ποῖαι τούτων αἱ ἀποδείξεις –73 a 4 f.).
Cebes reminds him of the questioning and answering, not unlike the exchange we have been witnessing between Socrates
and the young slave,[55] which provide excellent evidence for
Socrates' thesis. Upon Socrates' prodding, Simmias asserts
that he is not distrustful of Socrates' saying, but that he stands

---

69 b and *passim*—cf. Robin, *op. cit.*, p. 17, note 2; Hackforth, *Plato's
Phaedo*, 1955, p. 5, note 1), the doctrine of a spherical earth (cf.
Hackforth, *op. cit.*, p. 173, note 5), the "musical" themes (60 e – 61
a; 85 b – 86 d; 88 d), the examples taken from the τέχνη of Arithmetic (101 b – 106 c; cf. p. 139, note 98, and p. 145, note 115), and
the coupling of ethical terms with terms indicating "magnitudes" of
various kinds as well as their relations (cf. pp. 141 f., notes 104, 105,
106, and Diels-Kranz, 7th ed., I, 58 B, 4 and 5, p. 452, and B, 21 p.
456). Cf. also Olympiodorus *in Phaedonem* (Norvin), p. 205, 15–20;
p. 244, 9 ff., and Iamblichus *De vita pythag.*, 257 – Robin, *op. cit.*,
p. 102, note 1 to 117 e 1–2: ἐν εὐφημίᾳ χρὴ τελευτᾶν. The question
whether these various doctrines and themes are genuinely "Pythagorean" is irrelevant in the context of the dialogue. These doctrines
and themes appear, at any rate, associated—directly or indirectly—
with the Pythagorean legend. Hardly separable from some of these
doctrines and themes are those which underlie "orphic" rituals and
mysteries. Nor can the element of playfulness ever be divorced from
the seriousness with which the various arguments are being advanced and refuted.
53. Diog. Laert. I (Prooem.), 12; VIII, 8; Heraclides of Pontus in
Cicero, *Tusc. Disp.* V, 3 (Hackforth, *op. cit.*, p. 29).
54. Plato, *Rep.* X, 600 b 3–4.
55. But why should the words of Cebes (73 a 7 – b 2) imply an allusion
to the episode in the *Meno?*

in need of learning[56] what the saying is about, stands in need of learning to "recollect"; that Cebes' attempt to explain the matter to him has already refreshed his memory and convinced him to a degree; but that, nevertheless, he would like to hear how Socrates himself went about explaining it (73 b 6–10). Whereupon Socrates proceeds as follows (73 c 1 ff.).

"We agree, don't we, that if any one is to recollect something he must have known that something at some previous time" (δεῖν αὐτὸν τοῦτο πρότερόν ποτε ἐπίστασθαι). Simmias agrees. Socrates gives playfully simple examples of how recollection may come about through consequential association (lyre or cloak → beloved youth; Simmias → Cebes) and makes Simmias confirm that "that sort of thing is some kind of recollection" (τὸ τοιοῦτον ἀνάμνησίς τις ἐστι), "especially when some one experiences (πάθη) it with regard to things which he had already forgotten through time and inattention" (73 e 1–4). Up to this point the emphasis is on sequences of things not resembling each other, which can all be perceived through our senses and either are or were so perceived at some moment of time. Socrates then (73 e 5) changes the pattern of these sequences slightly, but significantly, by introducing "images" of things: picture of a horse or picture of a lyre → man; picture of Simmias → Cebes. Implied in these examples—and made explicit immediately afterwards—is the sequence "image of a thing → the thing of which the image is an image" (picture of Simmias → Simmias). This kind of sequence, involving visible images of visible things, belongs altogether to the domain of the visible in which our fundamental faculty of εἰκασία exerts itself. We have to note that in the sequences mentioned by Socrates the original (Simmias, lyre, horse) is, in each case, supposed to have been encountered before. With regard to those sequences we can indeed say that we are "reminded" of the original by the image and the term ἀνάμνησις is perfectly applicable here.

In what follows (74 a ff.) a new kind of sequence is brought up by Socrates, although the pattern "image → original" seems to remain unchanged. The sequence now given as an example is "equal things → the equal itself" (αὐτὸ τὸ ἴσον). The terms of this sequence are not comprehended within the confines of the visible domain: "equal things" are perceived

56. Heindorf's correction of μαθεῖν into παθεῖν (73 b 7) is as ingenious as it is unnecessary (in spite of πάθη – e 2). It disregards the deliberate playfulness of Simmias' remark (cf. p. 97 and *Rep.* III, 392 d 7 and 413 a 3).

through our senses, "the equal itself" or "equality" (ἰσότης) is not. There can be only *knowledge* (ἐπιστήμη) of the latter, acquired by means of our senses "out of" (ἐκ) our perceiving equal visible things and out of nowhere else (μὴ ἄλλοθεν – 75 a 5–7).[57]

How can this acquisition of knowledge be called "recollection"? The answer to that question, in the *Phaedo,* is made dependent on our realizing that the equality of apparently equal visible things is a deficient one, is tainted with "inequality": we realize that two visibly equal things are not quite equal, since sometimes they appear to one man equal and to another unequal, although each of these things remains the same.[58] To be able to recognize this deficiency, so the argument runs, means that we must have previously known (προειδέναι – 74 e 3, 9) perfect equality, which can never be found in visible things. And it is this previous, but forgotten, knowledge that we *recollect* when, in perceiving visibly equal things, we realize that their equality is merely an approximation, a copy, an "image" of perfect equality, of "the equal itself."

The act of "recollecting," then, enables us to "relate" (ἀνοίσειν – 75 b 7; cf. ἀναφέρομεν – 76 d/e) the apparently equal visible things to an intelligible "original." This act of relating is performed by our διάνοια[59] in the exercise of its faculty of *dianoetic eikasia:* as in so many other cases, we "liken" (ἀπεικάζομεν – 76 e 2) here properties of visible things to invisible, yet more precise, objects of thought.

In the λόγος presented by Socrates to Simmias, the familiar experiences of forgetting and recollecting are used to describe the working of our διάνοια. But these experiences are taken on an immeasurably enlarged scale.

We must have acquired (εἰληφέναι[60]) that knowledge of perfect equality, Socrates submits (75 c 4–5), before we were born (πρὶν γενέσθαι). Simmias agrees. That applies not only to equality but to any intelligible object on which, in our questioning and answering, we put the seal of "its being

---

57. Cf. 75 e 3: ταῖς αἰσθήσεσι χρώμενοι, 76 d 9: ἐκ τῶν αἰσθήσεων . . . .
58. Disregarding the version τότε . . . τότε (74 b 8–9). Cf. R. S. Bluck, *Plato's Phaedo,* 1955, p. 178, note 1; Robin, *Platon, Œuvres complètes* (Pléiade) I, 790.
59. Constantly used in this passage is the verb ἐννοεῖν (and the noun ἔννοια once): 73 c 8, 9, 74 a 6, b 6, c 8, d 1, 9, e 2, 75 a 1, 5 f., 11, 76 a 3. (Cf. Cicero, *Tusc. Disp.* I, 24.) Cf. 73 d 7 f.: ἐν τῇ διανοίᾳ, 66 a 2: τῇ διανοίᾳ, 65 e 7: αὐτῇ τῇ διανοίᾳ.
60. The perfect is used 75 b 5, c 2, 4 f., d 5, 76 b 2, the aorist participle 75 c 7, d 7, 9, e 2.

what it *is*" (αὐτὸ ὃ ἔστι – 75 d 2; cf. 65 d 13 f., 78 d 3–9, 92 d 9).⁶¹ "And if, after acquiring (λαβόντες) [such knowledges], we did not indeed, on each occasion (ἑκάστοτε),⁶² forget them, we must always be born with knowledge and always have knowledge (εἰδέναι) throughout life. For 'to know' (εἰδέναι) means just this: having acquired knowledge of something to keep it (ἔχειν) and not to have lost it. 'Loss of knowledge' (ἐπιστήμης ἀποβολή), that is what we mean by forgetting (λήθη), don't we, Simmias?" Simmias is in complete agreement (75 d 7 – e 1).

It appears, however,⁶³ Socrates concludes, that we do lose those previously acquired knowledges when we are being born and that, later on, using our sense perceptions, we recover (ἀναλαμβάνομεν – 75 e 4) them, those same knowledges which we at some former time (ποτε) already had. What we call learning would thus be the recovery of knowledge which is already ours (ἆρ' οὐχ ὃ καλοῦμεν μανθάνειν οἰκείαν ἂν ἐπιστήμην ἀναλαμβάνειν εἴη;). "And should we not be right in calling this 'recollecting'?" (75 e 6–7).⁶⁴ Simmias seems satisfied. But it takes some additional arguing to convince Simmias completely that learning is recollecting (76 a 1 – c 5) and that our souls existed without our bodies before we were born (76 c 6 – 77 a 5). With regard to the pre-existence of our souls, what is most convincing to Simmias is that, necessarily (76 e 2), the soul, even before our birth, has being (εἶναι – 76 e 3; 77 a 1) *just as* the intelligible objects have being (ἔστι – 76 d 7; e 3; 77 a 1–2). The point is stressed: there is an "equal necessity," there is "the same necessity" (ἴση ἀνάγκη – 76 e 5; ἡ αὐτὴ ἀνάγκη – e 8–9) for our soul to exist before our birth and for all the intelligible objects to have being. Still, the necessity of asserting the soul's pre-existence is understood to *depend* on the presupposed being of the intelligible objects. If *they* had no being, Socrates says, there would be no point in arguing the pre-existence of our souls (76 e 4; cf. e 7). And nothing is more clear to Simmias than that all those objects *are* in the strictest possible sense (πάντα τὰ τοιαῦτ' ε ἶ ν α ι ὡς οἷόν τε μάλιστα – 77 a 3 f.). The being of the soul in its prenatal state—a state characterized by φρόνησις

61. Cf. *Rep.* VI, 507 b 7; VII, 532 a 7.
62. Robin, *Phédon*, 1934, p. 31, note 2, and *Platon* (Pléiade) I, 1327, note 57, understands ἑκάστοτε as referring not to the acquisition of each particular knowledge but to each of our rebirths.
63. Cf. Hackforth, *op. cit.*, p. 71, note 1.
64. This last sentence seems to refer directly back to Simmias' request in 73 b 6–10.

(76 c 12; cf. 79 d 6 f.) [65]—appears to *follow* from the exalted **131** status of the intelligible. It is *this* dependence which provides Simmias, and also Cebes (87 a 3–4), with a sufficient proof (ἱκανῶς ἀποδέδεικται – 77 a 5) of the pre-existence of the soul.

Throughout the preceding λόγος the emphasis is on the existence of the soul *in time*, regardless of whether it is connected with, or separated from, a body. Accordingly, here again, as in the myth of the *Meno*, the knowledge that the soul possesses is knowledge *acquired at some moment of time*. Those of us who, in this life, pass from the state of ignorance to that of knowledge are said to "recollect" what they "once learned" (ἀναμιμήσκονται . . . ἅ ποτε ἔμαθον – 76 c 4). [66] In spite of the recollection thesis the soul itself is thus understood to be capable of, and at some period of time actually to have been engaged in, *learning*.

The immediately following λόγος, which deals with Cebes' concern about the status of the soul *after* death, has a very different pattern. The persistence of the soul in time is mentioned only in connection with certain mystery rites (81 a 8–9). The emphasis is on the soul's *unchanging* nature which suggests a timeless order of being (especially 79 d–e).

b) The recollection thesis reappears for the second time in the wake of Simmias' and Cebes' final objections concerning the soul's indestructibility, in the very middle of the dialogue, when the battle against Fear of Death is joined in earnest. Socrates begins the discussion by asking how Simmias and Cebes regard the argument which maintains that learning is recollecting and that consequently (τούτου οὕτως ἔχοντος) the soul must exist "somewhere else" (ἄλλοθι) before being bound to the body (91 e 5 – 92 a 1). Both, Simmias and Cebes, emphatically endorse the argument (92 a 2–5).

Socrates then proceeds to eliminate Simmias' objection first. This objection consists in bringing up the widely held (cf. 92 d 2 and 86 b 6 – c 2), and possibly also "Pythagorean," thesis that the soul might well be something like an appropriate arrangement or attunement (ἁρμονία) [67] of bodily characteristics. Socrates makes Simmias see that this the-

---

65. Φρόνησις is emphasized throughout: 65 a 9; 66 a 6; c 5; e 3; 68 a 7; 69 a 4; b 3, 6; c 2; 70 b 4; 80 d 7; 81 a 5; 94 b 5; 118 a 17.

66. Cf. 72 e 6–7 (Cebes speaking): . . . ἀνάγκη που ἡμᾶς ἐν προτέρῳ τινὶ χρόνῳ μεμαθηκέναι ἃ νῦν ἀναμιμνησκόμεθα and p. 129, note 60.

67. Cf. Hackforth, *op. cit.*, p. 97, note 1, and p. 98, note 1, Robin, *Phédon*, 1934, p. 49, note 2, also *Platon* (Pléiade) I, 1328, note 76. Augustine, *De trinitate*, IV, 2, and *De civitate Dei*, XXII, 24, translates ἁρμονία with "coaptatio."

sis cannot be reconciled with the one about recollection. Whereupon Simmias decides to abandon the former in favor of the latter. What prompts him to do that? The attunement thesis occurred to him, he says (92 c 11 – e 3) "without demonstration" (ἄνευ ἀποδείξεως), being somewhat plausible and decorous, while the recollection thesis has been argued on the basis of a supposition worthy of acceptance (δι' ὑποθέσεως ἀξίας ἀποδέξασθαι).[68] Simmias refers back to the relation of dependence between the being of the soul which is ours[69] even before it enters the body and the kind of being (οὐσία) the soul by itself attends to as to its proper[70] domain, the kind of being characterized by the appellation of "that which *is*" (92 d 7–9). That is the starting point which Simmias confidently accepts; and that is why he feels compelled to abandon the attunement thesis (92 e 1–3).

We note that Simmias does not quite follow Socrates: he does *not* base the pre-existence of the soul on the recollection thesis. It is the other way around: he accepts the recollection thesis because it seems to *follow* from the soul's pre-existence, and the soul's pre-existence, in turn, seems to follow from the kinship between the soul and its intelligible objects.[71]

c) It is now Cebes' turn (95 a 4). His objection is the crucial one. In warding it off, Socrates does not make any use of the recollection thesis. And yet, what Socrates has to say on this occasion bears heavily on the problem of learning.

According to Cebes, no convincing arguments have been advanced by Socrates so far to show that the soul will *everlastingly* exist after death. From the mere pre-existence of the soul we can certainly not infer that it will keep its existence forever. The λόγος which stressed the kinship (συγγένεια) between the soul and the unchanging character of the intelligible (78 b 4 – 80 c 1) had indeed ended with the conclusion that it is proper for the soul to be either altogether indissoluble or *nearly so* (ἢ ἐγγύς τι τούτου). Cebes now enlarges upon this "nearly so": the soul may well outlast the body for quite a while and yet finally cease to exist (86 e 6 – 88 b 8). Cebes' objection, we note, presupposes that a soul which lasts forever never ceases to exist in time.

68. As opposed to διὰ τῶν εἰκότων – 92 d 3.
69. Cf. ἡμετέραν – 76 e 1, 3; ἡμῶν – 77 a 1.
70. Keeping αὑτῆς (92 d 8) as against Mudge, Hirschig, Wohlrab, Schanz, Archer-Hind (p. 117), and Hackforth, *op. cit.*, p. 114, note 2. Cf. Heindorf (with reference to 76 e): ad mentem nostram pertinere; Robin, *Phédon*, 1934, p. 60, note 3; Bluck, *op. cit.*, p. 99, note 2. Αὑτῆς (d 8) and ἡμῶν (d 7) are parallel.
71. Cf. 79 d 3; 80 b 1–3; also *Rep.* VI, 490 b 1–4.

To meet this objection, Socrates—after looking back into himself for quite a while[72]—reaches far back into his own youth. He wanted very much, he reports, to find out, with regard to any single thing or occurrence (ἕκαστον), what was responsible for its coming into being, its passing away, its being the way it was (96 a 9–10; cf. 97 c 6–7). But he could not find any satisfactory answers. Nor could he learn them from anybody else, not even from Anaxagoras. The main difficulty lay in the very meaning of the question Socrates and so many others were asking.

What does it mean to raise the question of "responsibility," to ask what the reason (αἰτία) for something is? What does it mean to ask: "why is this so"? The question "why" or "wherefore" (διὰ τί) [73] comes up whenever we are unable to understand what presents itself in our immediate experience. The raising of this question indicates that our διάνοια has been aroused and called upon to disentangle the difficulty. Out of such natural questioning grows, among others, that special wisdom known by the name of the "story of nature" (περὶ φύσεως ἱστορία – 96 a 8). This story, variously told, persists in responding to that very question without discriminating between its possible meanings.

That is how Socrates decided, as he further reports, to embark upon a different journey, his "next best try," to find out "why" things are as they are (δεύτερος πλοῦς ἐπὶ τὴν τῆς αἰτίας ζήτησιν – 99 c 9 f.). This is the presentation (ἐπίδειξις – 99 d 2; cf. 100 b 3, 8) he makes of his new endeavor.

By looking directly at whatever presents itself in our familiar world, at things and their properties, at human affairs and actions, we run the risk of being blinded as people do who observe[74] the sun during an eclipse if they do not look at its image on some watery surface. That may well have happened to those investigators of nature. To avoid being "blinded," Socrates thought that he had to "take refuge in the spoken word" (εἰς τοὺς λόγους καταφυγόντα – 99 e 5), in exchanging questions and answers with himself and with others,[75] and in *them* search for the truth of things.

Any speaking, any λέγειν, is but the audible manifestation of the activity of our διάνοια. In the *Sophist* (263 e 3–5) the Stranger asks: "Well, then, is not thinking (διάνοια) and

---

72. Cf. pp. 92 f.
73. Cur, pourquoi, perchè, warum (cf. the dialectical play between ἕνεκά του and διά τι in *Lysis* 218 d – 221 d, esp. 220 d 4 – e 6).
74. Cf. Hackforth, *op. cit.*, p. 136 f. (d).
75. Cf. 100 d 9 – e 2: καὶ ἐμαυτῷ ἀποκρίνασθαι καὶ ἄλλῳ, and καὶ ἐμοὶ καὶ ὁτῳοῦν ἄλλῳ ἀποκρίνασθαι.

speech (λόγος) the same thing, except that the former, the silent inner discoursing of the soul with itself (ὁ μὲν ἐντὸς τῆς ψυχῆς πρὸς αὐτὴν διάλογος ἄνευ φωνῆς γιγνόμενος), has been given the name of 'thinking'?" Theaetetus answers: "Quite so."[76] The stepping stones in thinking as well as in speaking are the single silent or audible words, the ὀνόματα,[77] which seem to designate, more often than not, visible things as well as their properties and relations. But, in truth, these ὀνόματα signify the suppositions which the διάνοια makes and which help us understand what we perceive. That is to say, they signify the objects of thought, the νοητά, and the connections that seem to prevail or do necessarily prevail between them.[78]

Socrates' "next best try," then, consists in following the path which the διάνοια traces: the reasons for things being as they are and the truth about those things are to be found in the spoken, or silent, words and the νοητά they signify. That is not to say, Socrates warns, that the example of the sun, at which we can only look by looking at its image, is applicable here: if one compares a man who investigates things in words with one who investigates them directly, the former can hardly be said to be more concerned with images than the latter (100 a 1–3). On the contrary, we surmise, the former, in the exercise of *dianoetic eikasia,* sees things as images *of their intelligible originals,* in spite of the widespread opinion that "mere" words and their meanings do nothing but reflect, and possibly distort, "reality."[79]

Socrates gives the following outline of the way he proceeds. On each occasion (ἑκάστοτε) he chooses as supposition the most reliable statement[80] which, in his judgment, would make us understand what remains obscure and concealed in our immediate experience. Such a statement, a connection of words, would render manifest the connection of νοητά which underlie that experience. Whatever appears to be consonant with that

---

76. Cf. 264 a 9 and *Theaet.* 189 e 4 – 190 a 2, also *Phileb.* 38 e 1–8.
77. Cf. p. 57 and p. 136, note 88.
78. Cf. *Theaet.* 147 a 1 – c 2; *Laws* X, 895 d – 896 a.

    On the final level of insight, on that of ἐπιστήμη, the λόγος might fail, for the underlying νοητά, the εἴδη, might not be numerically related as the corresponding ὀνόματα are: the counting of the ὀνόματα might be misleading. Cf. *Soph.* 217 a – 237 c – 254 c – 257 a; also *Statesman* 257 a – b (see Jacob Klein, *op. cit.,* § 7, C). Not to be overlooked is the doubt cast on the "truthfulness" of ὀνόματα in *Cratyl.* 439 a – b and context; cf. also above p. 121, note 33.
79. Cf. *Tim.* 51 c 4 f.: . . . μάτην ἑκάστοτε εἶναί τί φαμεν εἶδος ἑκάστου νοητόν, τὸ δ' οὐδὲν ἄρ' ἦν πλὴν λόγος;
80. Cf. *Crito* 46 b 4–6.

statement is to be posited as genuinely true, whether it concern the αἰτία of something or anything else, and whatever does not conform to the statement is to be taken as untrue (100 a 3–7).

Cebes does not quite follow. He is not saying anything new, Socrates explains, but rather what he has never stopped saying, at other times as well as in the preceding discussion.[81] And now again he is going to revert to those much babbled-about words and make them his starting point, his initial supposition being that there *is* something named, itself by itself (αὐτὸ καθ' αὑτό), "beautiful" and also something itself by itself "good" and something itself by itself "big" and all the rest.[82] Each of these νοητά is understood to be *precisely what it is,* and nothing but that. And the most reliable statement chosen by Socrates on each occasion points to the necessary connection between any of those νοητά and Being itself (100 a 7 – b 7).

Consonant with any such statement is a further one of the following type: if there be anything else beautiful besides Beauty itself, it will be beautiful for no other reason than that it shares in, or partakes of (μετέχει – 100 c 5), Beauty itself. It is this kind of reason (τῆς αἰτίας τὸ εἶδος – 100 b 4) which is responsible for things being beautiful, which "makes" (ποιεῖ – 100 d 5) [83] them beautiful. Statements of this type provide the safest (ἀσφαλέστατον – 100 d 8) answer to the question: "why" are things as they are?

Inasmuch as Socrates' "next best try" is a deliberate attempt to follow up the ordinary, "natural," path of our διάνοια, Socrates can characterize (100 d 3–4), ironically and truthfully, his way of understanding why things are as they are as "simple" (ἁπλῶς), "artless" (ἀτέχνως), and "perhaps foolish" (ἴσως εὐήθως). His answer, with all its safety, is a simple-minded, "unlearned" one (ἀμαθής), as he later (105 c 1) —again ironically and truthfully—adds. Its safety is based entirely on the reliability of the underlying statement that the intelligible objects, the νοητά, have being. Socrates is not ready "as yet" (100 d 6) to state with any confidence how the "sharing" in a νοητόν is to be understood: Does the sharing in Beauty "make" things beautiful on account of Beauty's "presence"

81. 65 d f., 74 a ff., 75 c–d, 76 d – 77 a, 78 d ff.
82. Of the three named, Beauty and Bigness are chosen for further elaboration, the Good is left out.
83. Cf. *Phileb.* 26 e 6–9: ΣΩ. Οὐκοῦν ἡ τοῦ ποιοῦντος φύσις οὐδὲν πλὴν ὀνόματι τῆς αἰτίας διαφέρει, τὸ δὲ ποιοῦν καὶ τὸ αἴτιον ὀρθῶς ἂν εἴη λεγόμενον ἕν; ΠΡΩ. Ὀρθῶς. See also *Symp.* 205 b 8 – c 3.

(παρουσία) in those things? Or on account of its establishing a "community" (κοινωνία) among those things? Or on account of something else? In the exercise of *dianoetic eikasia* we understand, at any rate, that things beautiful *look like* the invisible νοητόν Beauty itself. Here, too, the seeing is doubled, as it were.[84] That is, indeed, how the word εἶδος or ἰδέα, applied in common speech to the looks or "aspects" of visible things can be—paradoxically—used to signify the invisible objects of the διάνοια.[85] In the *Parmenides* (132 d 1–4), Plato makes the very young Socrates declare with great confidence that "these εἴδη stand by themselves[86] like [unchangeable] models (ὥσπερ παραδείγματα), while the other [visible and changeable] things resemble them (τούτοις ἐοικέναι) and are [their] copies (ὁμοιώματα); as to the sharing in the εἴδη, which is the lot of those other things, it is nothing but their being cast in the image of those εἴδη." The very old Parmenides, "venerable and dreadful, too," like Priam,[87] points to the grave difficulties which arise from such an understanding and which demand for their solution a well disposed soul and an immensely laborious effort. But he also concludes (135 b–c) that, if one were to deny those εἴδη, "he will have nothing toward which his διάνοια may turn" and "will thus utterly destroy the power of discoursing" (τὴν τοῦ διαλέγεσθαι δύναμιν).

To meet Cebes' objection Socrates has to show *why* the soul can never "die." That is what he hopes to accomplish (100 b 7–9) and that is what makes it necessary to consider the very meaning of the question "why?"

The "demonstration" he offers resembles indeed a most intricate maze. It is ultimately based (1) on the underlying, and most reliable, statement that each of the εἴδη is something which has *being* (εἶναι τι ἕκαστον τῶν εἰδῶν – 102 b 1); (2) on its corollary that everything else, by "sharing" in those εἴδη derives its name from them (τούτων [sc. τῶν εἰδῶν] τἆλλα μεταλαμβάνοντα αὐτῶν τούτων τὴν ἐπωνυμίαν ἴσχειν – 102 b 1–2[88]); and (3) on the kindred corollary that this sharing in the vari-

---

84. Cf. p. 115. See also Anaxagoras, fr. 21a (Diels-Kranz, 7th ed., II, 59 B, 21 a, p. 43): "what is seen is the sight of the invisible" (ὄψις γὰρ τῶν ἀδήλων τὰ φαινόμενα).
85. Cf. pp. 49 f. and pp. 65–66 (the case of στερεόν). Cf. *Symp.* 210 b 2–3.
86. ἐν τῇ φύσει – cf. *Phaedo* 103 b 5.
87. Cf. *Theaet.* 183 e 5 f. and *Iliad* III, 172 (also *Soph.* 217 c 4–7).
88. Cf. 103 b 7 f.: . . . περὶ ἐκείνων αὐτῶν ὧν ἐ ν ό ν τ ω ν ἔχει τὴν ἐπωνυμίαν τὰ ὀνομαζόμενα. (Cf. also *Rep.* X, 596 a 6–7, *Tim.* 52 a 4–5.)

ous εἴδη can be safely understood as the reason (αἰτία) for
everything being as it is.

But, in addition, there are two prescriptions which have to guide the διάνοια on its new journey and therefore also in the pursuance of the task Socrates has now set himself.

The first is: consequences which, in a given case, spring from one of those safe suppositions concerning the reason for something being as it is must be scrutinized as to their mutual compatibility or incompatibility (101 d 4–5). The second is: the safe supposition itself must, in the case under consideration, be accounted for in the same manner (ὡσαύτως), that is, by recourse to another—"higher" (ἄνωθεν) —supposition chosen as the best one (βελτίστη), and this process must be continued until something sufficient (τι ἱκανόν) is finally reached (101 d 5 – e 1).

These two ways of proceeding, Socrates takes care to remark,[89] the one towards consequences which spring from the safe supposition (τὰ ἀπ' ἐκείνης [ὑποθέσεως] ὁρμηθέντα – d 4; τὰ ἐξ ἐκείνης ὡρμημένα – e 2-3),[90] the other concerning its source (περὶ τῆς ἀρχῆς – e 2), should not be "mixed up," if one wants to find something genuinely true.[91] We cannot fail to observe, however, that Socrates, in the very choice of his words (ὁρμᾶσθαι ἀπό or ἐκ . . . — ὑπόθεσιν ὑποθέμενος . . . τῶν ἄνωθεν . . .), does not separate clearly the downward and the upward motion of the διάνοια and merges the meaning of "supposition" with that of "source" in his use of the term ὑπόθεσις.[92] These ambiguities are tied to the general mythical character of the dialogue. Throughout the dialogue the invisibility of the νοητά is related by way of a pun to Hades (τὸ ἀιδές—ὁ Ἅιδης),[93] but the pun is more than a play on words. All the familiar connotations that Hades has as the dwelling-place of souls after death are conjured up. But whether going to that "other" place, "the true Hades" (εἰς Ἅιδου ὡς ἀληθῶς –

89. Cf. p. 122, note 37.
90. Cf. with ὁρμαί – Rep. VI, 511 b 6.
91. Cf. 101 e 1–3.
92. Cf. pp. 121–23.
93. Especially 79 a – 85 b; 107 a 1. Cf. Gorg. 493 b 4–5 and Cratyl. 403 a 3 – 404 b 4. In the Cratylus, Socrates playfully replaces that pun by another. But in deriving Ἅιδης from πάντα τὰ καλὰ εἰδέναι (404 b 3)—or, as Hermann suggests, ἀεὶ εἰδέναι (ἀϊειδέναι—Robin, Platon [Pléiade] I, 640 and 1305, note 47) Socrates, in effect incorporates the first into the second.
   The Platonic pun is but a variant of the pun implied in the Homeric phrase Ἅϊδος κυνέη (Iliad V, 845)—cf. Rep. X, 612 b 5. Cf. also Diels-Kranz, 7th ed., I, 28 B, p. 243, 14–15 (Simplicius about Parmenides).

80 d 5–7), means going "downwards" or "upwards" must perforce remain shrouded in darkness.[94]

Two *main* examples of the way to proceed are adduced by Socrates. The one is the case of bodies which are hot or cold (103 c 10 – e 5). The other is the case of things the number of which is either odd or even (103 e 5 – 104 c 10; 104 c 11 – 105 a 5).

The first example is supported by a discussion of the case of men who are big and small (102 b 3 – 103 a 3), which discussion is but an extension of a preceding argument on the same subject (100 e 5 – 101 b 3).

The second example is related to a discussion of unity and duality (101 b 9 – c 9).

There are, in addition, seemingly marginal examples about "multitude" and "magnitude" (101 b 4–8), about "sickness" (105 c 2–4), and also about fractional "parts" and the corresponding "whole" (105 a 6 – b 4).

In every one of these cases the "safe" and simple-minded supposition concerning the αἰτία can be made: a man is big and is called big, and not small, by reason of his sharing in "Bigness" or, as we may say, by reason of "Bigness" being "in" him; a body is hot and is called hot, and not cold, by reason of its containing "Heat" (105 b 8 – c 2) ; a body is sick and is called sick (and not healthy) by reason of "Sickness" inherent "in" it; a number of things is odd and is called odd, and not even, by reason of its sharing in "Oddness."

There is an important difference between the first main example and the second one.

Something is hot or cold only *in relation to* (πρός) something else: thus a body is *both* hot and cold, hot in relation to a colder body, cold in relation to a hotter one. The case of Simmias' being big *and* small was brought up by Socrates to point to this very circumstance (102 b ff.). And, as we learn from the *Republic*,[95] the apparent contradiction in our perceptions of big and small is resolved by the διάνοια, which separates and relates Bigness and Smallness as the two *intelligible* objects involved in the confusion of our senses. Indeed, Heat (θερμότης – 105 c 2, 106 b 6/7) and Cold are, just as Bigness and Smallness, intelligible objects, objects apprehended through the basic activity of our thinking (τῷ τῆς διανοίας λογισμῷ – 79 a 3). But they are invisible εἴδη of a pe-

---

94. Cf. *Iliad* XXIII, 103–4: Ὢ πόποι, ἦ ῥά τίς ἐστι καὶ εἰν Ἀίδαο δόμοισι ψυχὴ καὶ εἴδωλον, ἀτὰρ φρένες οὐκ ἔνι πάμπαν.
95. Cf. pp. 116–17.

culiar type: they are eidetic poles of infinitely extended sensible ranges; and these ranges, on their part, are held together by the sliding band of the "more and less."[96]

A number of things, on the other hand, can in no sense be odd and even at the same time: it is *either* odd *or* even. It is odd not in relation to an even number only but, primarily, in itself. Here the διάνοια is not called upon to clear up any confusion, but is active on its own grounds, as it were, expanding the suppositions to be made in the face of anything countable and numerable to "higher," to "technical" levels.[97] The distinction between the "odd" and the "even" yields the first set of εἴδη that the τέχνη of Arithmetic has to deal with. These two εἴδη divide the domain of everything numerable into two clearly recognizable "halves" (104 a 7 – b 4).[98] The "more and less" does in no way affect that domain.[99] That is presumably why the second example is clearer (σαφέστερον – 103 e 6) than the first.

Nevertheless, the first prescription, the one regarding the compatibility or incompatibility of consequences, is applicable to both examples.

A hot body may cool off and then again become hot, but the Heat "in" it can never become cold nor the Cold "in" it ever become hot (cf. 103 a 4 – c 9). For Heat and Cold, just as Bigness and Smallness, are by themselves (ἐν τῇ φύσει – 103 b 5) incompatible with each other.

In a similar way, an odd number of things can be increased or decreased so as to turn into an even number of those things, but the Oddness "in" a given odd number, in three apples, for example, cannot coexist with Evenness, since Oddness by itself is incompatible with Evenness by itself.

Consequent on, but quite distinct from, the pair of opposites "Heat – Cold" is another pair: "fire – snow." Now, "fire" and "Heat" are of necessity compatible, for fire is hot,

96. Cf. *Phileb.* 24 b 4–5 (and context).
97. Cf. pp. 118–22.
98. Cf. Philolaos, Diels-Kranz, 7th ed., I, 44 B, 5, p. 408, also Jacob Klein *op. cit.*, §§ 4, 6. In the "Pythagorean" table of opposites (Aristotle, *Met.* I, 5, 986 a 22–26) the "odd" appears on the "positive" side, the "even" on the "negative" side. This reversal of the colloquial meaning of περιττόν may well be labelled the "Pythagorean revolution." Cf. Plutarch, *De animae procreatione in Timaeo, Moralia* VI, 155 f. (Bernardakis)—see Diels-Kranz, 7th ed., I, 14, 11, p. 102, 6 and p. 489, 27–34, also II, 217, 5 and 218, 9 as well as J. Bidez et F. Cumont, *Les mages hellénisés*, 1938, I, 37 f., II, 35, 63–66, 80. (Cf., by way of contrast, *Critias* 119 d 2–4.)
99. Cf. Aristotle, *Cat.* 6, 6 a 19–25.

but "fire" and "Cold" cannot—in "fact" and in "thought"—possibly coexist. Nor can "snow" coexist with "Heat" (103 c 10 – e 5).

In a parallel way, the three-ness of any three things is of necessity compatible with Oddness, for three things are an odd number of things, but their being "three" precludes Evenness in them (104 d 5 – e 6). Nor is it possible that four things be an odd number of things.

So far, the two examples show the following parallelism: to the pair of opposites "Heat – Cold" corresponds the pair of opposites "Odd – Even"; to the pair "fire – snow" corresponds the pair "a given odd number – a given even number" (for example, three things – two things, five things – four things, and so on).

It is stressed by Socrates, we note, that "three" and "two" of something are not opposites (104 c 5; cf. b 8), while the relation of "fire" to "snow" is left undetermined. It can be said, however, that just as an odd number and Evenness or an even number and Oddness are not opposites, fire and Cold or snow and Heat are not opposites either (104 e 7 – 105 a 5). For fire and snow, on the one hand, and Cold and Heat, on the other, belong to different levels of being.

Beside or beyond (παρά – 105 b 6) that safe and simple-minded answer concerning the αἰτίαι of things there has thus come into sight another safe way of answering. Socrates gives the following examples: a body will be hot not only on account of Heat (θερμότης) entering into it but also, we may say, on account of "fire" (πῦρ); a body will be sick not only on account of Sickness entering into it but may become sick also on account of fever; a number of things will be an odd number not only on account of Oddness (περιττότης) entering into it but also on account of "unit" (μονάς)! It is from this kind of answer, a "more ingenious" one (κομψοτέραν[100] – 105 c 2), that the deathlessness of the soul is to be inferred (105 b 5 ff.) : soul (ψυχή) is going to join the rank of those new entities to account for Life.[101]

Let us look closely at the similarity and the difference between the old and the new answers.

100. Cf. 101 c 8: τὰς τοιαύτας κομψείας and the context. (Cf. also *Rep.* VI, 499 a 6 f.: τὰ δὲ κομψά τε καὶ ἐριστικά . . . ; *Gorg.* 521 e 1 f.: κομψὰ ταῦτα, which turns Callicles' quotation from Euripides, 486 c 6, upside down.)

101. It is not unimportant to note that the opposition between Life and Death resembles more that between Odd and Even than that between Heat and Cold (cf. pp. 138 f.).

1. In none of the new answers does the newly introduced
entity (πῦρ, πυρετός, μονάς, ψυχή) supply the appellation of
what is in question (θερμόν, νοσεῖν, περιττόν, ζῆν).

2. In both the new and the old answers the level on which
a hot body and a sick body—also a big man—present themselves
to our senses, to the sense of sight and the sense of touch, is,
of course, the same. This is also true of any odd number of
things, three apples, for example, inasmuch as numbers of visible things have "visible or touchable bodies,"[102] namely the
bodies of the numbered things.

3. In the old answers, "Heat," "Sickness," and also "Bigness," belong to the same level of intelligibility, "Oddness,"
however, to a higher one. What Socrates calls at one point
(104 d 5 f.) ἡ τῶν τριῶν ἰδέα (three-ness) may belong to the
level of "Heat" and "Sickness." But Oddness and Evenness
are more comprehensive than either three-ness or four-ness.

4. But to what level shall we assign fire, fever, unit, and—
soul?

This is not a marginal question. Socrates himself, after
pointing to that "something else" (ἄλλο τι – 103 e 4, 9 f.; ἀλλ'
ἄττα – 104 c 8) which does not "accept" (δέχεται) one of the
two opposites, even though, by itself, it is not "opposed" to it,
proposes to Cebes twice that they determine (ὁρίσασθαι) what
sort of entities (ὁποῖα – 104 c 11; ποῖα – e 7) those new ones
are. This determination is finally given in a rather involved
anacoluthon (104 e 7 – 105 a 5). It restates what was said before in a significantly descriptive way: the new entities, while
not "accepting" one of the two opposites, "bring up" the other
opposite and impose it on what they approach.[103] But what
their mode of being is remains undetermined. Let us attempt
some clarification.

Fire and snow are perceived by our senses. They may be
somewhat elusive, but they have more of the character of
"things" than hot and cold: "hot" and "cold" are adjectives,
the substantive bases of which our διάνοια has to find in the
eidetic domain; "fire" and "snow" are by themselves nouns.
But fire and snow are *not* εἴδη.[104] Nor are they sensible quali-

---

102. *Rep.* VII, 525 d 7 f.; cf. *Epinomis* 990 c 6; also Jacob Klein,
    op. cit., pp. 35, 53–55, 88.
103. Cf. Hackforth, *op. cit.*, p. 152, notes 4 and 5.
104. The examples of νοητά given repeatedly throughout the *Phaedo* are,
    as has been often enough remarked, most significant: δίκαιον, καλόν,
    ἀγαθόν (65 d 4–8), καλόν, ἀγαθόν, δίκαιον καὶ ὅσιον (75 c/d),
    καλόν and ἀγαθόν (76 d 8; 77 a 4; 100 b 6). In every case there
    is an addition analogous to "καὶ τἆλλα πάντα" which follows the

ties like hot and cold, or big and small. They are conspicuous denizens of the visible world. They are met with, such as they are, again and again. Each part of them is like any other part. They have *elemental* character.

Fever, akin to fire, is yet subject to the "more and less": being feverish is like being hot. Fever is not perceived directly but indicated by symptoms. Whenever it occurs it seems to be based on some *elemental* disturbance.[105]

What about "unit" (μονάς) which is introduced by Socrates quite casually at the end of his enumeration of the "more ingenious" answers (105 c 6)?

Is the μονάς the *one thing* which defies division whenever one tries to halve any odd number of things and which is thus, as a *part* of such a number, responsible for its oddness?[106]

Or is the μονάς, as Socrates had intimated before (101 c 2–7), a νοητόν, the sharing in which makes anything be one and be called one?[107] The sharing in it would be also responsible for the one-ness of that one "odd" thing which puts a limit to the halving of any odd number. The sharing in it would, therefore, be the ultimate αἰτία of the oddness of an odd number.

Or is perhaps the μονάς the "source of everything," as Philolaos taught,[108] the ἀρχή which keeps the "boundless" (ἀπειρία) in bounds?[109] And, if so, is it not close to the νοῦς which, ac-

---

example of μέγα (100 b 6–7)—65 d 12 f.: . . . περὶ πάντων οἷον μεγέθους πέρι, ὑγιείας, ἰσχύος, καὶ τῶν ἄλλων . . . ἁπάντων (μέγεθος, ὑγίεια, ἰσχύς being responsible for the ἐπωνυμία of μέγα, ὑγιής, ἰσχυρός —cf. *Meno* 72 d – e); 75 c 9–10: οὐ μόνον τὸ ἴσον καὶ τὸ μεῖζον καὶ τὸ ἔλαττον ἀλλὰ καὶ σύμπαντα τὰ τοιαῦτα . . . ; 76 d 8–9: καὶ πᾶσα ἡ τοιαύτη οὐσία; 77 a 4: καὶ τἆλλα πάντα; in 78 d 3 αὐτὸ τὸ ἴσον is linked with αὐτὸ τὸ καλόν. How far the meaning of τἆλλα πάντα, or of σύμπαντα τὰ τοιαῦτα, or of πᾶσα ἡ τοιαύτη οὐσία, can be stretched becomes a crucial question in the last argument provoked by Cebes' objection. As to fire and snow, in particular, the question whether we have to assume an εἶδος Fire and an εἶδος Snow (and beyond that, an εἶδος Σῶμα and an εἶδος Κίνησις)—and if so, how their manner of being ought to be understood—is, at any rate, one of the most difficult questions our διάνοια faces. Cf. *Parm.* 130 c 2 and context, *Tim.* 51 b 6 – e 6, *Soph.* 248 d 10 ff.

105. See *Tim.* 86 a 2–8.
106. Cf. Aristotle, *Top.* VI, 4, 142 b 8; *Met.* XIII, 8, 1083 b 29 f.; Nicomachus, I, 7, 2 (also Jacob Klein, *op. cit.*, pp. 47 f., 61 f.).
107. Cf. Euclid, *Elements* VII, Def. 1: Μονάς ἐστιν, καθ' ἣν ἕκαστον τῶν ὄντων ἓν λέγεται.
108. See Diels-Kranz, 7th ed., I, 44 B, 8, p. 410 (from Iamblichus).
109. Cf. *Phileb.* 16 c 7–10; Aristotle, *Phys.* III, 4, 203 a 10–15; *Met.* XIV, 3, 1091 a 13–18. (Cf. also Plutarch, *Lives, Numa XI*, where πῦρ is equated with Ἑστία and with μονάς.)

cording to Anaxagoras, "orders everything and is responsible for everything" (διακοσμῶν τε καὶ πάντων αἴτιος – 97 c 2),[110] presumably with a view to what is *best* in every single instance (97 c 4 – 98 b 6)?

How, then, does Cebes, and how do we, understand what the word μονάς stands for in the sequence presented by Socrates? Is μονάς subordinated to Oddness, as fire to Heat and fever to Sickness, or is it "higher," more comprehensive, than Oddness? Are we guided by the first or the second prescription in going from περιττότης to μονάς? Is the meaning of παρά (105 b 6) the same in all the examples cited by Socrates?

Finally, what about ψυχή? It is Cebes who, in this case, answers the question: what, entering into a body, will make it a living body (ζῶν)? He answers this question not safely and simple-mindedly by pointing to Life (ζωή), but in a more ingenious way, by invoking "soul" (105 c 9–11). Cebes does that upon Socrates' prodding and warning not to answer his, Socrates', question except[111] by imitating Socrates' own "more ingenious" answers (καὶ μή μοι ὃ ἂν ἐρωτῶ ἀποκρίνου ἀλλὰ μιμούμενος ἐμέ – 105 b 5–6). It is true, Cebes' answer follows the pattern set by Socrates: the opposite of Life is Death (105 d 6–9); ψυχή, by itself not "opposed" to Death, "brings up" Death's opposite, Life (105 d 10–11), brings Life to whatever it "occupies"[112] (ὅτι ἂν αὐτὴ κατάσχῃ) (d 3–5); and since, in analogy to Socrates' examples, "soul" does not "accept" Life's opposite, does not "accept" Death, "soul" cannot be touched by Death: the soul, therefore, will never "*die*." The demonstration seems to have reached its end (105 e 8–9).

We have to ask: does Cebes, in imitating Socrates' answers,

110. Cf. Diels-Kranz, 7th ed., II, 59 B, pp. 37–39 (from Simplicius).
111. For the use of ἀλλά in the sense of πλήν cf. the references to *Laws* IV, 710 c 7–8 and *Symp.* 181 d 1–2 in Ast, *Lexic. Platon., s.v.* ἀλλά, I, 102. Ast himself, taking into account the version ᾧ ἂν ἐρωτῶ . . . ἀλλὰ ἄλλῳ, paraphrases the sentence (*s.v.* ἀποκρίνω): cave ita respondeas ut eo utare quod interrogans posui. (Ficino translates: nec tamen per id quod nunc interrogo, sed per aliud quiddam mihi respondeas, me imitans.)
Denniston, *The Greek Particles*, 2nd ed., pp. 3–4, asserts that he can find no examples for the use of ἀλλά in the sense of πλήν outside Aristotle, except in Sophocles, *Oed. Tyr.* 1332. Jebb, in his note to this verse, mentions *Odyssey* 8, 311–12 and *Iliad* 21, 275–76. Denniston observes that in these cases "ἄλλος makes the ἀλλά normal, 'no one else, but.' " Does it? Cf. also Kühner-Gerth, *Ausführliche Grammatik der griechischen Sprache*, 1904, II 2, pp. 283 f. (I am grateful to Seth Benardete for his assistance in this matter.)
112. Cf. Hackforth, *op. cit.*, p. 156.

put ψυχή on the level of πῦρ and πυρετός? And also of μονάς? But may not μονάς belong to a "higher" level? Is the motion from ζωή to ψυχή a downward or an upward motion? No light is shed on this point in what either Cebes or Socrates says. It is up to the other witnesses of the conversation—and, thanks to Phaedo, we are now among them, together with Echecrates and his friends (cf. 102 a 8)—to decide this issue. The decision will depend on the very meaning we shall attribute to ψυχή.

Socrates himself raises the problem in a different, oblique, and "more ingenious" manner.

The entities the "sharing" in which is responsible for certain features of the visible world (according to the old answers or the new ones)—as well as those sensible features themselves—carry, by virtue of their *not* "accepting" one of the opposites in question, a negative appellation, for instance, "not-even" (ἀνάρτιον – 105 d 15; cf. 104 e 5), "not-just," "not-musical" (ἄδικον, ἄμουσον – 105 e 1), "deathless" (ἀθάνατον – 105 e 6 f.). But these negatives do not tell whether that which they signify "departs" or vanishes altogether whenever the negated opposite approaches. The alternative is mentioned repeatedly and well in advance[113] of the final conclusion: "Bigness" "in

---

113. And is already anticipated in 88 b 5–6 as well as in 95 b/c.

In a larger sense, the alternative is anticipated in the contrast between the early ἀνταπόδοσις argument (70 c – 72 d) and the final assertion of the incompatibility of opposites (102 d ff.). This contrast is underscored by the intervention of the unnamed listener who is amazed to discover that the latter assertion seems to contradict what the previous argument had advanced (103 a 4–10).

Socrates carefully disentangles the difficulty (103 b 2 – c 2): on the level of our common experience, which extends even to regions only heard of or imagined, we are dealing with things and states of things opposite to one another and yet capable of gradually changing into one another (a hot body into a cold body, and vice versa, a living thing into a dead thing, and—conceivably—vice versa); but when we turn our attention to what is responsible for that opposition, namely the sharing in the various pairs of opposites understood in their "purity" by our διάνοια, we also understand that, within each set, *these* opposites could not possibly gradually "change" into one another, each being nothing but what it is (Heat – Cold, Life – Death). These opposites are not subject to transmutation, whether they are taken as being "shared in" by things and thus as determining the character and the name of those things, or whether they are taken "by themselves" (cf. 103 b 5: οὔτε τὸ [ἐναντίον] ἐν ἡμῖν οὔτε τὸ ἐν τῇ φύσει).

It is conceivable, however, that the "sharing" in one of the opposites ceases and is "replaced" by the "sharing" in the other: that is how an ἀνταπόδοσις (72 a 12; b 8; also 71 e 8) may come about (cf. 106 b 7 – c 1, especially the expression "ἀντ' ἐκείνου"). Cf. Hackforth, *op. cit.*, pp. 153–54.

us" (ἐν ἡμῖν – 102 d 7) [114] *either* escapes, retires, goes away
(φεύγειν καὶ ὑπεκχωρεῖν – 102 d 9; ἀπέρχεται – 103 a 1) *or* perishes at the approach of Smallness; snow will *either* give
place to Heat (ὑπεκχωρήσειν αὐτῷ [*sc.* τῷ θερμῷ] – 103 d 8) *or*
perish; fire *either* withdraws (ὑπεξιέναι – 103 d 11) before the
Cold *or* perishes; and so in every case (104 b 6 – c 1).

Now, three things, inasmuch as they are three, are an odd
number of things and the "not-even" "in" this assemblage of
things may be said to be responsible for their being conjointly
odd. If, then, the "not-even" in this number of things were altogether indestructible, their being odd could not be destroyed.
But that is far from being the case since three things can,
through addition or subtraction, turn into four or two of those
things. The "not-even" "in" an odd number of things is *not*
"indestructible" (106 c 3).[115] If it were, we could indeed maintain without difficulty, that, at the approach of the "Even,"
the "Odd" and the "three," too, would simply go away (οἴχεται
ἀπιόντα – 106 c 5).

Similarly, if the "not-hot" in a cold body or in a cold medium were altogether indestructible, snow, at the approach of
Heat, would withdraw "safe and unmelted" (106 a 3–6). But,
as we know, that is not the case. Nor can fire in a hot body
safely "depart" (ἀπελθὸν ᾤχετο – a 10) when approached by
Cold. Neither the "not-cold" in a hot body nor the "not-hot"
in a cold body is indestructible.

Could not the same be true of "soul"? That is Socrates'
query. As something to which the appellation "deathless"

114. ἐν ἡμῖν – 102 e 6; 103 b 5; ἐνόντων – 103 b 8; τῇ ἐν αὐτοῖς οὔσῃ
– 104 b 10; ἐγγένηται – 105 b 9; c 3; 5; ἡ ἐν τῷ πυρὶ θερμότης –
106 b 6. The preposition (or prefix) ἐν embodies the problem of
"sharing," left "unsolved" by Socrates (see pp. 135 f. and 138).

115. The addition (or subtraction) of one thing to (or from) an assemblage of things is not the "reason" for this assemblage becoming
an odd or even number of those things (cf. 96 e 6 – 97 b 7); the
reason for its being either odd or even is its "sharing" in either
"Oddness" or "Evenness" (p. 135). The asserted destructibility
of either Oddness or Evenness does not contradict the impossibility
of their being transmuted into their opposites (note 113). But does
it not contradict what their eidetic character implies, namely their
intrinsic immutability and indestructibility?

The answer to this question seems to be: the εἴδη have unchanging and indestructible *being* only "by themselves" (ἐν τῇ
φύσει), not when "shared in" by what pertains to the visible world.
It is this distinction which Aristotle attacks and erases. In the context of the *Phaedo* this distinction appears directly tied to the
"Pythagorean" understanding of numbers (see Aristotle, *Phys.* III,
4, 203 a 6–7; *Met.* XIII, 6, 1080 b 16–20; XIV, 3, 1090 a
22–23; I, 6, 987 b 27–29). Cf. Hackforth, *op. cit.*, pp. 162–63.

(ἀθάνατον) applies, it might nevertheless share the fate of "three" and of "Odd" and of snow and of fire. It also could be "extinguished" (ἀπεσβέννυτο – 106 a 9) and perish at the approach of Death. It would be a "living" soul only as long as it exists in a body (cf. 103 e 5: ὅτανπερ ᾖ[116]) and no longer. The demonstration, with which Cebes was so much satisfied (105 e 9), amounts to nothing if one considers that possibility. Another λόγος seems to be needed (106 c 9 – d 1).

It is again Cebes who dismisses that possibility. Does not the "deathless" mean that which never dies? And must not that which never dies exist forever (ἀίδιον ὄν – 106 d 3)? If the "deathless" were subject to destruction (φθορά), Cebes exclaims in an "orphic" vein, could there be anything else (τι ἄλλο) that would escape it! Whereupon Socrates: "Deity, at least, and Life itself by itself (αὐτὸ τὸ τῆς ζωῆς εἶδος), and if there be anything else (τι ἄλλο) 'deathless'—that these never perish might, I think, be agreed upon by all (παρὰ πάντων ἂν ὁμολογηθείη[117])." There is as much ambiguity as solemnity in these words. Cebes catches the irony and chimes in: "By all men, to be sure, Zeus knows, and even more so by the gods, as I, for my part, suppose" (106 d 5–9). But Socrates and Cebes do agree (106 e 1 – 107 a 1): since "soul" does not "accept" Death, as has been shown, and *if* thus the "soul" is indeed deathless, there could be no alternative to its being indestructible, *once it is granted* (ὁπότε δή . . . ἐστιν.) that the "deathless" is also indestructible (ἀδιάφθορον). It seems, therefore, that when Death approaches man, what is mortal about him dies, while the "deathless," retiring before Death, departs safe and unimpaired (σῶν καὶ ἀδιάφθορον οἴχεται ἀπιόν, ὑπεκχωρῆσαν τῷ θανάτῳ – 106 e 7). "Soul, then, Cebes," Socrates concludes, "is most certainly (παντὸς μᾶλλον) something deathless and indestructible, and our own souls will truly (τῷ ὄντι) be in Hades." But, most certainly, *what* the "deathless" part of man is and what kind of place "Hades" is, remain unstated.

Both Cebes and Simmias declare that they are satisfied with what has been said. But Simmias feels bound to make a reservation: considering the weakness of man as against the mag-

116. Strato of Lampsacus' criticism in Olympiodorus, p. 183 (Norvin), quoted by Hackforth, *op. cit.*, p. 163 and p. 196 (m), does not add anything to what Socrates says in the dialogue. The misunderstanding of Platonic dialogues begins early. (Cf. also Hackforth, *Plato's Phaedrus*, p. 68.)

117. Cf. *Symp.* 202 b 6: . . . ὁμολογεῖται γε παρὰ πάντων . . . and the context.

nitude of the subject under discussion, he, for one, cannot
completely trust the argument. Socrates fully approves of Simmias' stand and even extends the distrust (ἀπιστία) to the very
first suppositions underlying the entire argument (τάς γε
ὑποθέσεις τὰς πρώτας – 107 b 5) : however trustworthy they may
appear, they ought to be looked into more thoroughly. There
is a final stage, Socrates intimates, at which no further search
will be needed. To reach that stage, the first suppositions must
be sufficiently (ἱκανῶς) articulated and then the consequences
have to be followed up in argument as much as might be
humanly possible (107 b 6–9). With this rather darkly phrased
prospect Socrates seems to come back to the prescriptions
which were to guide his course, reversing the order originally
indicated (101 d 3 – 102 a 2[118]). It is not hard to see: what
happened between that beginning and the end now reached
lacks clarity.

The inconclusiveness of the "demonstration" hinges on
Cebes' imitating Socrates' "more ingenious" answers. The assertion that sharing in ψυχή is responsible for ζωή in a body,
that "soul" is thus "life-bringing," is rooted in the common
identification of "living being" and "animate being" (of ζῷον
and ἔμψυχον). The emphasis in the preceding discussions lay
on the kinship between ψυχή and the intelligible. What characterized ψυχή was φρόνησις.[119] Cebes' "imitated" answer gives
ψυχή a radically different meaning, relating it not to φρόνησις
but to "living" (ζῆν). Moreover, this answer implies that sharing in ψυχή amounts to the existence of a soul "in" the body of
an animate being: this soul is understood to "occupy"[120] that
body and to dwell "in"[121] it. The indestructibility of this soul,
as the exchange between Cebes and Socrates shows, and as
Simmias confirms, is far from certain.

Does all this mean that the λόγος, intended to meet Cebes'
decisive objection and built up with so much care and cir-
cumspection, does not fulfill its task? Taken by itself, it fails
indeed: even though Cebes seems satisfied with it, it does not
quite dispel the fear that "the child in us" has, and cannot
help having, the fear of that "bugbear" (τὰ μορμολύκεια) –
Death (77 e 4–7). But had not Socrates said (77 e 8–9), playfully and truthfully, that daily incantations[122] are required for

118. Cf. p. 137.
119. Cf. p. 131, note 65.
120. Cf. p. 143.
121. Cf. p. 145, note 114.
122. Cf. *Charm.* 157 b.

that child until that fear is charmed away? Are not the λόγοι of the dialogue a series of such "incantations," including the very last tale (114 d 6–7)? But will they not, and necessarily so, remain ineffective unless supported by evidence more powerful than the evidence they by themselves are able to supply?

This supporting evidence is there, in the very δρᾶμα presented by Phaedo.[123] We witness Socrates' behavior during the long hours before he drinks the draught. For it is not only the content of the λόγοι, their cogency and insufficiency, that mark the struggle with Fear of Death, it is also, and more so, the adult sobriety, the serenity in gravity and jest, imposed by Socrates on the conversation. Φιλοσοφία is present. We witness its ἔργον. And it is the final scene that illuminates the wording, and failing, of that λόγος we were concerned about, the one prompted by Cebes' gravest objection.

The friends surrounding Socrates are made to apprehend directly the slow and gradual approach[124] of Death bringing cold and rigor in its wake: they watch[125] the hands of the executioner follow its path and so do we. When that cold and rigor come close to the heart, says the man, "Then he will have departed" (οἰχήσεται – 118 a 4).

The common euphemism echoes the words with which the λόγος abounds.[126] The imagery of "approach" and "departure" draws its strength from the world of visible and tangible things. It cannot do justice to what, of necessity, must remain invisible and intangible. It matches Socrates' exalted topography which assigns various dwelling-places (οἰκήσεις) on, above, and inside the Earth to the souls of men (107 c 1 – 115 a 8). This final tale and incantation competes with stories told about nature. In telling his own story, Socrates reverts to the kind of journey he claims to have undertaken in his youth.

123. Cf. *Rep.* X, 604 e.
124. The verb ἐπιέναι (with hostile overtone) was used throughout in the λόγος: 104 b 10, c 7, 106 a 9, b 8, c 4 (ἐπελθόντος), and finally e 5: ἐπιόντος . . . θανάτου ἐπὶ τὸν ἄνθρωπον . . . (προσιέναι is used 103 d 7, d 10; 106 a 4: ὁπότε τις ἐπὶ χιόνα θερμὸν ἐπάγοι . . .).
125. Burnet's interpretation (in his edition of the *Phaedo*, pp. 117 f., note to 118 a 2) of αὐτός (118 a 3) might be quite right. (See also Bluck, *op. cit.*, p. 142, note 2.)
126. 115 d 9 f.: οἰχήσεσθαι ἀπιόντα; 115 d 4: οἰχήσομαι ἀπιών . . . ; 106 e 7: οἴχεται ἀπιόν, ὑπεκχωρῆσαν τῷ θανάτῳ; 106 c 5: οἴχεται ἀπιόντα; 106 a 10: ἀπελθὸν ᾤχετο. Further back (102 d 9 – 106 a 4) the expressions vary (cf. p. 145) in striking contrast to the constant repetition of the verb ἀπόλλυσθαι (except for 106 a 9: ἀπεσβέννυτο). Early in the dialogue Socrates uses ἀπιέναι (61 a 8), ἐκεῖσε ἀποδημεῖν (e 1), and τοῦ βίου ἀπαλλάττεσθαι (85 b 7).

But what he has to tell is not a new version of περὶ φύσεως ἱστορία but a part of the ἱστορία περὶ ψυχῆς: it is a topography or, more exactly, an oecography of the soul.

Not that this πρῶτος πλοῦς, this first and last journey of Socrates, is safer than any other: it does not befit a man of sense to assert with confidence that things are as the tale depicts them (114 d 1–2). But once the indestructibility of the soul, with which the λόγος concluded, is accepted, it is also fitting to accept the content of this tale or of one like it: it is worthy of a man to run the risk of such acceptance, for it is a noble risk (καλὸς γὰρ ὁ κίνδυνος – 114 d 6).[127] The conclusion of the λόγος was uncertain. The λόγος failed because its motion took, unexpectedly, a turn downwards, towards the level on which Death can be even perceived to "approach" a man. On this level the brave assertion of the soul's "departure" becomes a manifestation of human excellence. That is what the *action* presented in the dialogue *shows*.[128]

But there the matter cannot rest. Human excellence itself demands that the effort of the διάνοια be kept up, that the λόγος continue. Immediately after Simmias and Cebes raise their gravest objections (89 c 11 – 91 c 5)[129] Socrates enjoins his hearers forcefully to forgo forever any "misology." The prescriptions laid down by Socrates must remain the guiding beacons in the search for a "sufficient" answer. This is well understood by the men surrounding Socrates and no less so by Echecrates and his friends (102 a 2–8). The indestructible "part" of Socrates, in whatever guise (cf. 78 a 1–9), may well be "present" whenever the search is undertaken. This "presence" may not even require any visible manifestation at all. Is it not secured by the very effort to keep the λόγος alive?

d) To continue the λόγος means to be earnest about the pleasures of *learning* (τὸ μανθάνειν – 114 e 4 and context). This learning, if Socrates' prescriptions are to be followed, demands a determined effort on our part, demands lengthy and laborious study.[130] We still have to ask: what light does the theme of "recollection" shed on that effort?

The theme came into play when the discussion dealt with the pre-existence of the soul: "recollection" was then mythically, and "naturally," understood as having its place within the temporal texture of our common experience. Accordingly, Cebes' doubt concerning the status of the soul *after* a man's

---

127. Cf. ἀκινδυνότερον (85 d 3) and the context.
128. Cf. *Rep.* VI, 486 a 1 – b 5.
129. Cf. Hackforth, *op. cit.*, p. 109.
130. Cf. *Theaet.* 186 c 2–5.

death could not be removed by invoking recollection which refers to the forgotten past. It is perhaps significant that in the midst of the conversation with Cebes Socrates takes the opportunity to remark (105 a 5–6) : "Do recollect once more; for we may as well listen many times [to the same argument]." This remark invites Cebes to recollect what he presumably had already learned from previously given examples. But Socrates does not imply that Cebes' previous learning had been an act of recollection.

It could be argued that the enterprise of learning presupposes, of necessity, a state of knowledge in which the truth of things is manifest. The recollection thesis would thus point to that "pre-existent" Truth, perhaps not to be grasped in the lifetime of a man, but enabling him to search for it. The process of "recollecting" would mean nothing but the very process of learning guided by Socrates' prescriptions. Later in the *Meno*, Socrates himself interprets "recollection" in that fashion.[131] But such an understanding of "recollection" changes its meaning as implied in the recollection thesis itself and as supported by the mythical frame in which that thesis is propounded.

No doubt, there is a profound discrepancy between the "natural" phenomenon of recollection, even if we enlarge it to a mythical scale, and the work of the διάνοια, the aim of which is understanding and learning. The effort of recollection, when directed toward the recovery of an insight, tends to reach a moment of time in the past at which that insight was first gained,[132] while learning, that is, the acquisition of knowledge, is in no way concerned with any past moment of time but is uniquely interested in the content of the knowledge to be acquired. The object of knowledge is, as such, independent of any time. To try to recover a lost insight means to try to repeat what happened at least once before. The effort to learn something is an effort to grasp something that is always true.

The gulf between the learning effort of the διάνοια and the effort to recollect a forgotten insight seems to become less deep, however, if either effort is seen as the continuous exercise of our faculty of *dianoetic eikasia*.[133] No explicit attempt is made by Socrates, or Plato, to take up that point. Instead, it is ἀνάμνησις which is singled out to throw light on μάθησις. Why do we need this mythical light?

131. Cf. Hackforth, *op. cit.*, p. 75.
132. Cf. pp. 109–11.
133. Cf. pp. 119, 129.

a) The dithyrambic words in the palinode of the *Phaedrus*
mention twice (249 b 5–6; e 4 – 250 a 1) that no soul can become a human soul unless it has seen the truth in the region
"above heaven" (247 c 3). It follows that we all had knowledge once, and that is why we can try to recollect (249 d 6;
250 a 1) that knowledge now. It is also said (248 a 2–6) that
the human souls, unlike those of the gods, are not quite able
to see *all* the truth: whatever knowledge they might have
gained and regained must, of necessity, be incomplete and
must, therefore, always be tainted with ignorance. No man
can be wise (cf. 278 d 3–6) and only in a few is remembrance
of what was once seen sufficiently present (250 a 5).

To become a *human* soul, the soul has to acquire the power
of speaking and of perceiving the meaning of the spoken
word. To perceive the meaning of whatever may be spoken
is to grasp the intelligible content of the spoken words, to
grasp the εἴδη and their connections, which the words signify
and to which they "refer." Whatever may be spoken is spoken
with reference to those εἴδη, described as "located" in the nowhere "outside" of heaven (cf. 247 c 2; 248 a 2–3). Whatever
may be spoken "refers" to the invisible domain of the intelligible. Man as man, therefore, cannot help following the lead
of his διάνοια: "For man must needs perceive the meaning
(συνιέναι) of whatever is being spoken, [spoken necessarily]
with reference to the intelligible (κατ᾽ εἶδος λεγόμενον[134]), by
going [in every case] from many perceptions (ἐκ[135] πολλῶν
ἰόντ᾽[136] αἰσθήσεων) to the unity (εἰς ἕν) comprehended in a
reasoned account (λογισμῷ συναιρούμενον); in this consists the
recollection (ἀνάμνησις) of those [εἴδη] which this soul of ours,
in its upward surge towards that which truly is, once beheld
while journeying with a god and looking down upon what

134. The interpretation of συνιέναι κατ᾽ εἶδος λεγόμενον by Stallbaum,
 Ast, Robin seems hardly tenable. On the other hand, to insert, as
 Heindorf, Schanz, von Arnim, Hackforth do, in accordance with
 common usage, τό before κατ᾽ εἶδος means—or could, at least,
 mean—to take κατ᾽ εἶδος in a restrictive sense, as if there could be
 some other kind or kinds of λεγόμενα. Is not that the reason why
 the article is omitted before the somewhat disturbingly—and pleo-
 nastically—interpolated κατ᾽ εἶδος?
135. Cf. 250 a 1 and *Phaedo* 74 b 4, 6, c 7; 75 a 5–7 (p. 129).
136. To read ἰόντ᾽ instead of ἰόν—with Badham and H. W. Thompson—
 seems indeed necessary (cf. Hackforth, *Plato's Phaedrus,* p. 86,
 note 1).

we now claim has 'being' (εἶναι)" (249 b 6 – c 4). This claim is possible because things down here look "like" those invisible εἴδη "outside" of heaven (cf. ὁμοίωμα – 250 a 6, b 3; εἰκόνας and εἰκασθέντος – b 4, 5). To "comprehend" an εἶδος is an exercise in *dianoetic eikasia.*

Later in the dialogue (275 a 2–5), in a context far removed from the "divine madness" (256 b 6) of the "mythic hymn" (cf. 265 b 6 – c 1), but still tied to an "Egyptian" tale about the invention of writing, the god-king Thamus is made to criticize that invention. Far from being a help to memory and craftmanship (μνήμης τε . . . καὶ σοφίας φάρμακον – 274 e 6), writing will promote forgetfulness in the souls of men engaged in learning (τῶν μαθόντων) by making them neglect the use of their own memory (μνήμης ἀμελετησίᾳ): relying on what is written, they will be led to their recollections from without, from imprints not their own (ὑπ' ἀλλοτρίων τύπων), instead of recollecting by themselves, from "within."[137] Writing does not help memory: it can only remind those "who know" of what the written words are about (275 a 5; d 1; 278 a 1). The written word could be justly called a sort of image (εἴδωλόν τι) of the one which is alive (ζῶν καὶ ἔμψυχος) and authentic (γνήσιος), of the one "which is being written with knowledge in the soul of the learner" (ὃ μετ' ἐπιστήμης γράφεται ἐν τῇ τοῦ μανθάνοντος ψυχῇ), while the process of examining and teaching (ἀνάκρισις καὶ διδαχή) what is true (276 a; 277 e 9; 276 c 9) goes on.

Learning is thus again identified with recollecting. We gather, however, that learning consists in reviving, as it were, the imprints left on our memory "within" the soul and—for the most part (250 a 1 – b 1) —"forgotten" after our journey to the ὑπερουράνιος τόπος. Thus, in the *Phaedrus,* not only the activity of recollecting but also memory acquires mythical dimensions. The soul of the "philosopher" is close, as close as it can be, to the highest region, the region of the divine, by virtue of its memory (μνήμη – 249 c 5–6; cf. 252 e 5 – 253 a 5, also 254 b 5). It is to memory, more than to recollection, that Socrates, somewhat apologetically, it seems (cf. 250 c 7–8), pays tribute in his dithyramb.

b) In the *Philebus,* Socrates introduces (33 c 8 ff.) the theme of memory and recollection by clarifying the meaning of "sense perception." He does this in the larger context of an investigation of pleasure (ἡδονή).

Our body is exposed to all kinds of encroachments from the

137. For the text cf. Hackforth, *op. cit.,* p. 157, note 1.

outside, which make it "shake" to a greater or lesser degree. Sometimes, perhaps most of the time, the "shock" (σεισμός) is absorbed and "quenched" by the body before reaching the soul, that is to say, it remains "imperceptible." But whenever the "shock" reaches the soul so as to make the soul shake, too, though in its own peculiar way, we say that we "perceive." "Sense perception" (αἴσθησις), then, is the name we give, not improperly, to the simultaneous agitation of body and soul, which are jointly affected (cf. 34 a 3–5).

Now, to "remember" means to "preserve a sense perception" (σωτερία αἰσθήσεως – 34 a 10), to preserve, that is, a certain agitation affecting body *and* soul. This power of "retention," which the soul seems to exercise only in conjunction with the body, we call memory (μνήμη). But the retentive power may weaken its grip: memories may fade and "go out." The "outgoing of memory" (μνήμης ἔξοδος) is what we call (33 e 3) "forgetting" (λήθη).

"Imperceptible" shocks suffered by the body alone and "quenched" in it cannot be said to have been "forgotten." For, as Socrates takes care to remark to Protarchus, "it is absurd to say that something which does not exist or has not yet come into being can be somehow 'lost'" (33 e 4–7). If nothing has been "retained" or "kept," there is nothing that can have been "lost." The term "forgetting" is altogether inapplicable in this case.

Socrates proceeds to describe "recollecting" by contrasting it with "memory" (34 b 2). In so doing (34 b 6 – c 3), he manages to enlarge the scope and the meaning of "memory" vastly.

That which the soul once experienced conjointly with the body (μετὰ τοῦ σώματος) may become lost or forgotten. But the soul has the power to recover (ἀναλαμβάνειν) that loss, though not completely, all by itself, "without the body" (ἄνευ τοῦ σώματος). When the soul is engaged, to the best of its ability (ὅτι μάλιστα), in this kind of recovery, engaged "by itself within itself" (αὐτὴ ἐν ἑαυτῇ), it is fair to say that it is engaged in "recollecting" (ἀναμιμνῄσκεσθαι).

What does the soul thus recover? Not the original agitation (κίνησις) of the body since the body is not involved in the act of recollection. The soul recovers the peculiar (ἴδιον – 33 d 5) state it itself was in when it "shook" conjointly with the body. That state of the soul, once restored, is once more made available for "retention": a "memory" of that state can be re-established.

Such a "memory" belongs altogether to the soul.[138] This becomes especially clear when one considers that acts of recollection need not only apply to previous sense perceptions. They may also apply to previous learning which has led to knowledge without the body being involved in the process. This knowledge may have been "kept" for quite a while, but it, too, was subject to forgetfulness. It, too, can be recovered and then again be kept or retained in our memory. Thus Socrates "adds" (34 b 10 – c 2): ". . . when [the soul], having lost (ἀπολέσασα) the memory of either a sense perception or, for that matter (αὖ), of something [once] learned (μαθήματος), turns it up again and anew (αὖθις ταύτην [sc. μνήμην] ἀναπολήσῃ[139] πάλιν) [and does this] by itself within itself, we do call all such happenings, don't we, recollections[140] and memories."[141] What is regained by ἀνάμνησις is the content of the lost μνήμη, but the reconstituted μνήμη itself is a new one. As Aristotle says,[142] ἀνάμνησις is not an ἀνάληψις of a lost memory as such. Diotima, in the Symposium, confirms this.

Our memory thus not only preserves sense perceptions, it can also retain something once learned and function as the repository of knowledge. Correspondingly, "forgetting" can be described not only as the "outgoing of memory" (μνήμης ἔξοδος), but also as "loss of knowledge" (ἐπιστήμης ἀποβολή) —the phrase Socrates uses in the Phaedo (75 d 10–11),[143] or as the "outgoing of knowledge" (ἐπιστήμης ἔξοδος) —the phrase Diotima uses in the Symposium (208 a 5).

Thus far, the functioning of our memory seems to have been restricted to a man's lifetime. But Socrates pushes the enlargement of the meaning of μνήμη still further. Memory is finally located, as in the Phaedrus, within mythical horizons.

The example which leads to that most comprehensive mean-

---

138. Cf. also Rep. X, 604 d 8–11.
139. Cf. R. G. Bury's edition of the Philebus, 1897, p. 68.
   It is noteworthy that Plato does not use ἀναλαμβάνειν with regard to μνήμη.
140. Cf. Laws V, 732 b 8 f.: ἀνάμνησις δ' ἐστὶν ἐπιρροὴ φρονήσεως ἀπολειπούσης.
141. There is no reason to delete καὶ μνήμας, as Gloël, Burnet, and Hackforth do, or to correct the phrase (cf. Bury, loc. cit.). See also Charm. 159 e 9, 176 b 1–4.
142. De memoria 451 a 20–21 (see p. 110); Freudenthal, op. cit., p. 404; H.-G. Gadamer, Plato's dialektische Ethik, Phänomenologische Interpretationen zum 'Philebos', 1931, p. 125. (In "recollecting" we are aware of our "having forgotten" – cf. p. 112. This awareness is an essential element in the phenomenon of recollection. Gadamer's analysis seems to neglect that element.)
143. See p. 130.

ing of memory is a specific case of desire (ἐπιθυμία), to wit, the desire experienced in thirst (34 e 9 – 35 d 7). The experience of being thirsty is in itself a double one: it comprises (a) the painful feeling of depletion (κένωσις) and *simultaneously* (b) the longing for replenishment (πλήρωσις) and for the satisfaction which accompanies the feeling of being "filled" again.[144] Socrates raises a teasing question (35 a 6–9) : how can a man who suffers from thirst for the first time (τὸ πρῶτον), that is to say, is being "emptied" for the first time, have any inkling (ἐφάπτεσθαι) of the opposite process, of that of replenishment? And how can he be longing for something which has never before been part of his experience, either through direct sensing (αἰσθήσει) or through memory (μνήμη)? At first glance the impossibility of desiring replenishment in such a case seems perfectly clear. But we should not forget: to be thirsty means *in any case* to need the opposite of what produces the suffering. If no direct experience of being filled again has ever occurred before, the conclusion is inescapable that there must be something else in man which makes him desire replenishment. It is also clear that the source of this desire cannot have anything to do with man's body, which merely undergoes the process of being emptied, but must belong to his soul and account for his anticipating the satisfaction to be derived from his being replenished again. It is obvious, Socrates claims, that this not ignorant, and hopeful (cf. 35 e 9 – 36 b 7 and 32 b 9 – c 6), anticipation in man's soul must be due to the Memory which is the soul's very own (35 b 11 – c 2).

The memory Socrates is talking about at this point (35 c 1; c 13; d 2; cf. 33 c 5–6) is not the memory mentioned before (33 c 8 ff. including 35 a 7), the one which arises from sensing or even from learning in one's lifetime. It has a mythical character. It hints at something experienced and retained not in this life. It is not something ever *renewable* by recollection, like the memories commonly at our disposal, but something forever *abiding*, like the memory of the "philosopher" in the *Phaedrus*.[145]

A little later in the dialogue (38 b 12 – 39 c 6), Socrates reverts to the understanding of memory with which he began. Our attempts to reach and to state definite opinions on various matters, our very ability to have any opinion (δόξα) at all, are rooted both in memory and sense perception. It is as if

144. Cf. *Lysis* 221 d 6 – e 5; *Symp.* 204 a 6–7.
145. See p. 152.

our sensing, our memories and our feelings (τὰ παθήματα – 39 a 2) about what we sense and remember were acting conjointly on our soul[146] like a scribe covering a scroll with written characters, sometimes truthfully, sometimes falsely. But, in addition, when we are detached from any direct sensing and feeling, we are capable of seeing in ourselves copies of what was once written in our soul, as if a painter (ζωγράφος – 39 b 6),[147] succeeding the scribe, had provided us with images (εἰκόνες – 39 c 1, 4) of what was previously opined and stated in spoken or silent words.[148] These images are, correspondingly, either truthful or deceptive. They are ever-renewable memory imprints. In "reading" them we exercise our faculty of *dianoetic eikasia*.[149]

c) Thus, considering what is said in the *Philebus* and the *Phaedrus*, memory has a triple aspect. It is understood (1) as capable of retaining our immediate experience, which is based on our outer and inner sensing; (2) as the repository of knowledge acquired in one's lifetime or even before that, on one's journey with the gods to the region "above heaven"; (3) as the source of our desires which depend, once more, on some mythically conceived previous fulfilment and insight. With regard to the first two aspects, our memories are not persistent but may be newly re-established by a process of "natural" or mythical recollection. With regard to the third aspect, memory is enduring and does not need the help of any kind of recollection: it seems, in the *Philebus*, to play itself the role assigned elsewhere to ἀνάμνησις.

There is a genuine tension between these various aspects of memory. Diotima, in the *Symposium*, reveals the main root of that tension.

Diotima had just enumerated everything in man that, strangely enough, is constantly changing. She then goes on to say (207 e 5 – 208 a 7): "And still much stranger than all those things [mentioned before] is what happens to our knowledges: not that some of them arise and some vanish in us and that we are never the same even with regard to our knowledges, but [the point is] that each single knowledge also suffers the same [predicament]. Indeed, what is called

---

146. Cf. Hackforth, *Plato's Examination of Pleasure, A translation of the Philebus, with Introduction and Commentary*, 1945, p. 75, note 1; Robin, *Platon* (Pléiade), II, 1490, note 108.
147. Cf. p. 110.
148. Cf. *Theaet.* 190 a 4–6; c 5; *Soph.* 264 a (see also pp. 104 f. (4) and 133 f.).
149. Cf. p. 109 f.

studying (μελετᾶν) carries the implication that knowledge has gone out (ὡς ἐξιούσης ἐστὶ τῆς ἐπιστήμης); for forgetting (λήθη) is the outgoing of knowledge (ἐπιστήμης ἔξοδος), while study (μελετᾶν) replaces the outgoing memory (ἀπιούση μ ν ή μ η) [of something once learned] by producing afresh a new one (πάλιν κ α ι ν ὴ ν ἐμποιοῦσα) and thus preserves (σῴζει) the knowledge so as to make it appear the same (ὥστε τὴν αὐτὴν δοκεῖν εἶναι)." Μελέτη here means the studious effort of learning and is at the same time clearly a pun on μη-λήθη: the effort of learning is interpreted as removal of forgetfulness.[150] What is being lost and renewed are memories, memory "imprints." It is of old and new μνῆμαι that Diotima speaks as of old and new "knowledges," that is, of knowledges committed to memory. A vanished image, a memory imprint, of something "known" is replaced by a new image, a new memory imprint, of that very same thing, again as a "known" one. The two images, the two "memories," are two *remembered* knowledges and are thus subjected to the vicissitudes of time, but they give the appearance of being *one and the same knowledge* because their *content* is the same, *unchanging and timeless*.[151] That is why this exchange of "knowledge" for "knowledge" is so much "stranger" (ἀτοπώτερον) than any other change or exchange in man.

6. THE AVOIDANCE OF THE ἀνάμνησις THESIS IN OTHER DIALOGUES, AND ESPECIALLY IN THE *Theaetetus*

In the *Symposium,* Diotima does not revert to the recollection thesis at all. Nor is it mentioned in the sixth and seventh books of the *Republic,* in the *Theaetetus,* or elsewhere. Yet in these dialogues the theme of learning either is or seems to be eminently present.

The "divided line" in the sixth book of the *Republic* points to an ascent in the domain of the intelligible and implies a way of genuine learning.[152] So does the image of the "cave" at the beginning of the seventh book. But neither the one nor the other brings up the theme of recollection.

150. Thus not only ἀλήθεια but also μελέτη appears to carry the connotation of the "un-forgotten." This kind of punning, in its playfulness and its seriousness, is hardly a matter for etymological considerations (cf. P. Friedländer, *Plato I,* English version, 1958, pp 221 ff.). In *Rep.* X, 621 a, the river Ἀμελής borders on the plain of Λήθη.
151. Cf. *Phaedr.* 247 d 6 – e 2.
152. Cf. pp. 117–25.

The bulk of the seventh book of the *Republic* deals with the education of the future guardians of the City. Socrates is explicit about what they have to *learn* so as to be led upwards into the light, "as some are said to have ascended from Hades to the gods" (521 c 2–3). The various μαθήματα those men have to master are thoroughly surveyed (521 c ff.) but μάθησις itself is nowhere linked with ἀνάμνησις.

It has often been remarked that, before Socrates begins speaking about the course of studies to be followed by the future guardians, he seems to allude to the *anamnesis* thesis. Rejecting an ever-present view concerning the nature of education, he criticizes those who claim to "put" knowledge "into" a soul in which that knowledge is absent (518 b 6 – c 2). In Socrates' view, to which Glaucon adheres, there is within the soul of each one of us the power of learning and the "instrument" by means of which each one of us acquires knowledge by himself so as to be able to reach up to the highest level of being and to endure the sight of what is most luminous (cf. 518 c 4 – d 2). Still, there is no mention of "recollection" in this passage.

Instead, the seventh book of the *Republic* again conjoins μάθησις and μελέτη (526 c 1–2; 535 c 3).[153]

So does the *Theaetetus*. Here (153 b 9 – c 1) Socrates asks: "Is not the condition of the soul (ἡ ... ἐν τῇ ψυχῇ ἕξις) [in analogy to that of the body (b 5–8)] such that it acquires and retains what can be learned (μαθήματα) and [thereby] grows better through certain motions, namely through learning and studious effort (ὑπὸ μαθήσεως ... καὶ μελέτης), while it does not learn anything or forgets what it may have learned by remaining motionless, namely by making no effort and [therefore] staying ignorant (ὑπὸ δ' ἡσυχίας, ἀμελετησίας[154] τε καὶ ἀμαθίας οὔσης) ?" "Certainly," says Theaetetus.

But while there is no mention of recollection in the *Theaetetus*, the emphasis given to Memory in the second part of the dialogue is most noteworthy.

The problem is: how can something be "mistaken" for something else?—"mistaking" being one of the fundamental errors our διάνοια is capable of (ἀλλοδοξία – 189 b 12; ἀλλοδοξεῖν – 189 d 5, 190 e 1; ἑτεροδοξεῖν – 190 e 2; ἑτεροδοξία – 193 d 2).[155] This problem is part of the more general one: what does it

---

153. Cf. *Tim.* 88 a 2–3: μαθήσεις καὶ ζητήσεις.
154. Cf. *Phaedr.* 275 a 3: μνήμης ἀμελετησία (cf. p. 152).
155. Cf. p. 28.

mean to "have in mind" something which is false, to "opine" **159**
something untrue (τὸ δοξάζειν τινὰ ψευδῆ – 187 d 6)? And in
the background looms the even more comprehensive problem: what is "opining" (δοξάζειν)?[156] The discussion of this
skein of problems is introduced by Socrates with the words:
"It is better, I suppose, to bring to an end a small task
(σμικρόν) well than a big one poorly" (187 e 2–3). To
bring to an end their "small"[157] task, Socrates and Theaetetus
cannot avoid taking into account Memory, that marvelous—
and, on occasion, perilous—gift of Mnemosyne, the mother of
the Muses (191 d 3–4). For Opinion (δόξα) and Memory
(μνήμη) appear closely and inextricably related.[158] It is this
relation which is emphasized in the second part of the *Theaetetus*. Μνήμη is seen here in its common, ubiquitous, role, without any mythical magnification.

We have to put the discussion which goes on in this second
part of the doxological mime[159] into its own proper perspective.

The discussion is based on Theaetetus' second tentative answer to the question, "What is knowledge?" The first, by now
refuted, answer was: To know is to perceive. The second is
(187 b 5–6): Holding a "true opinion" (ἀληθὴς δόξα) means
to be in the state of "knowing."

The second answer is no less tentative than the first one
was. In fact, the tentative character of his contributions is
stressed by Theaetetus himself and acknowledged by Socrates
(151 e 1–5; 187 b 5 – c 6; cf. also 201 c 8 – d 3). Each time
Theaetetus' tentative answer brings out a particular δόγμα
championed by others.[160] The discussion shows that all these
opinions are faulty ones.

As to his second answer, Theaetetus from the very beginning (187 b 4–5) brings into play not only "true opinion"
but also "false opinion" (ψευδὴς δόξα): for the entire domain
of opinions (πᾶσα δόξα – 187 b 4), Socrates and Theaetetus
agree, is divided into two areas, one "truthful," the other
"deceptive" (δυοῖν ὄντοιν ἰδέαιν δόξης, τοῦ μὲν ἀληθινοῦ, ψευδοῦς
δὲ τοῦ ἑτέρου – c 3–4). Instead of directing their attention
to the character of "true opinion," as Theaetetus' answer seems

156. This last problem, in all its comprehensiveness, is raised in the
  fifth book of the *Republic* (esp. 476 e 4 ff.) and dealt with in the
  sixth and seventh books (cf. pp. 112–25).
157. Cf. 145 d 6.
158. Cf. Gadamer, *op. cit.*, p. 135.
159. Cf. p. 18.
160. Cf. 157 c 9 – d 2.

to demand, Theaetetus and Socrates—Socrates leading the way (187 c 7 – e 2) —seem to sidetrack the issue and concentrate on the area of the "false." This amounts to taking up again (ἀναλαβεῖν πάλιν – c 7) a problem touched upon previously (167 a – d; 179 c 1–2) and to pursuing an old track anew (187 e 1–2). It is thus that Theaetetus and Socrates, in following up the identification of "knowledge" with "true opinion," happen to be talking in the main about the problem that "false opining" poses.

We cannot fail to see that Theaetetus and Socrates, while *discussing* the phenomenon of mistaking something for something else, are themselves *enacting* this kind of error. They are able to do this because of the tentativeness of the answer under consideration. For an answer given, and accepted, tentatively cannot help being a *pretended* answer. Thus Theaetetus and Socrates *enact* an ἀλλοδοξία, present a case of ψευδῆ δοξάζειν, in "mistaking" ἀληθὴς δόξα for ἐπιστήμη: the argument they are engaged in treats knowledge explicitly *as* something *"known,"* known *as* true opinion, while it implicitly appeals to some possible other, albeit *unknown*, meaning of knowledge, differing from that of "true opinion." The—unavoidable—"impurity" of such an argument, duly recorded by Socrates (196 d 2 – 197 a 7),[161] stems from that hidden appeal.

It is in this context of "mistaking" – ἔργῳ – knowledge for true opinion and of accounting– λόγῳ – for the possibility of false opinions that Memory assumes a peculiar significance.

The possibility of "mistaking" something for something else is rooted in our, on the face of it, "incredible" (cf. 188 c 4), ability not to know what we know and to know what we do not know (188 a 10–11; c 2 f. – 191 a 8 – b 1; b 7–8; 196 c 1–2; 198 c 7–8; 199 c 5–6). It is "incredible" because, as is made emphatically clear (188 a 10 – b 2), it appears quite impossible that one who knows should not know and one who does not know should know. But this ability becomes credible as soon as we differentiate between two ways of "knowing" (197 a 8 – 198 a 4): we may have stored up knowledge in our memory and in this sense "possess" (κεκτῆσθαι – 197 b 8) it and may yet not have the known "present" before us; we may, on the other hand, have direct insight into something by "grasping and holding" (λαβεῖν καὶ σχεῖν – 197 c 9; 198 a 2; d 3) it "right now," "in our hands," as it were (cf. 198 d 3 – 4). The difference between "possessing knowledge" (ἐπιστήμης κτῆσις) in the

161. See pp. 84 f.

first sense and "having knowledge" (ἐπιστήμης ἕξις) in the second sense[162] may amount to "nothing," as Socrates does not
fail to remark (ἴσως ... οὐδὲν [διαφέρει] – 197 b 6), but it seems
to account, at any rate, for our "mistaking" something for
something else. It seems to account for our opining "falsely"
instead of "rightly."

We may have direct insights in a twofold way. We either
perceive something clearly enough by means of our senses
(αἰσθάνεσθαι) or grasp something solely by thinking (διανοεῖσθαι
μόνον) without making use of our senses (cf. 195 d 6–10). Both
kinds of insight can be recorded on our memory, which Socrates describes by using two similes.

In one of them memory is compared (191 c 8 – e 1) with a
"lump of wax" (κήρινον ἐκμαγεῖον) [163] on which sense perceptions (αἰσθήσεις) and also thoughts (ἔννοιαι) [164] can "stamp impressions" (ἀποτυποῦσθαι). Our memory is thus the receptacle
of "imprints" the quality of which varies depending on the
quality of the wax, that is, of the particular memory in question. In terms of this simile we are said "both to remember
and to know" (μνημονεύειν τε καὶ ἐπίστασθαι) that which succeeds in being effectively imprinted, as long as the imprinted
"image" (εἴδωλον) of whatever produced the imprint persists.
We are said "both to have forgotten and not to know"
(ἐπιλελῆσθαί τε καὶ μὴ ἐπίστασθαι) that which is wiped out
through the disappearance of its image, or else that which was
not able to leave an imprint at all (191 d 7 – e 1). The "knowing" and the "not knowing" refer here respectively to the
"possession of knowledge" (ἐπιστήμης κτῆσις) and to its opposite, *not* to the "having of knowledge" (ἐπιστήμης ἕξις) and
to its opposite.

Throughout (192 b 3 – 194 d 4), Socrates calls a "memory
imprint" a "mark," a σημεῖον—in analogy to the mark left by
the signet of a seal ring,[165] also a τύπος (192 a 4; 194 b 5) or
ἀποτύπωμα (194 b 5), a σφραγίς (192 a 6), an ἐκμαγεῖον (194
e 6), and, most pregnantly, a μνημεῖον ἐν τῇ ψυχῇ (192 a 2 f.; b
6; cf. 196 a 3: μνημεῖα ἐν τῷ ἐκμαγείῳ). The "memory imprints,"

162. Cf. the twofold meaning of ἐντελέχεια in Aristotle, as exemplified
by the distinction of "possessing knowledge," ἐπιστήμην ἔχειν
(ἐντελέχεια ἡ πρώτη), and of "exercising" it, τὸ θεωρεῖν: De
anima II, 1, 412 a 10–11; 22–28; 412 b 27 – 413 a 1; II, 5,
417 a 22 – b 2. Cf. also Nic. Eth. I, 8, 1098 b 31–33 and the use
of ἔχειν in Phaedo 75 d 9 (p. 130). Cf., on the other hand,
Aristotle, Phys. VIII, 4, 255 a 33 – b 5.
163. Cf. 194 c – d.
164. Cf. pp. 153 ff., also p. 129, note 59.
165. Cf. p. 110.

the μνημεῖα, the "memorials," do not belong to the domain of the visible and tangible. They belong to the medium in which our διάνοια does its work, to the stuff out of which what we call "mind" is made. Whenever we misjudge sensible things, mistaking one for another and thus opining falsely, we fail to correlate properly our perceptions and our memory imprints; we fail "in the adjustment of perception to thinking" (ἐν τῇ συνάψει αἰσθήσεως πρὸς διάνοιαν – 195 d 1–2). On the other hand, whenever the adjustment is made in the proper way, we opine rightly.

But we can also make "mistakes" which have nothing to do with sense perceptions. We can be mistaken in our thinking. The theme of "opining" (δοξάζειν) came up, in fact, after it had become clear that knowledge could not be found in what we call αἴσθησις, but had to be sought in that state of the soul, whatever its name, of which the soul becomes aware "when engaged all by itself (αὐτὴ καθ' αὑτήν) in considering what there is" (187 a 3–8). It was Theaetetus who ventured to submit that such a state of the soul is the one we are wont to call "opining."[166]

The possibility of mistakes in our thinking makes Socrates introduce another simile for memory. He now compares the memory in every soul with an aviary (197 c ff.) in which birds of all kinds and habits are kept. The birds are supposed to represent "knowledges"—"kept" knowledges. The very phrasing of the distinction between "possessing knowledge" and "having knowledge" was chosen to fit this new simile. The birds, or knowledges, are there; we own them, but we "have" them, strictly speaking, only if, after putting our hands into the cage, or applying our thinking in earnest, we "catch" them (θηρεύειν – 197 c 3; d 1; 198 a 2; a 7; d 2; 199 b 2) for the second time (διττὴ . . . ἡ θήρα); we can indeed do this whenever we so desire; we can also let them go again and repeat this operation at will (197 c 7 – d 2; 198 a 1–2). But it may well happen that, in performing this operation, we catch the "wrong" bird, a knowledge we were not after, that is to say, we make a "mistake" and thus obtain a ψευδὴς δόξα (199 a 9 – b 3).

This simile, then, helps us to imagine vividly the possibility of "mistakes" which our thinking makes all by itself. If, however, catching the wrong bird is equivalent to gaining a "false

166. In the *Republic* (477 e 1–3) δόξα is taken as a faculty or power (δύναμις) of the soul: it is that "by means of which we are able to opine" (ᾧ . . . δοξάζειν δυνάμεθα). *What* we opine is the δοξαστόν (cf. p. 113).

opinion," catching the "right" bird must be equivalent to gain- **163**
ing a "right opinion." This is the consequence Socrates himself draws (199 b 7–8): "When, on the other hand, [a man]
really gets hold of what he is trying to get hold of, he [can be
said] not to be mistaken (ἀψευδεῖν) and [therefore] to opine
what truly is (τὰ ὄντα δοξάζειν)." It thus indeed appears
possible for a man not to know what he knows (199 c 5) and
to go on relearning from himself what he already knows
(πάλιν ἔρχεται μαθησόμενος παρ' ἑαυτοῦ ἃ ἐπίσταται –198 e 4–5), as
Socrates had suggested previously (198 d 4–8) in a rather
involved phrase: "It is thus possible for a man to learn anew
(πάλιν ἔστι καταμανθάνειν) the very things the knowledge of
which was long before in him, after he had learned them so
that he knew them; [it is possible for him to relearn them]
by recovering the knowledge (ἀναλαμβάνοντα τὴν ἐπιστήμην) of
each of them and holding fast (ἴσχοντα) to it, which knowledge he had possessed long ago but did not have at hand in
his thinking" (πρόχειρον δ' οὐκ εἶχε τῇ διανοίᾳ).

At this point (199 c 7), however, a grave difficulty arises: if
one catches the "wrong" bird which, in any event, represents
a *"knowledge,"* is it conceivable that such a catch results in
our *not* having a knowledge "in our hands"?[167] Theaetetus
tries to overcome that difficulty by suggesting (199 e 1–6) that
among the birds there may be some which stand for
"knowledges," while others may stand for "ignorances"
(ἀνεπιστημοσύναι), so that the catch may sometimes end in
one's holding a true opinion, that is, in knowing, and sometimes in one's holding a false opinion, that is, in not knowing.
Socrates praises Theaetetus for his suggestion (199 e 7) and
then proceeds to show him that it, too, leads to insuperable
difficulties.

Yet Socrates' praise of Theaetetus on this occasion seems to
be more significant than his comment regarding Theaetetus'
suggestion. For this suggestion amounts not only to supple-
menting the identification of "knowledge" and "true opinion"
with that of "false opinion" and "ignorance," but also to interpreting the aviary, that is, our *memory*, as housing nothing
but "opinions," both true ones and false ones. The birds, being
of two kinds, can only stand for opinions, not for knowledges.
Socrates himself, indeed, in pursuing the simile of the aviary
and in taking the τέχνη of Arithmetic as an example, leaves
us in no doubt as to what he thinks the birds represent. A man

167. Cf. 199 d 1–2; also 189 c 5 – d 1.

who is proficient in the art of Arithmetic, Socrates intimates, "possesses" all the "knowledges" about numbers and is able to pass them on (παραδιδόναι) to someone else (198 a 10 – b 2). This now is how Socrates continues: "And we proclaim[168] the man who passes them on to be teaching (διδάσκειν) and the one who takes them over [from the first] to be learning (μανθάνειν) and him who has them, in the sense of keeping them in that aviary, to be knowing (ἐπίστασθαι)" (198 b 4–6). We do indeed. Such "teaching" and "learning," however, can only be understood as a passing on and a receiving of "opinions," at best of "true" ones, at worst of "false" ones. Such "teaching" and "learning" is constantly going on. We cannot dispense with it. The acquisition of a variety of skills, the gathering of information of all kinds, the convictions and practices which govern the conduct of our lives, all depend on it. For we live, and cannot help living, from childhood on, in the medium of accepted opinions. Our memory is to an overwhelming degree the repository of those opinions. When we are children, this receptacle, the aviary, must be considered empty (κενόν – 197 e 2 f.). Gradually we fill it up, we claim to be "learning" or to be "finding out" and finally to be "knowing" (cf. 197 e 2–6). What this means is that, all the while, we are "receiving" other peoples' opinions. Theaetetus' second answer and the discussion it provokes rest altogether on this fundamental human experience and on the common understanding of teaching and learning derived from it.[169]

That discussion led to an impasse, says Socrates (200 c 8 – d 2), because it concerned itself with the problem of "false opinion" before dealing with that of "knowledge": it is impossible to understand "false opinion" without having sufficiently grasped what "knowledge" is. Since the underlying assumption in all that discussion was the identity of "knowledge" and "true opinion," we understand Socrates to be saying that prior to investigating how false opinions come about one ought to try to investigate what is meant by "true opinion." In making Theaetetus' second tentative answer to the question "what is knowledge?" the basis for their discussion of "false opinion," Socrates and Theaetetus had left the most difficult problem of "true opinion" itself untouched, had not considered the relation of opinion to truth. In what sense can an opinion be "true" and still remain an "opinion"?

168. καλοῦμεν is rather emphatic (cf. 189 c 3).
169. Cf. p. 106. See also Cornford, *Plato's Theory of Knowledge,* 1935, pp. 135 f.

As to our memory being to an overwhelming degree the **165**
repository of opinions, it is hard to deny that our memory *also*
preserves genuine knowledge which we once acquired. The
question of how this first acquisition, this *initial* learning,
comes about is not even raised in the *Theaetetus*. In the
Meno as well as in the *Phaedo,* in the *Phaedrus* as well as in
the *Philebus,* the tale of mythical recollection or of mythical
memory at least hints at, or takes into account, in a more
or less elaborate way, the problem of initial learning, but
the *Theaetetus* ignores that problem altogether. Instead, the
Theaetetus takes up, in connection with the aviary simile, the
theme of relearning. The possibility of relearning seems to be
asserted: we are indeed able to catch the right bird. But this
ability is matched by our ability to catch the wrong one. Is it,
then, a matter of chance whether we succeed or fail in our
catching? If it were, how could we reconcile the serious effort
of learning with such haphazard catching? The phrase μάθησις
καὶ μελέτη seems to preclude an acquisition of knowledge based
on anything but deliberate search.

In fact, the *Theaetetus* does not try to *account* for learning
of any kind. For, although the dialogue raises the question of
knowledge, it deals with the ways we err: its immediate concern are "false opinions," notably false opinions about knowledge and learning. To bring those false opinions into the light
of day is the primary purpose of Socrates' "maieutic" art, so
much talked about in this dialogue (cf. esp. 157 c 7 – d 3; 210
b 4 – d 1).

It is tempting to consider Socrates' ironic insistence on his
being a "midwife" for young men (149 a 1 – 151 d 3; 157 c
7 – d 3; 160 e 2 – 161 a 6; 161 b 1–6; 184 a 8 – b 2; 210 b 4 –
d 1) as complementing his recollection story from the point of
view of the one who assists others in their effort to "recollect."[170] But as far as the *Theaetetus* is concerned, and it is
only in this dialogue that Plato makes Socrates characterize
his own dialectical art as "maieutic," Theaetetus is delivered
not of any insights but of false opinions spread over his memory.[171] It is true, this kind of deliverance is indispensable for

170. This is the view of the Anonymous Commentator (quoted with approval by Cornford, *op. cit.,* p. 28). Because it appears strongly
supported by the passage 150 d 6 – e 1, it has remained ever since
the prevalent view.
171. Cf. Aristophanes, *Clouds* 137 (and 139), where a pupil of Socrates
says to Strepsiades, who knocks violently at the door: "you have
made a thought, just excogitated, miscarry," φροντίδ' ἐξήμβλωκας
ἐξηυρημένην (quoted by Cornford, *loc. cit.*).

future "positive" learning.[172] The *Theaetetus*, however, does not show such learning and, if for no other reason than this, need not invoke the ἀνάμνησις thesis. Not ἐπιστήμη but her bastard sister δόξα dominates the scene. That is why opinion's faithful nurse, memory, is also constantly in sight.[173]

The ἀνάμνησις story presupposes, on the face of it, that there is knowledge "in" us, which proper questioning on the part of the "teacher" might bring to light. This knowledge "in" us is not supposed to be "fathered." But the false opinions, of which Theaetetus is unburdened by Socrates' maieutic skill, all have their "fathers": they are all "begotten." That is why they can be compared to infants whose birth needs the assistance of a μαῖα. This crucial circumstance seems to lie at the basis of the "midwifery" image.

7.

From what is said in the *Phaedo*, the *Phaedrus*, the *Philebus*, the *Symposium*, the *Republic*, and the *Theaetetus*, about learning, forgetting, recollecting, and remembering, we can infer:

1. The nature of the tie between the thesis of the soul's indestructibility and the thesis of recollection is by no means clear. This unclearness is not unrelated to the ambiguous use of the term ψυχή itself, the connotations of which range from φρόνησις to ζωή.

2. The central difficulty of the recollection thesis lies in the discrepancy between the timeless target of all learning and the temporal character of any recollection.

3. Memory, on its part, is curiously "in touch" with what happens to the body, on the one end, and no less curiously "in touch" with the domain of the intelligible, on the other end. Thus memory can be understood as preserver of sense perceptions, as repository of knowledge, and, most importantly, as recipient and dispenser of all kinds of opinions.

4. Whenever learning is identified with recollecting, or remembering, the problem of *initial* learning is held in suspense, unless the first beholding of the εἴδη on the part of the souls, as described in the *Phaedrus*, be taken as indicating initial learning.

172. Cf. p. 173.
173. The theme of μνήμη was first brought up in 163 d 1 – 164 d 6, where initial learning is indeed implied.

5. The link between learning and "studious effort" (μελέτη) **167**
is conspicuously emphasized.

With regard to the second and fifth points, we may well ask:
does not the studious effort involved in learning, does not
learning itself take time, occur in time? And is not the character of temporality common to both, learning and recollecting?

The effort of learning, however, does not aim at some point
back in time, it rather anticipates the acquisition of knowledge
at some future point of time. Does, then, the *repetition* involved in ἀνάμνησις and μελέτη, with their contrary motions,
tend toward the same goal? At the moment of insight, after a
period of learning, we cognize that what we have learned is
true. Can this cognition be anything but re-cognition? Does
not thus learning ultimately indeed merge with recollecting?
And must not then, conversely, the "yet unknown" and "unlearned" be equated with the "forgotten" (as Diotima's pun
intimates) and the state of ignorance with that of forgetfulness?

In the *Sophist* (229 b – c) the Stranger distinguishes different aspects of ignorance (ἄγνοια). One kind of ignorance, however, outweighs all the others. It consists in thinking that one
knows something while not knowing it (τὸ μὴ κατειδότα τι
δοκεῖν εἰδέναι). This kind of ignorance is properly called ἀμαθία.
This word points to the state men are in when they have not
learned what they are supposed to have learned. When we
blame a man for being ignorant we do so, indeed, not simply
because he does not know but because he has not exerted his
faculty of learning. We call him therefore ἀμαθής—"unlearned." On the other hand, having forgotten what we once
learned and knew, we also find ourselves in a state of ignorance, which could be removed by an effort of recollection. If
"being ignorant" and "not knowing" were altogether identical
with "having forgotten,"[174] any process of learning would indeed be a process of recollection, as the recollection thesis
maintains.

But does not Socrates claim in the *Philebus* (33 e 4–7)[175]:
It is absurd to say that something which does not exist or
has not yet come into being can be somehow 'lost' "? That
means: knowledge not yet acquired cannot be "forgotten."
Again, does not Socrates, in the *Theaetetus* (188 a 2–4),
mention, in passing, that learning (μανθάνειν) and forgetting

174. Cf. *Theaet.* 191 e 1: ἐπιλελῆσθαί τε καὶ μὴ ἐπίστασθαι (see p. 161).
175. See p. 153.

(ἐπιλανθάνεσθαι) have their place "between" (μεταξύ) knowing (εἰδέναι) and not knowing (μὴ εἰδέναι) so that "ignorance" does not appear to be equated with "forgetfulness." The discussion of learning and forgetting does not belong to the argument he and Theaetetus are pursuing at this point,[176] Socrates remarks. Conceivably, then, a more thorough investigation of learning and forgetting could throw more light on their "intermediate" position and therefore also on the relation of "forgetfulness" to the state of "not knowing." But this investigation is nowhere to be found. It would amount, at any rate, to an argumentative examination of the *anamnesis* thesis itself.

Are we not led to the conclusion: we have to withhold our assent to the thesis that learning is recollecting?

But would not such a conclusion miss a most important point?

Does not the thesis itself of necessity preclude any didactic argument about its validity? Was not that the reason why Socrates refrained from *telling* Meno more about it? What Meno asked, and we are asking now, is: how can we ascertain that what the thesis claims is true?

Socrates introduced the *anamnesis* story as stemming from people conversant with the highest order of things and capable of speaking about it. How adequate can this speaking be? Must not any *telling* about the highest, that is, the all-comprehensive, levels of things be marred by opaqueness and ambiguity, not because on those levels "things" are necessarily "dark" in themselves, but rather because their integrity and luminous clarity cannot help being broken in the fragmenting medium of speech. Even the most precise "technical" way of speaking could not alter this situation, because speech, like knowledge, reflects the inescapable plurality of a "world" subjected to the rule of "The Other."[177]

Speech is not quite capable of coping with "wholeness."[178] This theme of "wholeness" was reached in the dialogue, we remember, just before Meno refused to continue the search[179] and was present in the myth told by Socrates. In that myth, it actually provided the link between the theme of the soul's undying nature and the theme of learning.[180] But like any other

176. Cf. p. 165.
177. Cf. p. 86.
178. Cf. *Epist. VII*, 343 a 1: τὸ τῶν λόγων ἀσθενές (also pp. 17, 122, 146 f.).
179. P. 80.
180. P. 96.

kind of speaking, mythical speech detracts from the clarity of what is "whole," it cannot *tell* the whole truth.

There is a tendency to interpret a myth told in a Platonic dialogue, especially one told by Socrates, as a lever of persuasion more potent than any other way of speaking, appealing to less and yet to more than our understanding, a unique means of conveying the incommunicable. Is that what Alcibiades means in the *Symposium* (215 d 3–6) when he exclaims: "Listening to you [Socrates] or to your words spoken by somebody else, even though that one be a very poor speaker, we are overwhelmed and captivated, whoever be the listener, a woman, a man, a boy"? Does he refer to Socrates' sometimes exasperatingly ironic and mocking inquiries and never disguised dialectical power that may induce "torpor" in the one Socrates questions, but may also engender an unquenchable desire to search for the truth?[181] Or does Alcibiades have in mind Socratic myths of the kind we find in Platonic dialogues? If the latter be the case, is it true that the primary purpose of such myth-telling and mythmaking is the conveying of the incommunicable? To deal with that question properly we cannot refrain from reflecting, as Plato seems to be constantly doing, on the nature of myths the origins of which are unknown and which are passed on to us through innumerable generations of men.

Are not myths of that kind exalted opinions, human δοξάσματα[182] of a most impressive and unforgettable stature? Do they not serve as an insufficiently or too brightly illuminated background for all the opinions in which and by which we live?

What ought to be stressed is that myths never stand by themselves. That is their weakness and their strength. It is not a matter of chance or of some particular historical development that myths, at all times and in all lands, are found transposed into, or embodied by, or enacted in rituals, ceremonies, customs, institutions, presentations, tragedies, all of which cannot exist unless we have a stake and a share in them. Conversely, the fragmented and mute *actions* of man find a language of their own in myths.

In the *Phaedrus* (229 c 4 – 230 a 6) there is a brief conversation about the truth of familiar myths. Socrates dismisses as a sort of "boorish wisdom" (ἄγροικός τις σοφία – e 3) the attempts to reduce their respective content to some "natural"

181. Cf. pp. 92–95, 106 f., and VI, 1.
182. Cf. *Phaedr.* 274 c 3.

and trivial event magnified out of all proportion. It would be difficult, at any rate, says Socrates, to "set straight" (ἐπανορθοῦσθαι – d 6) mythical monsters like Centaurs and the Chimaera and the Gorgons and Pegasus in a similar way, according to what is "probable" (κατὰ τὸ εἰκός – e 2). He, Socrates, has no time to spare for this sort of guessing game: he is preoccupied with the all-absorbing task of "knowing himself," of finding out whether he is a beast even more complex, more inflated and fiercer than the monster Typhon or else a gentler and simpler living being to whose lot has fallen something of a lofty and serene nature.

Socrates is not interested in that "boorish wisdom" about mythical stories, but he is quite evidently interested in those stories themselves and in everything connected with them. Phaedrus asks him (229 b 4–9) whether a particular spot on the Ilissus is the site of the alleged seizure of Oreithyia by Boreas. "No" (οὐκ), Socrates replies with remarkable definiteness, and he indicates with equally remarkable precision where the event is said to have taken place and where the altar dedicated to Boreas is located (c 1 – 4).[183] This is the same Socrates who is supposed never to have set foot outside the walls of the City (230 c 6 – d 2),[184] at least in time of peace, because, so says Socrates, the countryside and the trees will not teach him anything (d 4). The list of monsters given by Socrates suggests the reason for his profound interest in myths. In the ninth book of the *Republic* (588 b 10 – e 2) Socrates fashions such a monster as an *image of the soul* (εἰκὼν τῆς ψυχῆς), Glaucon listening all the while in a somewhat amused mood of disbelief. Here, Scylla and Cerberus are added to the list. Are not myths, in Socrates' understanding, great luminous mirrors which throw reflected light on the condition and the predicament of human life and are not mythical monsters always images of the soul itself? Even though the ultimate source of that reflected light remains hidden, to "know oneself" means, among other things, to look at oneself and at one's actions in the mirrors with which those familiar, and mostly dreadful, myths have surrounded us.

A myth provides some measure for our actions. Platonic dialogues are set to measure that measure. To try to *find* the right yardstick for this task, to try to *find* the source of that reflected light, means to be engaged in Philosophy. To *combat* the

183. Cf. Herodotus VII, 189.
184. Phaedrus exaggerates slightly: cf. *Crito* 52 b and Robin, *Platon* (Pléiade), II, 1408, note 22.

pernicious effect of a false yardstick, to *combat* the distortion
which those mirrors produce, requires the setting up and telling of new myths. Myth-telling is indeed the paradigm of all
rhetorical art: it tends to initiate an *effort* in the soul of men
and to beget action. It is in actions that human excellence and
its opposite reveal themselves.

A new myth, a Socratic-Platonic myth, will always speak of
the Soul and will always be concerned about the undistorted
Whole. But its truth will not be found in its words.

In the case of the myth of recollection, the very fact of *telling* it as a means of conveying its "teaching" clearly defeats its
purpose. In this sense the myth of recollection is the prototype
of all myths. More than any other myth it *requires* transposition into a medium in which our own action or reaction
may embody its content.

In the *Republic,* after having *almost* completed the drawing
of the outline of the best πόλις, Socrates faces the question
(V, 471 c ff.) : how can this best πόλις be instituted on earth;
is it something at all *possible?* The answer to this question—
an "incredible" answer (472 a 6; 473 e 4) —is the "third wave"
which threatens, according to Socrates himself, to drown him
in laughter and contempt (472 a 4; 473 c 6–8) and, in
Glaucon's version, to subject him to capital punishment (473
e 6 – 474 a 4). The answer itself deviates "slightly" from the
path which the *speaking* about the most desirable πόλις had
pursued up to this moment: it entrusts the power to rule, here
on earth (δύναμις πολιτική), to men engaged, here on earth, in
philosophizing. The anticipated result of such a merger of political might and φιλοσοφία is but an "approximation" of the
"model" of the truly good state (παράδειγμα ἀγαθῆς πόλεως
– 472 d 9–10; c 4) which perhaps resides in heaven (IX, 592
b 2) and which was dealt with all along *in speech* the way one
tells a myth (ἡ πολιτεία ἣν μυθολογοῦμεν λόγῳ – VI, 501 e 4;
cf. II, 376 d 9). The anticipated result is but an "approximation" because actions of men can, at best, only approximate
what the spoken words intend. Socrates, before rushing into
his "third wave," seeks Glaucon's agreement about this relation of *action* to *speech.* He asks (473 a 1–3) : "Is it possible
that anything be *done* the way it is *spoken of?* Or is it rather
in the nature of things that *acting* be less in touch with truth
than *speaking,* even if someone disagrees on that?" Glaucon
does not disagree. Yet there might be—well or ill founded—
reasons for disagreement.

In the case of *learning,* at any rate, speaking about it, telling what it consists in and how it may be achieved, cannot live up to its actual exercise. It is *the action of learning* which conveys the truth about it. The answer to the question about the possibility of learning is not a "theory of knowledge" or an "epistemology" but the very *effort* to learn. The answer is the deed, the ἔργον, the μελέτη of learning, which, in turn, may lead to the ἕξις of knowing. Is not that the significance of Socrates' repeated injunction addressed both to Meno and to the young slave: πειρῶ, "make an attempt . . ."?[185] And is not that the weight of the conditional clause at the end of the myth about the necessity of having courage and of not growing tired of searching, as well as of the renewed emphasis on that very point in Socrates' final prodding of Meno to join with him in the search for human excellence?[186] Meno is now offered the opportunity to "verify" the myth by his own action, and correspondingly, so are we.

We shall have to see whether the exhibition of Meno's way of learning will bear out what we have been trying to learn about "recollection"—and also about memory.

185. Cf. pp. 91–92, 100–1.
186. Cf. pp. 94, 96–97.

VI

1.

Twice during the conversation with the young slave Socrates turns to Meno for a comment: the first time, after
the boy's first attempt to answer the question about the side
of the double square; the second time, after the refutation of
the boy's second answer.

[82 e 4–13;
84 a 3 – d 2]

On the first occasion, Socrates, who had just elicited the first
false answer from the boy, wants Meno to notice that he, Socrates, is not teaching the boy anything but just keeps asking
questions; also, that the boy, at this very moment, thinks he
knows the answer to the question about the double square,
while he clearly does not know it and is merely misled by the
aspect of "doubleness." Meno agrees *(nai)*. And Socrates exhorts[1] Meno to observe how the boy will continue recollecting
"in orderly succession" *(ephexês)*, "as one ought to recollect"
(hôs dei anamimnêiskesthai) .[2]

On the second occasion, the young slave having just emphatically asserted his ignorance, Socrates points out to Meno
how much better off the boy is at this stage of his "recollecting": he is now genuinely disturbed and perplexed and does
not think that he knows the right answer of which he is in
fact ignorant. Meno agrees. The torpor induced by Socrates'
questioning, similar to the effect produced by the numbfish,
has apparently done no harm to the young man. "It does not
seem that it did," says Meno. On the contrary, it could help
him to find the right answer, Socrates suggests: for now, aware
of his own ignorance, he may, because of, and in addition to,
that awareness, be glad to take on the burden of the search,
since the successful completion of that search promises to re-
lieve him of his perplexity. Meno, we remember, felt merely
the sting of ridicule[3] when *his* second attempt to answer the
question about human excellence had failed. Instead of trying

1. Cf. p. 98.
2. Cf. Aristotle, *De memoria* 451 b 16 ff.
3. In a similar situation, in the *Charmides* (169 c 6 – d 1), Critias
felt "ashamed" *(ᾐσχύνετο)* and tried to conceal his perplexity. Cf.
above p. 25, also pp. 29, 88, 89, 105 f., and *Soph.* 230 c 3 – d 5.

to solve the difficulty by continuing the search, he tried to extricate himself from the ridiculous position he judged himself to be in by mocking, and even threatening, Socrates. Not so the young slave, it seems. And Socrates, discounting the fact that he was talking to a slave, and to a young and inexperienced one at that, sarcastically underscores the contrast between the slave and Meno by attributing to the boy an initial confidence in his own ability to speak easily (*rhaidiós*) and well (*eu*) and often (*pollakis*) and to many people (*pros pollous*) about the double square as requiring a side double in length. Socrates is quoting Meno's own words,[4] but Meno does not seem to mind. Has he forgotten what he himself said?

Socrates insists on the importance the induced torpor has to the boy. Could the boy have tried to search for or to learn (*zêtein ê manthanein*) what he believed he knew? Could he have tried to search or to learn as long as he persisted in that erroneous belief? Could he be ready to engage in the search before he had reached a dead end (*aporia*), fallen into a state of perplexity, become aware of his ignorance and thus experienced a craving for knowledge? "I do not think so," says Meno, who is now willing to admit that the young slave not only was not harmed by, but may even have profited from, the state of torpor Socrates induced in him.

Socrates invites Meno to observe how, out of and because of that perplexity, the boy will, in addition,[5] discover something, when searching jointly with him, Socrates (*met'emou*),[6] while he, Socrates, will merely ask questions and not "teach." Socrates' statement, we note, is quite categorical: The boy *will* discover (*aneurêsei*) an answer. And, once more, Meno is urged to watch Socrates' behavior closely so as to catch him if he ever tries to "teach" and to instruct the boy instead of eliciting the boy's own "opinions" by mere questioning. It is the first time, we note, that the noun *doxa* appears in the dialogue, although the verb *dokein* was often used before, most significantly perhaps in Socrates' very first attempt to make Meno repeat what Gorgias had said about human excellence[7] and also in Socrates' marginal "pedagogic" remark during his conversation with the young slave.[8] This word *doxa* will henceforth keep reappearing all the time.

4. Cf. pp. 46 and 88.
5. καί in 84 c 10 = καί in 84 b 10. Thompson (p. 137) seems to miss the point entirely.
6. Cf. 81 e 2: μετὰ σοῦ.
7. Cf. pp. 43 and 45.
8. Cf. pp. 102 and 104 f.

Immediately after the *epideixis* of the boy's learning has [85 b 8 – c 8] reached its end, Socrates turns to Meno again. It is up to us now to be especially watchful. For the conversation which follows will presumably mark the completion of the third stage in the *epideixis* of Meno himself.[9]

Socrates wants to know Meno's opinion on what had just happened before his eyes and ears (*ti soi dokei, ô Menôn?*). Could Meno notice, in the boy's answers, any opinion (*doxa*) but the boy's own?

If that question were put to us, what should we say? Should we not have first to counter Socrates' question by asking him: what do you mean by the boy's "opinions"?[10]

Do you mean the "propositions" which were contained implicitly or explicitly in the questions you put before the boy and which required either some simple computations on his part, his assent, or his denial? If that is what you mean by the boy's opinions, then our answer will be: they were not his own.

Or do you mean by the boy's opinions the results of the boy's own computations or his assent to, or his rejection of, those propositions, that is, the completion of his thinking about them (*dianoias apoteleutêsis*)? If that is what you mean, our answer will be: they were indeed his own. For the correct arithmetical answer as well as the "yes" or the "no" he arrived at in each case seemed to us the result of his bowing to the necessity revealed in his own thinking, since we ourselves, keeping up with your questioning, had to confirm in each case, silently, under the compulsion of *our* own thinking, the boy's correct arithmetical answer as well as his "yes" or his "no."

We had to do this notwithstanding the possibility, which we did envisage, that the boy's replies might have been given somewhat haphazardly or with the purpose of pleasing you.

Or do you mean by the boy's opinions the false numerical answers he arrived at and uttered? In that case our answer will be: those opinions were not his own for, in giving them, he did not "look into himself" at all—as we clearly saw by looking into ourselves—but simply succumbed to the superficial plausibility suggested by the manner of your questioning.

Meno's reply is simply that the opinions manifested in the boy's answers were his own.

A while ago, Socrates reminds Meno, they were both agreed

9. Cf. p. 99.
10. Cf. pp. 104 f. (4).

that the boy did not know the right answer to the question about the side of the double square (82 e 8–9) .[11] But now, says Socrates, it turns out that those opinions were "in him" (enêsan . . . autôi), meaning, we presume, those opinions which finally led the boy to the right answer. Again, without asking Socrates for greater precision in the matter of the boy's opinions, Meno agrees. His answer is a straight "yes."

Socrates' next question offers to Meno a generalized conclusion: does not, therefore, he who may lack knowledge of certain things have "true opinions" (alêtheis doxai) about those very things he does not know? Meno has no objections to that conclusion.

We note that the term alêtheis doxai may have the connotation of opinions not subject to forgetfulness, of "unforgotten" or even "unforgettable" opinions.[12] The paradoxical nature of what is called "true opinion" is not even alluded to by Socrates.[13]

[85 c 9 – d 2] Going back to the case of the young slave, Socrates remarks that, as of now, those true (or unforgotten) opinions have been merely stirred up in him, like in a dream; but, asked the same things more than once (pollakis) and in more than one way (pollachêi), the boy will end up knowing (epistêsetai) [14] those things with no less precision than anyone else. Socrates expects Meno to know that this is so and Meno again raises no objection.

We, on our part, can readily agree to Socrates' description of the event as consistent with our understanding of the nature of the boy's opinions. For the clarity and precision with which the boy assented to, or rejected, the propositions offered to him by Socrates must indeed have had a dreamlike quality. Beyond being affected by the intrinsic limitation imposed upon the activity of the dianoia which comprehends its noêta as underlying visible things—a limitation that, by itself, makes the activity of the dianoia akin to dreaming[15]—the boy was given only a fleeting opportunity to submit himself to the compelling impact of his dianoia. The level of clarity and precision his own thinking could thus reach had to fall short even of the level of lucidity usually provided by the technê of Geometry: facing the visible lines drawn in the dust before him, he did

11. Cf. p. 173.
12. Cf. p. 157, note 150.
13. Cf. p. 164.
14. Cf. p. 178, note 19.
15. Cf. p. 122.

not ascend to those more comprehensive suppositions from which he would have been able to demonstrate, step by step, in a strictly regulated and transparent manner, the construction presented to him by Socrates. At best, we may say, he has gone through an initial "analytical" exercise in mathematics.[16] At best, he has thus formed no more, indeed, than a not very stable, although "true," "opinion." Only repeated and varied further *practicing* could help him win the clarity and precision required by Geometry as a *technê*, could make him look more persistently "into himself" and bow with more awareness to the necessity inherent in his thinking. It is in that sense that he may end up "knowing," as Socrates had said.

Socrates presses his main point: nobody having taught the [85 d 3–8] boy, he *will* acquire knowledge (*epistêsetai*) merely by being questioned, recovering (*analabôn*) that knowledge (*epistê-mên*) himself out of himself (*autos ex hautou*). "Yes," says Meno. He does not seem to be bothered by Socrates' projecting the boy's state of "knowing" into the future, beyond what Meno could have observed during the exhibition he witnessed, nor does he seem to pay any attention to the shift from "opinions" to "true opinions" and now to "knowledge," successively described by Socrates as residing "in" the boy. In simply assenting to Socrates' last proposition he has, however, assented to much more. For it is hard for anyone to deny that recovering something within oneself by oneself is just what we commonly call "recollecting." That holds for recollecting knowledge (knowledge once had, that is), too, as Socrates does not fail to point out by asking: "And is not recovering knowledge within oneself by oneself—recollecting [that knowledge]?" (*To de analambanein auton en hautôi epistêmên ouk anamimnêiskesthai estin?*) Meno cannot help answering in the affirmative. Socrates thus seems to have "shown" in a way satisfactory to Meno what the exhibition performed "on" the boy[17] intended to show him.

3.

Yet Socrates continues the questioning of Meno. He begins [85 d 9 – 86 a 11] with the assumption, which Meno has just accepted, that the boy recovers "knowledge" which resides "in" him "now"

16. Cf. pp. 83 f., 85.
17. Cf. p. 98.

(*nyn* – d 9). In what follows, Socrates shifts back from the term "knowledge" to that of "opinions" (e 7) and then again to "true opinions" (86 a 7).

There can be only this alternative,[18] Socrates suggests, with regard to that "knowledge" which the boy "now" has: either he acquired it at some time (*pote*) or he always (*aei*) had it. "Yes," says Meno. If the latter is true, the boy always "knew." If the former is true, he could not have acquired that knowledge in his present lifetime (*en* . . . *tôi nyn biôi*) for, as Meno confirms, nobody had ever taught (*dedidache*) him any Geometry or, for that matter, anything else that can be learned (*kai tôn allôn mathematôn hapantôn*), Socrates taking this opportunity to point to the universal applicability of his questioning procedure. But since the boy, as Meno agrees, undoubtedly "has these opinions" now (here the shift from "knowledge" to "opinions" is made) and since he has not acquired them in his present life time, he, obviously, says Socrates, had them and had learned them (*eiche kai ememathêkei*) at some other time (*en allôi tini chronôi*), at a time when he was not a living human being (*hot' ouk ên anthrôpos*). "Yes," says Meno.

"All time" (*ho pas chronos* – 86 a 9) can be divided into the period when the boy is a living human being and the period when he is not a living human being. If, then, during *both* those periods of time, "true opinions" (here the shift from "opinions" to "true opinions" is made) are to exist[19] "in him" (*enesontai autôi*) —which true (or "unforgotten") opinions, when awakened by questioning, become "knowledges"— does it not follow, Socrates asks, that his soul (*hê psychê autou*) must be in possession of all that can be learned (*memathêkyia estai*)[20] always at all time (*ton aei chronon*)? Meno agrees.

We observe that Socrates, in his continued questioning of Meno, keeps avoiding the precision which he displayed in the questioning of the young slave. In fact, Socrates is merely expanding on the myth of recollection previously reported by him. The mythical way of speaking prevails throughout.

a) The meaning of "opinion" remains obscure. This obscurity is intensified by the way in which Socrates uses the

---

18. Cf. Thompson, pp. 140 f.
19. εἰ . . . ἐνέσονται is not a "real future condition" nor is the time in the apodosis really future—see Thompson, pp. 142–43 and Exc. IV. (The case is different for 85 c 10 – d 1; ἐπιστήσεται is repeated two lines later.)
20. Thompson, p. 142: "be in a condition of having learnt."

terms "opinion," "true opinion," and "knowledge," interchangeably.

b) The phrasing of Socrates' questions seems to assume that a human being exists "individually" even before he is born. This assumption amounts to the—mythical—assertion that the soul of a man exists before his birth.

c) The alternative that the boy's soul must either have acquired knowledge at some time or always have had it turns out to be no alternative at all or, at least, a highly ambiguous one. As previously in the myth itself,[21] the verb *manthanein* is again used ambiguously in the perfect tense. And to heighten the ambiguity, it is now explicitly intimated that the awakening of slumbering "true" (or "unforgotten") opinions through questioning may occur even in the prenatal past. Thus, the assumption that the boy acquired knowledge "at some time" (*pote*), that is, at some time before his birth, is made ambiguously equivalent to the assumption that the boy's soul possesses that knowledge throughout all time (*ton aei chronon*). Does, then, the alternative suggested by Socrates reduce itself to the alternative of possessing knowledge always "throughout all time" (*ton aei chronon*) or possessing it always (*aei*) in a way which is not susceptible of any temporal measure, that is, strictly speaking, possessing it at "no time"?[22] But is that latter possibility compatible with the mythical identity of the boy's soul before and after his birth?

Socrates proceeds to draw four conclusions from what has [86 b 1–6]
been agreed between him and Meno so far. Two of those conclusions are stated explicitly by Socrates, the other two are contained implicitly in what he says. These latter ones are: (1) since the young slave's soul is always (*aei*) in possession of true (or "unforgotten") opinions about all that can be learned, it is always in possession of the *truth* (*hê alêtheia*) of things; (2) since this can be said of the young slave's soul, it can also be said of any soul, more properly, of the soul in anyone of us (*hê alêtheia hêmin tôn ontôn estin en têi psychêi*). With these two implicit conclusions as premises, Socrates draws the following two explicit conclusions, the second being derived as a consequence of the first: (1) since the soul is *always* in possession of the truth of things, the soul can be assumed to be deathless (*athanatos an hê psychê eie*); (2) it is, therefore (*hôste . . .*), incumbent upon (*chrê*)

21. Cf. p. 95.
22. Cf. pp. 131, 150, 156, 157.

Meno to attempt confidently to search for what he happens not to know now (*nyn*), that is to say, for what is not now in his memory (*ho mê* [*tynchaneis*] *memnêmenos*); his searching (*zêtein*) will amount to recollecting (*anamimnêis-kesthai*).

The formulation of the first explicit conclusion (about the undying nature of the soul) marks it as a hypothetical one. It has a general character, and that is also the character of the two implicit conclusions. The second explicit conclusion is addressed directly to Meno. We note in particular that it distinguishes clearly between the state of "remembrance" and the action of "recollecting";[23] and that, while "recollecting" is equated to "searching," "knowing" is identified with "remembering."

It thus seems that Meno, in being urged to search for what he does not now know (it happens to be *aretê*), is invited to try to revive in his soul a *mnêmeion* of one of those "un-forgotten" opinions, in other words, to replace a worn-out imprint on his memory by a fresh one.[24]

The point at which we find Socrates and Meno at this moment is the same that Socrates had reached when he was finishing telling, and commenting on, the myth of recollection.[25] There is this difference, though: while in the original myth the identification of searching and learning with recollecting was derived from the undying nature of the soul, it now appears that the postulation of the latter *follows*[26] from our ability to learn, an ability exhibited by the young slave and interpreted as the ability to recollect the truth "within" us. The final conclusion is the same in both cases: it is possible to search for that truth and, with special reference to Meno, one ought to make the effort to do so.

Meno's reaction to what Socrates has just said is this: "I think you are right, Socrates, I know not how" (*eu moi dokeis legein, ô Sôkrates, ouk oid'hopôs*). Socrates seconds him: "I think so *too*, Meno" (*kai gar egô emoi, ô Menôn*).[27]

4.

Let us turn our attention to Meno's general, if somewhat qualified, acceptance of Socrates' comment on the young

23. Cf. pp. 109 ff.
24. Cf. pp. 156 f., 161 f.
25. Cf. pp. 94 f., 97.
26. As in the *Phaedo* (91 e – 92 a).
27. We should not overlook the irony of Socrates' words. They seem to refer no less to the second than to the first part of Meno's statement.

slave's performance under questioning, a comment which amounted to a restatement or an expansion of the original myth of recollection on the level of the myth itself. Meno had asked for a clarification of the meaning of that myth. And his demand seemed quite justified, considering the obscurity and ambiguity of the myth's terms as well as of its content. But now, in the face of the same—and even heightened—obscurity and ambiguity, Meno seems to be satisfied. (It is worth noting that, in his conversation with Socrates about what happened to the young slave, Meno uttered a simple and straight "yes" almost as many times as he had done in all the preceding and much more extended conversation.) Has Meno understood what went on during the "exhibition" of the slave? Has Meno learned his lesson as the slave has learned his?

Meno, we remember, had raised a strong objection to the very possibility of searching and learning. To counter that objection Socrates told or retold a myth which purported to justify the effort of learning. The exhibition of the young slave's acquiring geometrical knowledge in the process of being questioned by Socrates was meant to support the myth, was meant to show that "learning" *is* "recollecting" and that recollecting had actually taken place "in" the boy. If we were to assent to Socrates' comment on that event and to accept his interpretation of it, disregarding all the obscurities and ambiguities in his account, as Meno had done, we would have to agree to at least this much:

1. only that can be taught and learned which is somehow "within" the learner himself;

2. the process of learning appears as a process of recovery or recapture or repetition of what either has been learned once before or was always in some way "known" to us and slumbers "within" us as a true or "unforgotten" opinion;

3. to lift this slumbering opinion to the level of actual "knowledge," more than one effort of repetition is required, the effort itself must be repeated or "practiced";

4. above anything else, learning requires a serious and continued effort on our part.

In agreeing with Socrates now, must not Meno, too, even without understanding all the implications of Socrates' account, have understood at least those listed corollaries of the mythical proposition that "learning is recollecting"? Must he not have learned the lesson that "teaching and learning" is not opposed to "being given by nature," nor, for that matter, to "acquisition by practice"; that rather only what is given

182 "within" us and thus constitutes our "natural" possession can be taught and learned and practiced, while, on the other hand, without the effort of learning and practicing that natural possession of ours will remain submerged and inaccessible? Are we entitled to take Meno's last utterance as a sign of his—it is true, somewhat hesitant—willingness to accept those consequences? What he said was: "I think you are right, Socrates, I know not how."

We cannot be surprised at Meno's imperviousness to the lack of clarity and consistency in Socrates' way of presenting the story of recollection. Reasoned discourse, we remember, could not move him, and Socrates had to fall back upon habitually accepted opinions to be able to continue the conversation.[28] The mythical way of speaking, whatever obscurities it may contain and however much it may be removed from the immediate intentions of ordinary speech, is still close enough to our common experience and to the views habitually and hazily derived from it. We need not be surprised, therefore, if this way of speaking should have had some effect on Meno, even to the extent that he might now be willing to accept views not commonly held; we need not be surprised if Socrates' art of persuasion, of which the *expideixis* of the young slave was a part, were to bear fruit. This art is not maieutic; it may rather "beget" in the soul of the one who listens to Socrates' words the willingness or even eagerness to follow, with little reason perhaps, the path of reason; it does not necessarily make the listener learn a great deal, yet it may prepare him for a genuine effort of learning.[29] Are we witnessing an example of such persuasion, such "begetting" now, in the case of Meno? Meno might indeed have "learned" what consequences the mythical proposition about "recollection" entails; but, beyond that modicum of learning, might he not be willing now to engage actively in searching for something he does not know, abandoning his claim that any such search, any attempt to learn, is inherently impossible? Is not the main purpose of Socrates' telling, and expanding, the *myth* of recollection this: to induce Meno to "verify" that myth by his own action, by his own effort to search and to learn?[30]

[86 b 6 – d 2]   This, at any rate, is what Socrates quite clearly indicates immediately after agreeing with Meno that what he, Socrates,

28. Cf. pp. 52–53, 73, 79.
29. Cf. pp. 106 f.
30. Cf. pp. 171 f.

has just said seems to have been well said.[31] For he goes on **183**
asserting, forcefully and without any ambiguity, that in all
that was said there was only one point (81 d 5 – e 1; 86 b
2 – 4)[32] for which he would fight strenuously, in word and
deed (*kai logôi kai ergôi*), whenever he was able to do so.
This one point is the clear advantage of his *anamnêsis* story
over Meno's argument about the impossibility of learning:
the thought that one ought to search out (*dein zêtein*) what
one does not know would make us better men, more manly
and less slothful, than the thought that it is neither possible
for us to find what we do not know nor necessary to search
(*dein zêtein*) for it. As for the rest, Socrates says—sweepingly,
if not surprisingly—he would not, in defense of what was
said, uphold any other point with any confidence (*kai ta men
ge alla ouk an pany hyper tou logou diischyrisaimên . . .*).

May not the courage and the eagerness to engage in a tireless search (81 d 3 – 4)[33] have now been infused into Meno
directly by Socrates' words, which thus would have played the
role that the torpor and perplexity, induced by Socrates'
questioning, had played in the case of the young slave?[34]
Judging from Meno's reaction to Socrates' words, this may
indeed have happened. For Meno says: "There again I think
you are right, Socrates" (*kai touto men ge dokeis moi eu
legein, ô Sôkrates*).

Socrates' words, moreover, have brought back to the fore
the theme of *aretê*, which, in the myth, as told by Socrates,
appeared "enveloped" by the theme of learning[35] and was
mentioned only once again, somewhat marginally (81 d 6 –
e 1), just before Socrates' renewed prodding of Meno to
join with him in the search for human excellence.[36] If, indeed,
the main and only defensible point of the *anamnêsis* story is
that the acceptance of the truth of that story and its consequences makes us *better* men, then the theme of *aretê* was
ever-present, though on the surface somewhat forgotten, in all
the talk about learning and recollecting.[37] And as to Socrates'
avowed resolve to fight, in word and deed, whenever he can
do so, for the proposition that searching and learning improves
us, that is, brings us closer to what we ought to be, does it not

31. Cf. p. 180, note 27.
32. Cf. pp. 94, 97.
33. Cf. pp. 96 f. (6).
34. Cf. pp. 173 f.
35. Cf. p. 95.
36. Cf. p. 97.
37. Cf. p. 99.

reveal the peculiar excellence of Socrates himself? Does it not perhaps even contain the "whole" of human excellence?

Is Meno, then, ready to follow Socrates now? The query is put to Meno by Socrates himself: "Since, then, we are agreed that what one does not know ought to be searched out (*hoti zêtêteon peri hou mê tis oiden*), would you have us try, in common, to search for [the answer to the question]: what is human excellence?"

Meno was asked to join in that search before; he did not refuse, but preferred to be instructed more fully about the *anamnêsis* story. This wish has now been fulfilled, apparently to Meno's satisfaction. The situation seems quite changed: Meno has given up his objection to the possibility of learning. Socrates' words appear to have had some effect upon him. We might expect him now to embark upon that common search proposed by Socrates.

Indeed, we hear him say, in answer to Socrates: "By all means" (*pany men oun*). But then we hear him make this addition which indicates—again—a "preference": "Still, so far as I am concerned, it would please me best to examine the very question I asked first and also to hear [that is, to be told] about it (*kai skepsaimên kai akousaimi*), [namely,] whether human excellence should be dealt with as a thing that can be taught or as something accruing to men by nature or in some other way."

5.

No, Meno has not budged.[38] His continued assent has been a spurious one. He may have committed the story told by Socrates, as so many other *logoi,* to his memory,[39] but he has not learned his lesson, and his failure is a double one: (1) he is by no means ready to follow Socrates; (2) he has not understood at all what he heard, in spite of his assenting to Socrates' words. These two *failures* are interrelated in a manner comparable to the way in which the slave boy *learned* two interconnected geometrical theorems at once.[40]

Meno simply reverts to his original question with which the dialogue so abruptly began and which now, had he understood what he assented to, should have lost its meaning. He

38. Cf. pp. 44 f.
39. Cf. pp. 69–73.
40. Cf. p. 107.

changes the wording of the question only to the extent that he omits any reference to "learning" and to "practicing." A rather significant omission!

We, on our part, need not go back on the impressions we received of him earlier in the dialogue.[41] They have been confirmed—and amplified—by Meno himself. The third stage of the *epideixis*, in which Meno is the main participant, has come to an end.[42] This end parallels the end of the third stage in the exhibition of the young slave's learning. There Socrates had drawn lines which represent the diagonals of squares and which provide the solution of the problem posed by Socrates to the slave. This solution cannot be expressed numerically: the length of each of those lines is "unspeakable," is an *arrêton*. It can only be pointed at. But we comprehend, as the slave does, that this inexpressible length *is* the length of the sides of the double square.

Here, in the exhibition of Meno's learning, Socrates' exhortation and Meno's response to it correspond to the mute language of the lines drawn by Socrates in the previous exhibition: Meno's unspeakable soul has been finally unveiled. We see Meno now *as he is*, in the nakedness of his soul.[43] And we comprehend *who* he is[44] in relation to learning: a man unwilling to learn and incapable of learning, although endowed with a peculiarly powerful memory. We can also discern now what is wrong with that memory of his, what is "deranged" about it.[45]

Meno shifts his "opinions" or positions with the greatest of ease without realizing that, when one of them supplants another, it might contradict or repudiate that other.[46] This happens to him because, as we have had enough occasion to observe, either somebody else's utterances or commonly expressed views have left "imprints" on his memory, which he has no difficulty in translating into words, regardless of whether those utterances and views are consistent or inconsistent with each other. Thus, each of his professed opinions, taken separately, may well have some "reason" behind it,[47] but it is precisely that reason, and certainly the relations

41. Pp. 45, 69, 71 f., 78 f., 80, 91, 97.
42. Cf. pp. 99, 175.
43. Cf. p. 90. (Cf. also R. G. Hoerber, "Plato's Meno," *Phronesis*, 5 (1960), 89, 91.)
44. Cf. pp. 35–38.
45. Cf. pp. 45, 73.
46. Cf. pp. 67 f., 73 f., 75 f., 78 f.
47. Cf. pp. 47, 51, 52, 54, 73.

which those opinions of his may have to each other, that escape him. But now, at last, we have seen him giving his assent to Socrates' mythical account of the reason that made it possible for the ignorant young slave to learn his lesson. That assent, as we have also seen, did not reflect any understanding on Meno's part, contrary to what we were led to believe for a while. What, then, did it indicate?

Since Socrates merely restated and expanded, though in a somewhat modified manner, the *anamnêsis* story he had told before, he gave Meno the renewed opportunity to flatter his own memory, to flatter himself.[48] Socrates' comment on the slave's learning served, like the—not too reliable—quotation from Empedocles,[49] as an echo of the words Meno had already heard and, not quite distinctly, recorded "on" his memory. In this case, we actually witnessed the recording as well as the re-echoing of Socrates' words in Meno's soul. What Meno assented to were his own memory "imprints." No effort of understanding and learning, no "looking *into* oneself," was needed for that assent. Understanding and learning require more than an echo can provide and must, of necessity, descend beneath the "surface" of those imprints to get to their underlying "reasons" or "suppositions." Meno is not capable of such a descent.

We have to conclude that Meno's soul lacks the dimension which makes learning and the effort of learning possible.[50] The "derangement" of his memory consists in its being unsupported by a "third dimension" of his soul. No learning can occur without memory, but no memory fulfills its proper function unless related to some learning. Meno's soul is indeed nothing but "memory," an isolated and autonomous memory, similar to a sheet or to a scroll covered with innumerable and intermingled characters,[51] something of a two-dimensional and shadow-like being: it is a repository of opinions but it cannot become a repository of knowledge.[52] It has no "depth" and no "solidity" at all.[53] Plato has a name for this kind of soul. It is a "little" or "shrunken" soul, –a *psycharion*.

The word appears in the *Theaetetus* (195 a 3) in the context of the description which likens our memory to a lump of

48. Cf. p. 69.
49. P. 68.
50. Cf. pp. 59, 62, 66 f., 92, 97, 98, 171 f., 181.
51. Cf. pp. 71 f.
52. *Rep.* VI, 486 c 7–9.
53. Cf. pp. 65–66 and also the peculiar irony in the use of the word στερεώτερον in *Rep.* I, 348 e 5.

wax (191 c 9).[54] Depending on the quality of the wax in
their souls, men are wise or foolish, slow or quick to learn, in
possession of a good or a bad memory (194 c ff.). For the
quality of the wax accounts for the character of the "imprints" made on it. Thus, the memories of some men carry
imprints that are dim and unclear (*asaphê*). This happens
when the purity of the wax is contaminated by some undesirable admixture, or when the wax is too hard, or when
the wax is too wet and soft. The hardness of the wax, in particular, causes the imprints to be indistinct because, in this
case, "there is no depth in them" (*bathos gar ouk eni* –
194 e 7; cf. c 5, d 1). And if, in addition, on account of the
too narrow space available (*hypo stenochôrias* – 195 a 3), the
imprints impinge one upon another, they become even more
indistinct. Such is the condition of a soul that lacks the proper
"dimensions,"[55] the condition of a *psycharion*.

In the seventh book of the *Republic* (535 a – 536 b) there
is a discussion of the criteria that should govern the selection
of young men who might later become rulers in the *polis*.[56]
With a view to the studies they would have to undertake and
which would demand from them a great deal of learning and
practicing (*mathêsis kai askêsis*), a whole list of requirements
is given. And next to keenness of mind (*drimytês*) with regard
to what is to be learned, to facility in learning itself (*mê
chalepôs manthanein*), to the possession of a good memory and
stubborn tirelessness (*mnêmôn kai arratos*), the heaviest emphasis is on the necessity of being laborious (*philoponos*),
of being inclined towards learning (*philomathês*) and towards
attentive listening (*philêkoos*), of being disposed to search
(*zêtêtikos*), and of hating all falsehood, be it deliberate or in-
voluntary,[57] because of a zealous concern about truth. By contrast, a man who hates any laborious effort (*misoponei*) and
wallows in ignorance, that is, in a state brought about by
neglect of learning (*amathia*),[58] should not, and cannot, be
among the selected ones. He is characterized as defective or
"lame" (*chôlos*) and his soul as a mutilated soul (*anapêros
psychê*). Not only the lameness and spuriousness of such a
soul with respect to the effort of learning have to be considered in the selection, but also the same kind of defective-

54. P. 161. (Cf. also Aristotle, *De memoria*, 450 a 32 – b 11.)
55. Cf. also 173 a 3 and 175 d 1.
56. Cf. *Rep.* II, 374 e 6–9.
57. Cf. *Hipp. min.* 370 e 5 ff.
58. Cf. p. 167.

ness with respect to "all parts of excellence" (*panta ta tês aretês merê*). The "parts" explicitly referred to or listed in this connection (535 a 10 – b 1; 536 a 2–3) are: steadfastness (*bebaiotês*), courage (*andreia*), also, as much as possible, good looks (*eueideia*), and furthermore soundness of mind (*sôphrosynê*) and loftiness (*megaloprepeia*).[59] A special type of soul, that of men called "base, yet clever" (*tôn legomenôn ponêrôn men, sophôn de*), is mentioned earlier in the seventh book of the *Republic* (518 e – 519 a). It has sharp eyes for what it is interested in; it shares, therefore, to some extent at least, in the excellence of wise thinking (*hê aretê tou phronêsai*). No wonder, for this excellence, compared to any other human excellence, seems to come from an altogether more divine source whose power is never completely lost. That is why even "base cleverness" (*panourgia*) can be called a kind of thoughtfulness (*phronêsis tis*).[60] But the "base, yet clever" soul perverts the excellence of thoughtfulness to serve evil ends, the more so the keener its eyesight. And here again *psycharion* is the name attached to this type of mutilated soul (519 a 3).

Meno's soul seems to be the prototype of all those mutilated and shrunken souls. Any thoughtful judgment Meno is capable of exercising is part of his *panourgia*.[61] What characterizes him most is his insuperable reluctance to engage in any learning effort (*misoponia*) and the ensuing state of ignorance (*amathia*) he is in. In the dialogue these traits of Meno's soul are intimately connected with the character of his memory. While the slave exhibits a genuine learning ability, mythically called the power of "recollection," Meno exhibits a peculiar mnemonic skill which, in accordance with the jingle in the beginning of the dialogue,[62] could be properly called "menonic." (And do not all of us have a share in this menonic memory?)

There is another aspect to Meno's deficiency. Just as his answers are not *his* answers, his judgments, but merely reproduce opinions of others,[63] his questions are not really *questions* since they do not stem from any desire to know. Nor do they grow out of a background of continued exploration which may give rise to problems and alternative solutions. If they have any "background" at all, it is provided either by

---

59. Cf. *Rep.* VI, 486 a – 487 a; 490 c 9–11.
60. Cf. *Hipp. min.* 365 e 2–5; *Menex.* 246 e 7 – 247 a 2 (also Aristotle, *Nic. Eth.*, VI, 12, 1144 a 23–29).
61. Cf. pp. 89 f., 97 f.
62. Cf. pp. 44 f.
63. Cf. pp. 104 f. (4).

Meno's desire to avoid such exploration and search[64] or by his habit of bringing his memories into play.[65] His questions reflect the "surface" character of his being. They cannot help being "abrupt."[66]

6.

Can we understand more precisely now the insistence on "recollection" in the exhibitions we have witnessed? Why the theme is taken up by Socrates in a *myth* is perhaps sufficiently clear, considering the myth's main *purpose*, the enticement of Meno into the effort of learning.[67] But is there not another reason for making *anamnêsis* the *explicit theme* of Socrates' endeavor to teach Meno and us? Whatever the role of the *anamnêsis* theme in the *Phaedo* or the *Phaedrus*, the context of the drama played out in the *Meno* seems to link that theme directly with the character of Meno himself.

Whatever else *anamnêsis* might imply, it certainly connotes a looking *back,* not only back into the past, but also back into oneself. It means a recovering or recapturing (*analambanein*) of something "within" or "inside" us, and this was stressed by Socrates throughout the dialogue.[68] The repetition invoked by the term *anamnêsis* was contrasted, throughout the dialogue, with the verbal repetition of somebody else's utterances, the kind of repetition Meno, the pupil of Gorgias, so skillfully indulges in. As to the other kind of "repetition," the one suggested by the myth of recollection, it is, as we have seen, out of Meno's reach. For to be able to look back *into* oneself, one has to possess something "within" oneself susceptible of being looked into: there must be present a dimension of "depth," a "third dimension" (*tritê auxê*), and it is precisely this dimension, this "augment" that Meno lacks. Meno's soul has no "inside." It is a mutilated or shrunken soul, a "dead" soul, we should perhaps say, akin to those phantoms in Hades when they emerge from the floods of total forgetfulness.[69]

But does not that similarity mean that Socrates has, after all, presented us with an *image* of Meno, reciprocating Meno's

64. Cf. pp. 62, 65, 66 f.
65. Cf. pp. 41, 67, 69, 71 f., 91, 97.
66. Cf. p. 38.
67. Cf. pp. 97, 106 f., 172, 182.
68. Cf. pp. 96, 104, 105, 175, 179 f.
69. Cf. the "plane" number representing the tyrant's shadowy pleasure in *Rep.* IX, 587 d 6–7 and context.

drawing of Socrates in the image of a numbfish?[70] That is *not* what Socrates has done.[71] He has made *us* see Meno as Meno is, and has thus put *us* in the position to draw a picture of Meno's soul. The "description" of a "soul" cannot escape the use of imagery. Socrates did not describe Meno's soul. The action presented in the dialogue revealed that soul in its whole emptiness without any imagery.

Yet an image of the soul (not Meno's soul) is suggested by the *anamnêsis* myth. It is not as elaborate an image as we find in other Socratic myths, but seems to furnish the foundation for all the others. It shows the soul as having a "third dimension"—an indispensable condition for its learning, that is, for its growth—as having "depth" (*bathos*) and, therefore, the character of what is called in technical geometrical language a "solid." For it is not only the mythical way of speaking that provides us with "images"—technical speech can do that as well.

It is necessary, and possible, to find support for this implied image of the soul in other Platonic dialogues.

---

70. Pp. 88–90.
71. Cf. *Rep.* VI, 487 e 6. Adeimantus' remark (Σὺ δέ γε [ὦ Σώκρατες] . . . οἶμαι οὐκ εἴωθας δι' εἰκόνων λέγειν) is meant to be gently ironic. But another gentle irony, unsuspected by Adeimantus, is that his remark reflects in all truth a genuine Socratic "habit" at crucial moments of a conversation. (Cf. p. 90.)

VII

1. THE τέχνη OF SOLIDS IN THE *Republic*

In discussing with Glaucon (in the seventh book of the *Republic*) the sequence of studies in which the future guardians of the πόλις would have to engage, Socrates deals with the science of "solids" in a most peculiar way. Socrates himself introduces (527 d 1) astronomy as the third kind of discipline to be taken up after (plane) geometry and the sciences of numbers. Glaucon immediately launches into a praise of astronomy because of its utility in agriculture, navigation, and warfare, but is rebuked by Socrates who reminds him of the more important purpose of all those contemplated studies. Glaucon himself is supposed to explore the matter under discussion not for anybody else's sake but for his own sake (σαυτοῦ ἕνεκα – 528 a 2), that is, for his soul's sake, and Glaucon agrees (ἐμαυτοῦ ἕνεκα – a 4). "Retreat then" ("Ἄναγε τοίνυν εἰς τοὐπίσω – a 6), says Socrates, for it was not right to let astronomy, which deals with the revolution of "solids" (the heavenly spheres), follow geometry without having taken up first the subject of "solid" by itself: after plane geometry, which had brought in the second dimension, one ought to consider the third dimension (αὔξη τρίτη – 528 b 2), the dimension of depth (βάθους αὔξη – d 8). Glaucon objects: the matter has not been found out yet. Socrates agrees that the investigation in this field has barely, though promisingly, begun and gives two reasons for that fact. One, in no political community, in no πόλις (b 6), is this difficult matter held in esteem; two, there is nobody to supervise and direct the investigation, and even if such a one could be found, the experts would not be willing to follow his lead. If, however, Socrates adds, an "entire political community" (πόλις ὅλη – c 2) were to direct those studies in a common resolve (συνεπιστατοῖ), the situation would change. Finally, about to resume the discussion of astronomy, Socrates mentions (e 4) once more (for the third time, in fact) the political community's interest in pursuing the investigation of the "dimension of depth," that is, of the field of the "solid," in contrast to that of the "plane" (ἡ τοῦ ἐπιπέδου πραγματεία – d 3), as a precondition for its flourishing.

To assume that this episode, with its curious double step of premature advance and subsequent withdrawal (ἀνάγειν εἰς τοὐπίσω – 528 a 6; ἀναχωρεῖν – d 6[1]), is merely meant to promote stereometric studies is to overlook the emphasis that binds the theme of the "solid" to the theme of the πόλις. In the case of the other disciplines discussed in the context, we do not find a corresponding emphasis. The study of *all* the subject matters mentioned by Socrates is, of course, inseparably linked to the main purpose of the construction of the best possible πόλις in Books II to VII of the *Republic*. The link is explicitly stated in the case of the sciences of numbers (525 b 11 f.), of plane geometry (527 c 1 f.), of astronomy (530 c 5), and is perhaps also referred to when the πόλις is mentioned for the third time in connection with the study of solid geometry (528 e 4–5). But in the case of the "solids," the references to the πόλις, especially the first two, seem to be much more meaningful. We cannot forget that the theme of the πόλις in the *Republic* includes the theme of the "soul" as well as that of the "whole." The assigning of stereometry, instead of astronomy, to the third place in the sequence of required studies necessitates a *regress* in the enumeration of those studies. Is not this regress comparable to the *reflexive* motion of the soul looking into itself? The emphasis on the neglect of the "dimension of depth" so far as studies are concerned seems to imply a similar neglect with regard to the soul on the part of both city and citizens. What people do, what cities do, manifests what they are. A πόλις can shrink too. The life of a city may become a surface phenomenon: its soul, the πολιτεία, may lose its "depth."

The dimension of "depth" is usually understood as an attribute of a body (σῶμα). The question of what constitutes a "body" is *the* theme of the *Timaeus*, where Timaeus gives an answer to this question in the context of a mythical account of the "whole" and the "soul," which account, in turn, is tied, at both ends, to the theme of the πόλις. It seems that Timaeus' answer elucidates what was only hinted at in the stereometric episode of the *Republic*.

1. These are again military terms (cf. p. 123, note 42). For ἀναχωρεῖν cf. *Crito* 51 b 8, *Symp.* 221 a 2, *Menex.* 246 b 5; for ἀνάγειν see Lidd.-Scott, *s.v.* II. 10: "perhaps nautical."

The *Timaeus*, no less, and perhaps more, than any other Platonic dialogue, combines seriousness with playfulness, utter solemnity with fanciful mocking. The point is not that quite a few passages in Timaeus' account, as, for example, the mention of the traditional gods (40 d – 41 a; cf. 27 b–d), the description of the liver in its relation to divination (71 a – 72 c), the reference to the birds (91 d–e), are highly amusing or sarcastic; the dialogue as a whole, the character of the personages involved in it, the nature of the feast offered by Timaeus, Critias, and Hermocrates to Socrates in return for the latter's hospitality the day before, are altogether both soberly weighty and comically ambiguous.[2] We must be aware, therefore, that we again[3] run a great risk in dealing with the text in a fragmentary fashion.

Timaeus sets out to describe mythically the "generation" of the visible world around us. For this purpose a threefold distinction has to be made in thought (Χρὴ γένη διανοθῆναι τριττά – 50 c 7), the distinction between father, mother, and offspring.

The role of "father" is given to the "source" of what is generated in its likeness (τὸ ... ὅθεν ἀφομοιούμενον φύεται τὸ γιγνόμενον – 50 d 1 f.), to the "model" (παράδειγμα) of all the things that either live or sustain life. The model comprises all that *is* (27 d – 28 a; 52 a 1–4), that is to say, all that remains always unchangeably the same, ungenerated and indestructible, accessible only to intellect and thought (νοήσει μετὰ λόγου).

The role of "mother" is assigned to something the nature of which is extremely difficult to catch (δυσαλωτότατον – 51 b 1; cf. 49 a 3 f.). It is of the kind that cannot be seen at all (ἀόρατον – 51 a 7), can hardly be trusted to exist (μόγις πιστόν – 52 b 2), can only barely be "touched," without the aid of any sense perception, by "some spurious reasoning" (λογισμῷ τινὶ νόθῳ – 52 b 2), because it has no shape whatsoever (ἄμορφον – 50 d 7, 51 a 7), is in no way determined, and, therefore, not determinable at all. We understand, however, that for this very reason it is able to "receive" all possible

---

2. A. E. Taylor (*A Commentary on Plato's Timaeus*, 1928) and F. M. Cornford (*Plato's Cosmology*, 1937), not to mention other commentators, strangely—though traditionally—ignore this aspect of the dialogue completely.

3. Cf. p. 125.

shapes or determinations (πανδεχές – 51 a 7). It can indeed be named the "receptacle" of all generation and decay (πάσης γενέσεως ὑποδοχή – 49 a 5 f.), the "room" (χώρα) *"in"* which all change "takes place" (cf. 49 e 7, 50 c/d, 52 c 4), that is to say, *"in"* which all the "copies" (μιμήματα – 50 c 4–5, 48 e 6 f.; cf. 30 c 3 – 31 a 1, 29 b 1–2) of the model's content can emerge and disappear. The preposition "in" carries the entire weight of the problem we are confronted with. Lacking any shape or determination of its own and perpetually undergoing change, the "receptacle" still remains the indestructible matrix (ἐκμαγεῖον – 50 c 2) for everything (cf. 52 a/b) and must, therefore, be called "always the same" (ταὐτὸν . . . ἀεί – 50 b 6–7). That is why it can be faintly reached in our thinking and thus,[4] as Timaeus says (51 a/b), "partakes in some very perplexing way of the intelligible" (μεταλαμβάνον δὲ ἀπορώτατά πη τοῦ νοητοῦ), not too differently perhaps from the ἀρχή of "The Other."

Neither the "model" by itself, the "father," nor the "receptacle" by itself, the "mother," have either "body" or "soul."[5] It is only "between" (μεταξύ – 50 d 3) these two "extremes" that Soul and Body make their appearance. Soul and Body characterize the "offspring" (ἔκγονον – 50 d 4), the visible world around us, the domain of perpetual change (27 d 2 – 28 a; 52 d 3 f.), the domain of everything we sense, the subject matter of Timaeus' "likely story" (29 d 2; 30 b 7; 48 d 2; 53 d 5 f.; 56 a 1; 59 c 6; 68 d 2; 72 d 7). In the main, the story narrates the "making" of the visible gods (the Stars, the Planets, the Earth, and the Whole) and the "making" of men with their bodies, powers, and faculties, the healthy ones as well as the diseased ones. Thus, Timaeus, a stranger who, unlike the Stranger in the *Sophist* and the *Statesman,* and the one in the *Laws,* has a name, acts in the dialogue—though "in words" only—as the "father of gods and men." His contribution to the feast that Socrates is to enjoy is the ever-changing "offspring," the sum total of the "copies" of the Intelligible (cf. 59 c 9– d 2). A rather strange and debatable treat! How can Socrates enjoy it?

Taking his starting point from the "source" of the "offspring," Timaeus builds the Soul out of incompatible ingredients which can be brought together only by compulsion,

---

4. Cf. Cornford, *op. cit.,* p. 187 f.
5. The expressions ζῷον ἀίδιον and ἡ . . . τοῦ ζῴου φύσις (37 d) which refer to the "model" are disturbing. But they cannot, at any rate, imply the "soul" as Timaeus' story describes it.

"by force" (βίᾳ – 35 a 8). Taking his starting point from the "receptacle" of generation, Timaeus frames the Body by letting that over which the intellect has no control (and the name of which is Necessity) be at least "persuaded" by the intellect to follow, as much as possible, the direction towards the "best" (48 a 2–5). Persuasion is but a milder form of compulsion.[6] It is indeed simpler to deal with the body, which, at worst, is unruly, than with the soul, which, by its very constitution, is truly "monstrous."

Timaeus begins (31 b 4) with the Body, then (34 b 3) shifts to the building of the Soul and its distribution throughout the "Whole," and then (47 e 3) resumes and completes his account of the Body. Thus, the story of the Soul finds itself "enveloped" by the story of the Body.[7] Timaeus takes care, however, to stress (34 b 10 – c 5) that the sequence of the narrative, tainted as it is by human insufficiency, and, we should add, the very character of the subject matter (cf. 29 c–d), ought not to obscure the higher rank of the soul which, both in birth and in excellence (καὶ γενέσει καὶ ἀρετῇ), is prior and more venerable (προτέρα καὶ πρεσβυτέρα) than the body and is destined to rule over the latter. At the point of the narrative when the description of the building of the soul has been completed it is stated (36 d 8 – e 1), with some emphasis, that "after this" (μετὰ τοῦτο) the framing of all that is "bodily" (σωματοειδές) was taken up, and, what seems even more important, that this framing went on "within" the soul (ἐντὸς αὐτῆς [sc. τῆς ψυχῆς]).[8] We also note that twice in the narrative (34 b 3–4 and 36 e 2–3) the soul is described as wrapped around the body of the Whole "on the outside" (ἔξωθεν), in spite of the inconsistency this image seems to entail.[9] It does not seem clear whether the soul is "in" the body (ἐν σώματι – 30 b 4–5; cf. 43 a 5, 44 b 1, 69 c 5–8) or the body "in" the soul.[10]

The building of the Soul involves the ultimate "beginnings" (ἀρχαί) of all that is and comes to be (35 a–b; 37 a 2–3). The stretching of the Soul across the Whole, which

6. Cf. 56 c 5 f.: . . . ὅπῃπερ ἡ τῆς ἀνάγκης ἑκοῦσα πεισθεῖσά τε φύσις ὑπεῖκεν . . . .
7. Cf. p. 95.
8. Cf. 37 c 3–5: "ἐν ᾧ," referring (indirectly) to ψυχή.
9. Cf. Taylor, op. cit., pp. 58, 93.
10. There is a curious parallelism in the verbal expressions τὸ σῶμα αὐτῇ [sc. τῇ ψυχῇ] περιεκάλυψεν (34 b 4) and τὸ . . . σῶμα αὐτῇ [sc. τῇ ψυχῇ] περιετόρνευσαν (69 c 6), although their meaning is quite different (cf. 73 e 6–7).

stretching amounts to the very *constitution* of the Universe as a "whole," is achieved by means of numbers and ratios of numbers (35 b – 36 d), the subject matter of the τέχναι of arithmetic and logistic (and harmonics). So is the distribution, within the Whole, of earth, water, air, and fire, the so-called "elements," taken as *bodies* (46 d 6–7; 53 c 4–5) already available. But the construction of those bodies is done with the help of geometrical plane surfaces, more precisely, with the help of *two* types of triangles (53 c – 54 b). This construction is identical with the framing of Body in general, since all tangible and visible bodies are diversified compounds of those very small, and therefore not perceptible (56 b 7 – c 3), elementary bodies (58 c – 61 c; 73 b – e; 81 c 2–3; 81 e/82a).

The framing of the Body, then, is done according to geometrical and stereometrical patterns. The τέχναι of geometry and stereometry know indeed how to construct "solids," notably *regular solids* "contained by equilateral and equiangular figures equal to one another."[11] Here, in the *Timaeus*, however, this *technical* construction (54 d – 55 c) is used, mythically, to bring about *bodily solidity* (55 d – 56 c) of varying degree and of an altogether transient nature.[12]

Even before the "elements" with their uncontrollably disordered motions could be "persuaded" (56 c 3–7) to be properly and wholly balanced and distributed throughout the Whole (30 a; 31 b – 32 c; 34 b 2; 57 c 1–6; 58 a–c), a more profound disorder, which characterized the primordial state of the "receptacle," had to be cleared away. At this—only mythically conceivable and describable—stage the "receptacle" was "filled" (ἐμπίμπλασθαι) with dissimilar and unbalanced "traces" (ἴχνη) and "powers" (δυνάμεις),[13] *not* bodies, of the not yet existing four "elements" (53 b 1–4), and, swaying unevenly back and forth, it added to the agitation of those "powers" and "traces" and distributed them roughly in different places (52 d – 53 b). The decisive "persuasion of necessity by the intellect" consisted in just this: "limits" were provided by varying combinations of each of those two kinds of plane surfaces, of each of the two kinds of triangles. These limits were regularly shaped boundaries, of different size (57 d 1–2), which brought a certain regularity, if not constancy, to the chaotic condition of the "receptacle," for they made the "elements," in spite of their transient nature, be complete *bodies*

11. Euclid, *Elements*, XIII, Prop. 18.
12. Cf. pp. 65–66.
13. Cf. Cornford, *op. cit.*, p. 199.

(cf. 34 b 2), which they were not before. There is nothing
stable about these bodies either, because of the shifting nature
of the boundaries which keep combining, dissolving, and re-
combining all the time (54 b–d; 57 b).[14] Timaeus insists (48
b–c; 49 b – 50 a) that the so-called "elements" have no permanence whatever, that the nouns we use to designate them
should not mislead us to think of each of them as being "something" (τι). We should not point at them by saying "this" or
"this here" (τόδε καὶ τοῦτο). By far the safest way would be to
use expressions of the type "such and such" (τοιοῦτον), namely
"earthy" or "watery" or "airy" or "fiery."[15] These words carry
the implication that there is something else which we perceive
now *as* "watery," and now *as* "fiery," and so on. This "something else" is the "receptacle" (51 b 2–6). What distinguishes
the "civilized" state of the "receptacle" from its primordial
chaotic state is nothing but the presence of complete, if transient, *bodies*.

Thus "persuasion" (πειθώ) brought about Body, as "force"
(βία) brought about Soul. Persuasion and force initiated the
two opposite, yet converging, "generating" processes which led
to the emergence of the visible Whole. These processes came
to an end when the visible body of the whole (τὸ τοῦ παντὸς
σῶμα – 31 b 7, 32 a 8; cf. 32 c 1, 36 e 5[16]) was fused with the
invisible soul (30 b 4–5; 34 b; 46 d 6). The fusion was possible
because of the similarity in the composition of both. Both depend on factors of invariableness and on factors of change:
the soul lastly on "Sameness" and "Otherness" (35 a–b; 37
a 2–3), the body lastly on the equality of its constituent surfaces and its perpetual variability.[17] In this manner the world
became both "bodily" (σωματοειδές – 31 b 4, 36 d 9) and
"living" (ζῷον – 30 b 8, d 3; 32 d 1).

In Timaeus' account, then, the regularly shaped (mathematical) surfaces mediate between the uncontrollable disorder
of the "receptacle" and a planned order conceived as the
"best," mediate, in other words, between Necessity (ἀνάγκη)
and Intellect (νοῦς) (cf. 48 a 1–2), as numbers do in the case
of the Soul. The result of that mediation is the appearance of
Body. The "elements" and, therefore, all tangible bodies, as
well as the body of the Whole, owe their bodily status, their

14. Cf. Cornford, *op. cit.*, pp. 230–39.
15. Cf., on the other hand, 51 b 6 – e 6 and above pp. 141 f., note 104.
16. Also *Phileb.* 30 a 6.
17. Cf. in particular the references to σώματα in the description of the
    composition of the soul (35 a 2 and a 6).

bodily "solidity," to a regular configuration of plane surfaces, a configuration of two-dimensional entities. So does the "dimension of depth."

Timaeus introduces the discussion of this subject by saying (53 c 4–7) : "It is clear first of all, I suppose, to everyone that fire, and earth, and water, and air, are indeed bodies. Now, any kind of body has also depth. Depth, in turn—it is surface that encompasses it, and necessarily so" (τὸ δὲ βάθος αὖ πᾶσα ἀνάγκη τὴν ἐπίπεδον περιειληφέναι φύσιν[18]). The last sentence is not without ambiguity.

A body and its surface or surfaces are always conceived as inseparable from each other. We are inclined to think of a "surface" as a necessary attribute of a "body," not the other way around. It is peculiar, and essential, to Timaeus' account, however, that a body—and, consequently, the dimension of depth—is to be understood as an outgrowth (αὔξη) of a regular configuration of place surfaces. In this view, the bodily solidity of visible things is not their primary character. It is rather *derived* from an orderly combination of two-dimensional entities. This combination is done intelligently and artfully. It has a purpose. "Body" with its "third dimension" is a *device* to "receive" and to "carry" the "Soul,"[19] a device to let the "body of the Whole" be permeated by the soul in its original "arithmetical" and "logistical" composition, to let the body of man "house" that "part" of the soul which is not subject to death and destruction, and "contains" its intellectual powers (30 b 1–4; 37 c 1–5; 44 d 3–6; 46 d 5–6) as well as the soul's somewhat deteriorated "mortal parts" (41 d – 42 a; 43 c–e; 61 c 7–8; 69 c–e; 72 d 4–5; 73 b–d). It is only from this "receiving" function of the body that we are at all able to come closer to the meaning of the preposition "in" of which Timaeus' account makes such ambiguous use.

The main difficulty that Timaeus' "likely story" encounters in describing the "generation" of the visible world around us (a difficulty shared in one form or another by any myth) is that it cannot help using speech attuned to this world as one *already* "generated." For our διάνοια, manifested in our speech, is indeed turned towards this familiar world of ours, turned in the main, that is, towards visible bodies, which our διάνοια, in

18. Even if the phrase ἐπίπεδος φύσις, as it is used here, may have a generic meaning (cf. Taylor, *op. cit.*, p. 362; Cornford, *op. cit.*, p. 212; also above pp. 59–60) so as to be applicable to a spherical or any other curved surface as well, the emphasis in the construction of Body is on straight surfaces, the "faces" of regular "solids."

19. It is a "vehicle," an ὄχημα (69 c 7; 44 e 2; also 41 e 2).

the exercise of its power of *dianoetic eikasia,* understands as "copies" of what is intelligible only.[20] Accordingly, the preposition "in" cannot help referring primarily to the "inside" of bodily things. The pristine role of the bodiless "receptacle" can, therefore, be only conceived ("spuriously") *in the image* of the "receiving" function of the body. That is how the "receptacle" is spoken of as the "room" "in" which the copies of the intelligible appear and disappear again.

On the other hand, while the preposition "in" cannot help referring primarily to the "inside" of bodily things, to *their* dimension of depth, this very dimension of depth is required by the complex nature of the soul. It is required, above all, by the "capacity" of the soul to *learn,* which is *its* capacity to grow on proper nourishment (44 b–c; 47 b–c; 87 a–b; 90 d).[21] Hence it is possible to attribute a "dimension of depth" to the soul itself, to make the soul "contain" intellect. That is why, when using the expression "looking into ourselves," we unhesitatingly mean to refer to the "inside" of our soul and not to the inside of our body. What we do, and hardly can avoid doing,[22] is to speak of the invisible soul, too, *in the image* of the visible body.[23] Timaeus' account justifies this way of speaking.

Socrates might, after all, find some enjoyment in the feast offered to him, not only in Critias', the old Athenian's, story out of the "good old days," but also in the "likely story" of Timaeus, the Locrian. Timaeus' narrative is an ἱστορία περὶ ψυχῆς in the guise of a περὶ φύσεως ἱστορία.[24] What Timaeus presents to Socrates in this story is a disembodied body housing a soul capable of learning the truth.

It does not seem inappropriate for us, then, to draw an image of Meno's soul as one lacking the dimension of depth.

3.

The title of the dialogue prompted us to raise the question: who is Meno? The dialogue has now answered this question. Meno in the dialogue is a clever man totally incapable of learning. Is there any relation between this unique personage

20. Cf. 51 b 7 – c 5 and above pp. 118–19, 120, 129, 134, 152.
21. Cf. also p. 60.
22. Cf. p. 104.
23. Cf. Xenophon, *Memorab.* III, 10, 8.
24. Cf. 27 a 4, 47 a 7 (and Taylor, *op. cit.,* pp. 58 and 294), also above p. 149.

and Meno the Thessalian, the darling of Aristippus, the "hereditary friend of the Great King," the lover of wealth,[25] known to us, and presumably to his contemporaries, from other sources as well?[26] Is there any relation between the image we have just drawn of Meno's soul, as revealed in the dialogue, and the image of the "historical" Meno as that of an arch-villain?

Unwillingness and inability to learn lead to *amathia*, to ignorance. This defect is called in the *Timaeus* (88 b 5) the greatest disease (*hê megistê nosos*) of the soul.[27] A disease of the soul is "badness" or "depravity" or "viciousness" (*kakia, ponêria*).[28] It is hardly possible not to draw the conclusion that the reputed villainy of Meno the Thessalian is but an outward manifestation of his now revealed *amathia*. In truth, his *amathia is* his villainy. His lack of the "dimension of depth" is directly related to his lack of *aretê*. If his soul can be said to be "filled" with anything, it is "full of both forgetfulness *and* vice" (*lêthês te kai kakias plêstheisa*).[29]

Early in the dialogue, Meno, expressing surprise at Socrates' profession of ignorance in the matter of human excellence, seemed, for a moment, at least, to assume tacitly the truth of the proposition that "human excellence is knowledge" and, by the very fact of making this assumption, to put his detractors to shame.[30] We understand now that, if, indeed, this Socratic thesis can be supposed to have underlain Meno's expression of surprise at all, Meno could not have grasped its meaning and its consequences, sharing, as he does, the habitual incomprehension with which this thesis is so often tacitly implied in our speech. But we may now suspect that that thesis and Meno are bound together in a very different way. Meno provides an *example,* a paradigm,[31] for the assertion that ignorance (*amathia*), the opposite of knowledge (*epistêmê*)[32] is depravity (*kakia*),[33] the opposite of excellence (*aretê*). And it is up to us to "convert" this assertion, by "contraposition," into the Socratic one. In fact, we have been led to this very point, we

25. Cf. pp. 40, 41, 78.
26. Cf. pp. 36–37.
27. Cf. *Tim.* 86 b 2–4 and *Laws* III, 691 d 1; also *Hipp. min.* 373 a 1–2.
28. Cf. p. 46 and *Rep.* IV, 444 e 1 f., *Gorg.* 477 b 3–8, *Soph.* 228 b 8–10, d 4–11, 229 c 1–10.
29. *Phaedr.* 248 c 7.
30. P. 43.
31. Cf. *Statesman* 277 d.
32. As well as of wisdom (σοφία) and of the exercise of wise judgment (φρόνησις) — *Symp.* 202 a 2–10.
33. Cf. *Soph.* 228 d 6–11 and 229 b–c.

have been led to "recognize" the Socratic dictum "human excellence is knowledge" by recognizing *who* Meno is. Our *anagnôrisis* is a two-fold one.[34]

Socrates seemed to intimate, in a sober vein, that he would be satisfied to hear excellence described as something always "accompanied" by knowledge, in the same way in which color can be said to be always "accompanied" by surface.[35] This sober description could now be matched by the "simple" statement that ignorance is, of necessity, a "companion" of vice. But the "simplicity" of this statement would be deceptive. For Meno's case shows that ignorance is not a "vacuum": what provides "color" to Meno's depravity and "fills" his ignorance are all the *doxai* accumulated on his "surface" memory.[36]

Throughout the preceding conversation, Socrates and Meno counter-image each other, Socrates putting the effort of learning above everything else,[37] Meno never relenting in his unwillingness to make that effort, an unwillingness compensated by his readiness to rely on his memory, Socrates justifying his stand by recourse to a myth, Meno justifying his by bringing up an argument. But while it remained doubtful whether the *anamnêsis* thesis was part of the myth about the undying soul told by other people or Socrates' own contribution to it,[38] it could be safely assumed that Meno's argument was not his own.[39] What was at stake, we remember, in the peculiar exchange of threats, which preceded Socrates' and Meno's respective justifications, was each one's *aretê*.[40] We see now the outcome of that uneven competition: Socrates' excellence shines in his declared resolve to fight, in word and deed, at every opportunity, for the proposition that searching and learning improve us,[41] on which resolve he has acted throughout the dialogue; Meno's depravity, of which we previously had had only glimpses,[42] has, through his own words, come into full light.

Since we perceive Meno now as he is, we can also tell whether he is "beautiful, or wealthy, or again highborn, or else the reverse of these."[43]

34. Cf. pp. 107, 184, also pp. 115, 136.
35. Pp. 59–60.
36. Cf. pp. 71–72.
37. See pp. 94, 97, 183.
38. P. 97.
39. P. 91.
40. P. 90.
41. Pp. 182–84.
42. Pp. 62, 66 f., 78, 88 f., 91, 97 f.
43. P. 38. Cf. also *Rep.* IX, 577 a–b.

Beautiful as Meno's body might appear,[44] the deficiency of his soul makes him ugly. Timaeus, for one, goes into detail to explain (87 c – 88 b) that the due relation (*symmetria*) of soul to body is all-important and that too imposing a body which carries but a small and feeble mind (*dianoia*) robs the "whole living being" (*holon to zôion*) of all beauty,[45] makes what pertains to the soul dull (*kôphon*), slow at learning (*dysmathes*), forgetful (*amnêmon*), and thus brings about the greatest disease, ignorance (*amathia*).

However much wealth Meno might already have acquired and however much more he might still desire, he cannot have gained, and will not gain, any wisdom because of his unwillingness and inability to learn. He is truly poor.[46]

In Thessaly as well as in Attica he may be thought of as highborn and high-minded. That might well be, therefore, his own opinion of himself. Indeed, he does not think it possible that a slave could be a ruler and still remain a slave.[47] We now understand the sarcasm of Socrates' response: "It is not likely [that you do], my excellent man." The boy who learned his first lesson in geometry, though a slave, has shown an excellence that Meno does not possess. Which of the two, then, has a slavish soul?[48]

The dialogue about human excellence will continue, with Meno still a participant; but his role in the conversation, we suspect, will be henceforth different from the one he has played so far.

44. Pp. 58, 67, 89.
45. Cf. *Charm.* 154 c 8 – e 1 (and *Rep.* IX, 591 c 1 – d 5).
46. Cf. *Phaedr.* 279 c 1–3 (and *Rep.* VII, 521 a 3–4; IX, 578 a 1–2; 579 e 2–3; 591 d 6 – e 5).
47. P. 55.
48. Cf. *Clitophon* 408 a 4 – b 5.

PART TWO

DOXA

VIII

1.

Meno had indicated that he preferred to go back to *his* original question rather than to join Socrates in the search for an answer to the question: what is human excellence? Socrates pretends to be compelled to comply with Meno's wish and, in so doing, rebukes Meno for the last time. He contrasts his own power to "rule" (*archein*) with that of Meno. He, Socrates, is able to rule over himself but not over Meno; Meno, on the contrary, is trying to rule, and actually succeeds in ruling, over him, Socrates,[1] but is not even trying to exert any rule over himself. And Socrates suggests that Meno adopts this attitude to assert his noble "freedom" (*hina dê eleutheros êis*).[2] This is the way of tyrants who imagine that to do as they like[3] is to be happy and free: they do not know that they are in truth nothing but slaves.[4] In point of fact, which escapes Meno, it is Socrates who has power over Meno, more so, presumably, than the Great King will ever have: has not Socrates compelled Meno to reveal himself as he truly is?

If only he could control Meno, says Socrates, the examination of whether excellence is teachable or not would not take precedence over the examination of what excellence is. But he has no choice in the matter: it seems that they just cannot avoid considering[5] "how" something is without first knowing "what" it is (*poion ti estin ho mêpô ismen hoti estin*). As we have seen,[6] there are good reasons to assume that this procedure is not at all objectionable to Socrates; it was rather Meno who did not favor it.

[86 d 3 – e 1]

---

1. Cf. pp. 58, 67.
2. Cf. *Rep.* VIII, 562 e 9: ἵνα δὴ ἐλεύθερον ᾖ, also *Gorg.* 491 d 4 – e 1, and Thompson, pp. 145 f.
3. *Gorg.* 473 c 6–7.
4. *Rep.* IX, 579 d – e; 577 d (cf. Xenophon, *Memorab.* IV, 5, 5).
5. Cf. p. 42.
6. P. 85.

Given Meno's reluctance to follow Socrates, Meno is asked to relax the reins of his rule just "a little" so as to allow them to explore the question whether excellence is achieved by teaching or in some other way "from a supposition" (*ex hypotheseôs*). Meno seemed well acquainted with the ways of geometry,[7] and Socrates need not expect him to object to any accepted procedure and, above all, to any terminology of that *technê*. Indeed, there is no objection on Meno's part. Nevertheless, Socrates explains what he means by an exploration "from a supposition."

Geometricians do often adopt the following kind of procedure. If, for example, one of them has to answer the question whether a certain amount of space (whatever its—rectilinear— boundaries) is capable of being fitted as a triangle[8] into a given circular area (so that the three vertices will touch the circumference of that circular area), he may say: while I do not know whether this particular amount of space has that capability I believe I have something of a supposition (*hôsper . . . tina hypothesin*) at hand which might be useful for the purpose. It is this: if that amount of space (which can always be transformed into a triangular or rectangular area) were to be such that he who "stretches it along" (*parateinanta*) its (*autou*) given line "runs short" (*elleipein*) of a space *like* the very one which had been "stretched along" (the given line), then, it seems to me, one thing would be the result, and another again, if it were impossible for him to go through this experience. And so I am disposed to tell you what will happen with regard to the inscription of your amount of space (*autou*) into the circle, whether it is impossible or not impossible, by way of "hypothesizing" (*hypothemenos*).

The geometrician whom Socrates conjures up is a very cautious one; but the precision of his speech does not quite reach technical lucidity. He is made to use terms which Socrates elsewhere[9] criticizes. Moreover, he is made to use them in a way which seems to interfere with their "technical" relevance. Above all, it may be asked, are we really presented here with something resembling a geometrical "hypothesis"?

Recent commentators,[10] who do not seem to be aware of

---

7. Pp. 64–66, 99.
8. See Thompson, p. 149 (25); A. Heijboer, "Plato, 'Meno' 86E – 87A," *Mnemosyne*, 4th series, VIII (1955), 101, 103.
9. Cf. pp. 121 f. and *Rep.* VII, 527 a 66 ff., where the term παρατείνειν is explicitly mentioned (cf. also Heijboer, *op. cit.*, p. 109).
10. Heijboer, *op. cit.*, pp. 89 f., surveys the literature on the subject. Bluck gives a summary and critical appraisal of this literature in his

the gentle hoax perpetrated by Socrates at this point, have tried to throw some light on the geometrical problem that might possibly be hinted at here. The problem mentioned by Socrates may perhaps, as some of the commentators[11] think, amount to the problem of finding out whether one of the branches (or conjugate branches) of a rectangular hyperbolic curve with a given transverse axis[12] will or will not intersect, or at least touch, the circumference of a given circle, the diameter of which is taken as the line of "application," i.e., the line along which the given area is "stretched." Other interpretations which have been proposed are no more plausible. Only this much seems clear, the problem hinted at must be solved by "analysis":[13] the "inscription," the possibility of which is in question, has to be considered as "done" so that a sufficient condition for its being feasible can be inferred as a *consequence*. It turns out that one way to formulate such a condition is precisely this: two rectangular areas, the applied one and the other one by which the first is "deficient," must be "like" each other, must be "similar." In fact, to know that the "inscription" is feasible means to recognize the "similarity" of those two areas.

The lack of precision in Socrates' presentation of this geometrical problem is hardly due to the unsettled character of mathematical terminology in Plato's time.[14] The problem and its "indeterminate" solution[15] are not presented here by Socrates for their own sake. They are meant to provide, as once before the examples of *schêma* and *chrôma* had done, a pat-

---

Appendix, pp. 441–61. Bluck acknowledges (pp. 75 f., 322 f., 441, 460) the obscurity and ambiguity of the text as well as the relative unimportance of whatever specific solution the text may hint at, as others have done before him (notably R. Robinson, *op. cit.*, p. 126, Heijboer, *op. cit.*, p. 121); nevertheless, he pays special attention to the interpretations given by A. S. L. Farquharson, "Socrates' Diagram in the Meno of Plato, pp. 86E – 87A," *Classical Quarterly*, XVII (1923), 21 ff., and by A. Heijboer, *op. cit.*, pp. 89 ff.

11. E. F. August, *Zur Kenntnis der geschichtlichen Methode der Alten in besonderer Beziehung auf die platonische Stelle in Meno*, 1844; S. H. Butcher, *Journ. of Philol.*, XVII (1888), 209–25 (cf. Thompson, pp. 148 ff.); J. Cook Wilson, *Journ. of Philol.*, XXVIII (1903), 222–40, esp. 235 f.; Th. L. Heath, *A History of Greek Mathematics*, 1921, I, 298–303.

12. The square on the semi-transverse axis will cover double the amount of the given space.

13. Cf. A. S. L. Farquharson, *op. cit.*, p. 21.

14. As Heath, *op. cit.*, p. 300, note (and also p. 303, note), intimates. But Heath adds: "and he [Plato] allows himself some latitude of expression."

15. Cf. Jacob Klein, *op. cit.*, Bd. 3, Heft 2, 1936, pp. 139 f.

tern for the discussion of the problem of human excellence. Accordingly, the main emphasis is on the "similarity" of two areas, the precise shape of which is unknown.[16] (It is perhaps not without significance that the word *hoion* stands out in the passage; from 86 d 5 to 87 a 5 it is used four times, each time with a totally different meaning, to be sure, only the last of which has an affinity to the technical term *homoion* as it appears later in Euclid.[17]) The emphasis on the term "supposition," on the other hand, which term, in this case, points to a sufficient condition for the feasibility of the "inscription," does not lack ambiguity, as the analytical procedure teaches, as the seventh book of the *Republic* and the *Phaedo* show, and as will become even clearer in a short while.

[86 e 1 – 87 b 2]   Socrates proceeds immediately to draw the analogy with the case of *aretê*. Since we know neither "what" it is (*outh' hoti estin*) nor what it is "like" or "how" it is (*outh' hopoion ti*),[18] we have to make use of a "supposition" (*hypothemenoi*) in this case, too, in exploring the question whether excellence is teachable or not.

Does the co-ordination of "what" and "how" in the last sentence mean that the ignorance of the latter follows necessarily on the ignorance of the former, as was ambiguously asserted all along by Socrates? Or does it not rather mean that this distinction, at this moment, is not at all what matters? For the analogy to be drawn is as follows: the given space is (or is not) "inscribable" into the given circle, *if* the area which is equal to the given space has (or has not) the relation of "similarity" to another area; excellence is (or is not) "teachable"—inscribable into the soul, as it were—*if* it has (or has not) the relation of "similarity" or "likeness" to something else in the soul. What is this "something else"? It is playfully treated by Socrates as an unknown "fourth proportional" in his next

16. This, above all, militates against Heijboer's interpretation. Heijboer reduces (*op. cit.*, p. 120) the ambiguous meaning of the crucial word "οἷον" to simple "identity" (or rather "equality")—mainly by unduly stretching the meaning of αὐτὸ τὸ παρατεταμένον (87 a 5–6). See also R. Catesby Taliaferro's review of Robert S. Brumbaugh, *Plato's Mathematical Imagination*, 1954, in *The New Scholasticism*, XXXI, 2 (1957): ". . . the problem of application presented here reflects within itself the problem of the *Meno:* how to find a rectangle deficient by a rectangle similar to the rectangle to be found, how to wish for and to recognize something we do not know," and the context.

17. Elements VI, Def. 1 and Heath's comment, *The Thirteen Books of Euclid's Elements*, 2nd ed., 1926, II, 188.

18. Cf. p. 42.

sentence. This analogically hypothetical statement about excellence, embodying the "supposition," could read: "If excellence is (or is not) *like* something within the soul, then it is (or is not) teachable." But Socrates chooses to give an interrogative twist to the protasis of that sentence. He says: "Excellence would be teachable or not teachable, if it is like what (*poion ti*) among the things pertaining to the soul (*tôn peri tên psychên ontôn*) ?" And the formulation of Socrates' immediately following question brings the emphatic, if oblique, answer: "To begin with, if it is unlike (*alloion*) or like (*hoion*) knowledge (*epistêmê*) , is it teachable or not . . . ?"

The interrogative twist (*poion ti*) underscores that what is being considered "from a supposition" is the "likeness," not identity, of *aretê* and *epistêmê*. Not only the apodoses of the preceding sentences speak about "how" excellence may be, namely teachable or not teachable, the protases speak about that too, namely about excellence being "like" or "unlike" knowledge. The "how" and the "what" in this case, however, might well turn out to be hardly distinguishable.

We have to note, furthermore, that excellence is classed succinctly, if again obliquely, among "the things pertaining to the soul," which was implied in the myth of recollection and perhaps elsewhere in the dialogue, but was certainly not stated explicitly before.

For the first time also we see the link between excellence and knowledge emerging as an explicit theme, not hidden in the background of an exchange between Meno and Socrates,[19] not merely hinted at, as in the examples of "bounded surface" and "color,"[20] not dramatically mirrored in Meno's ignorant and depraved soul,[21] but introduced as the positive side of a two-pronged "supposition."

The myth of recollection, on the other hand, with its implications regarding both knowledge and excellence, recedes into the background. The myth has fulfilled its function, not that it had any effect on Meno, but it has helped us to understand Meno's soul. Socrates mentions "recollection" only briefly and parenthetically in continuing the sentence, in which he explicitly introduces the link between excellence and knowledge: ". . . is it [excellence] teachable or not, or, as we were just saying, recollectable—but which of the two words

19. P. 43.
20. P. 60.
21. Pp. 200 f.

we use should not make any difference to us so then, is it teachable?"

What does Socrates mean by his parenthetical remark that it should not make any difference to him and to Meno whether they refer in speaking to "recollecting" or to "teaching"? The "teachable" is what is learned or can be learned. Does Socrates then imply that he still upholds the identity of "learning" and "recollecting"? Does he mean that, since anything which is to be learned has, at any rate, to be understood, mythically or otherwise, as something to be recollected, the words we choose do not matter? Or is he implying that for the present purpose, the answer to Meno's question, the recollection thesis is irrelevant and could even be abandoned altogether? This retraction would in a rather large way counterbalance Meno's "small" concession about the use of a "hypothesis." It would, among other things, make Socrates willing to consider the benefits of teaching and learning as quite divorced from what is given to us "by nature."[22] The commonly accepted view of teaching would dominate the discussion to follow. According to this view, teaching means putting knowledge into somebody's soul,[23] an operation comparable to inscribing a triangle into a circle.

Omitting any further, apparently unnecessary, enumeration of "things pertaining to the soul," Socrates himself answers his question with the rhetorical query: "Or is not *this* indeed obvious to anyone, that man is *taught* nothing but *knowledge?*" So it seems indeed, replies Meno. But is it altogether clear that this is so?

Socrates concludes his "hypothesizing" with the statement: "If then [we were to assume that] excellence is knowledge of some kind *(epistêmê tis)*, it is obvious that it would be teachable." Meno: "How else?"

The way is cleared for the next step. Socrates remarks, and Meno agrees with him, that they have thus quickly disposed of this point, to wit, that excellence is teachable *if* it is of "such" a nature *(toionde)*, namely "like" knowledge, and not teachable *if* it is of "such" a nature, namely "unlike" knowledge. We can now turn our attention to the very content of the "supposition," the relation of excellence to knowledge.

[87 c 11 – d 1]   "So what one has to investigate after this *(meta touto)*," says Socrates, "is, it seems, whether excellence is knowledge or

22. Pp. 181 f.
23. Pp. 97, 106.

different (*alloion*) from knowledge." And Meno agrees that
after this that (*touto meta touto*) has to be considered.

What has actually happened in this exchange? Socrates has
brushed aside Meno's question (for the time being at least)
and returned to his own, for which he had claimed priority.
He has done that obliquely and rather playfully, however
serious the intent, by means of mathematical devices and—not
quite transparent—mathematical language, the authority of
which Meno is not wont to challenge.

The crucial theme, the nature of human excellence, is finally
before us—in words. The *logos* embedded in the conversation
to be held now will reflect what the drama we have been witnessing, the mimetic *ergon* of the dialogue, had presented to
us directly. The conversation, we should not forget, proceeds
now in the shadow of Meno's *amathia,* and that means in the
shadow of the innumerable accepted opinions which crowd his
memory.

What ought to be investigated now, "it seems," Socrates has
just said, is "whether excellence is knowledge or different
from knowledge." On the affirmative side of this alternative
"knowledge" is not qualified at all. *Tis,* for example, used
only a short while ago (87 c 5), is omitted. Nor is it suggested that excellence may be "like" (*hoion*) knowledge. The
negative side of the alternative, on the other hand, which
envisages the possibility of excellence being "different" from
knowledge, does this ambiguously. The word *alloion* was used
previously (87 b 7) in opposition to *hoion,* "unlike" contrasting with "like." The same word seems now to be used to
contrast the possibility of excellence being—simply—"knowledge" with the possibility of excellence being—simply—"not
knowledge." The phrasing of the alternative, in other words,
blurs the distinction between the "how" and the "what."
This haziness will persist in different guises throughout the
logos Socrates is about to present.

As for Meno, comically unaware of Socrates' lead, he will
serve reliably as a sounding board for Socrates' words.

2.

Socrates begins oddly as follows: "Let's see then, do we say [87 d 2–8]
that this thing 'excellence' is anything but a good thing, and
do we abide by *this* supposition, that it is a good thing?" "We
certainly do," is Meno's reply. And so is ours, and it cannot

help being everybody's. For difficult as it may be to determine the nature of human excellence, whenever we attribute excellence to a man, we mean to praise him, we mean to praise his "goodness." An affirmative answer to Socrates' question amounts to an approval of a tautology. No supposition underlies either the question or the answer. No "supposition" of this kind was ever stated in the preceding conversation, nor did it need to be stated.

It seems, however, that the use of the term "supposition" in this tautological frame has a double purpose: it casts a decidedly ironic light on the previous, ambiguous, use of that very term[24] and it prepares us for an exercise of our "hypothesizing" power which will imply a more genuine, and colloquial, meaning of *hypotithesthai*, namely, the act of "supposing" in the sense of "suspecting" (*hypopteuein*).[25] For Socrates continues: If there also were some other good severed (*chôrizomenon*) from all knowledge, excellence might perhaps not be knowledge of any kind (*epistêmê tis*); but if there is no good which is not encompassed by knowledge, our suspicion (*hypopteuontes*) that this thing (*auto*), excellence, consists in knowledge of some kind (*epistêmê tis*) would be a justifiable suspicion (*orthôs hypopteuomen*).

While previously, in analogy to the geometrical example, the question whether excellence is teachable or not was reduced, "hypothetically," to the problem of the relation between excellence and knowledge, the solution of that very problem is now made dependent on whether there is anything "good" outside the domain of knowledge. The genuine supposition (or "suspicion"), which is to be tested now, is that the domain of knowledge completely encompasses (*periechei*) the domain of "goodness," and therefore human excellence, the alternatives being that these two domains are completely separate or only partially overlapping spheres or circles.

[87 d 8 – 89 a 5] The testing and verifying of this supposition or "suspicion" proceeds in six main steps, Meno's continuous approval providing the echoing accompaniment.

Step one. Excellent men are good men (*agathoi*) by virtue of their excellence. And their being good men makes them "beneficial" (*ôphelimoi*), for everything that is good (*panta*

24. P. 206 (cf. pp. 120 f.).
25. The relationship between ὑποτίθεσθαι, ὑποπτεύειν and εἰκάζειν seems to be a close one—cf. pp. 114 f., 120, 129, 156.

tàgatha) does us good. It follows, necessarily, from what has been agreed on (*ek tôn hômologêmenôn*), says Meno, who does not want to shame his memory, that excellence, too, is a beneficial thing.

Step two. Surveying the things that do us good (*ha hêmas ôphelei*), taking them up one by one, we find them to be things such as health and strength,[26] and beauty,[27] and, of course,[28] wealth,[29] and their like.[30] But we also say that these very things are sometimes definitely[31] harmful to us (Meno fully agreeing). The "things" mentioned so far (including beauty) are understood to relate to our bodily existence. If we ask ourselves on what their being beneficial or harmful in various circumstances depends, we have to answer: on the way we use them. If we use them in the right way, they do us good; if we do not use them in the right way, they do us harm. The "right use" (*orthê chrêsis*) provides the "right lead."

Step three. If we turn to what pertains to the soul (*ta kata tên psychên*), we can enumerate what is known, and praised, as moderation or exercise of self-control, justice, courage, docility (*eumathia*), memory (*mnêmê*), loftiness,[32] and everything else of that kind. We are asked to distinguish among these qualities those that can be equated with knowledge (*epistêmê*) and those that are different from knowledge (*allo epistêmês*). The latter sometimes harm us and sometimes benefit us. Take "courage": "if courage is not the exercise of wise judgment (*phronêsis*) but is like (*hoion*) some kind of blind boldness (*tharros ti*)," a man who is senselessly "courageous" without any insight (*aneu nou*), is going to be hurt, but if he is sensibly courageous, realizing what he is up against (*syn nôi*), it will be to his benefit. And so it is with self-control (*sôphrosynê*) and docility (*eumathia*): depending on whether something is being learned or brought under control[33] with or without insight (*meta nou—aneu nou*), it is beneficial or harmful. In short, all that the soul attempts or endures, when

26. Cf. pp. 51, 78.
27. P. 67.
28. Thompson, p. 156 (3).
29. P. 78.
30. Cf. *Rep.* VI, 491 c 2–4.
31. Thompson, p. 156 (7).
32. Pp. 41, 56 (cf. *Rep.* VI, 487 a 4–5, 490 c 5, 10–11, 491 b 9 f.).
33. About the inversion see Thompson, pp. 159 and 244 f. (Thompson's insertion of πάντα seems wholly unnecessary.)

led by wise judgment (*phronêsis*), ends in happiness (*eis eudaimonian*), when misled by lack of judgment (*aphrosynê*), in the opposite (*eis toúnantion*), in misery.[34]

Step four. If then excellence is of necessity a thing beneficial (step one) and one belonging to the soul (*tôn en têi psychêi ti*),[35] that what it is must be the exercise of wise judgment (*phronêsis*). For it cannot be any of those qualities of the soul which by themselves are neither beneficial nor harmful but are made so when either wise judgment or lack of judgment accompanies them (*prosgenomenês . . . phronêseôs ê aphrosynês*). With respect to those "indifferent" qualities of the soul everything depends again on how we *use* them: the exercise of wise or unwise judgment is therefore decisive. The argument thus shows: since excellence is beneficial, it must be some exercise of wise judgment (*phronêsis tis*).

Step five. What holds for "wise judgment" or "lack of judgment" in relation to the rest of the soul, namely that their respective lead makes all that pertains to the soul either beneficial or harmful, holds also for the soul in relation to all the other things, wealth and the like, of which it was said that they are sometimes good and sometimes harmful; depending on whether or not the soul uses those other things rightly and asserts its right lead, it makes them beneficial or harmful. And it is the sensible, intelligent (*emphrôn*), soul which leads in the right way, while the senseless, foolish (*aphrôn*) one leads in a faulty way.

Step six. The following comprehensive (*kata pantôn*) statement can, therefore, be made: as far as man is concerned (*tôi anthrôpôi*), all other things depend, for their being good, on the soul that makes use of them, and all the qualities of the soul itself depend in turn, for their being good, on the exercise of wise judgment (*phronêsis*).

According to this argument then, the beneficial would be ultimately "the exercise of wise judgment." And, since excellence is a thing beneficial, we finally have to say that excellence is the "exercise of wise judgment," either all that there is of such exercise or "some part" of it (*êtoi sympasan ê meros ti*).

Here the Socratic *logos*[36] ends. Meno is inclined to approve

34. Cf. pp. 75–77.
35. P. 209.
36. Cf. Aristotle, *Nic. Eth.* VI, 13, especially 1144 b 17–32 and 1145 a 1–2.

of it wholeheartedly (*Dokei moi kalôs legesthai, ô Sôkrates, ta legomena*)! Let us consider it in some detail.

3.

1. The argument is presented in "simple" colloquial terms. The relevant ones cover a range of related meanings which permit a shifting of the terms themselves without, however, affecting the argument's broad persuasiveness. There are two striking examples of such shifting of terms.

a) Step one of the argument consists in nothing but the exchange of the term "beneficial" (*ôphelimon*) for the term "good" (*agathon*). This exchange is based on the common understanding that "everything that is good does us good" (*panta . . . tâgatha ôphelima* – 87 e 2) : in saying that something is "good," we usually do mean that it is "good for something else" and mostly and ultimately that it is good for us or for others or for all men. The words "good," "good for . . . ," and "beneficial" are indeed synonymous in common speech.[37] What any of them implies or what all of them imply is a matter of "philosophical" reflection in which we may engage, if we are ready to follow Socrates' lead.

b) Step three of the argument brings a rather decisive shift from *epistêmê* to *phronêsis*; *phronêsis* in turn is linked with *nous*. Now, *phronêsis*, the exercise of wise judgment, although *not identical* with *epistêmê*, knowledge, always appears *linked with* "knowledge." A man who judges people, situations, things wisely, so as to be able to counsel, to behave, or to act well, is a man not without "knowledge." In this sense, *phronêsis* may be said to be "knowledge of some kind" (*epistêmê tis*). Nor is *phronêsis* (and not only in common understanding) far away from *sôphrosynê* with its range of meanings.[38]

---

37. This is especially clear in 88 d 5, where ἀγαθά is used for ὠφέλιμα in opposition to βλαβερά. Something "good for one thing" may not be good "for another thing," something beneficial for one man may not be good for another, but that does not alter the general synonymity of the terms (cf. *Protag.* 333 d – 334 c, also *Charm.* 169 b 4 and *Symp.* 204 e – 205 a).

38. Cf. for instance Critias' tentative definition of σωφροσύνη, *Charm.* 163 e 10, as ἡ τῶν ἀγαθῶν πρᾶξις and Socrates' comment: καὶ οὐδέν γέ σε ἴσως κωλύει ἀληθῆ λέγειν. Cf. also, taking into account all the satirical playfulness of the passage, *Cratyl.* 411 e 4 f.: σωφροσύνη δὲ σωτερία . . . φρονήσεως, and Aristotle, *Nic. Eth.* VI, 5, 1140 b 11–12; furthermore, *Symp.* 209 a 5–8, *Laws* IV, 712 a 1: . . . τῷ φρονεῖν τε καὶ σωφρονεῖν . . . .

2. The argument shows that whenever something beneficial comes into being, this is ultimately due to the exercise of wise judgment. *Phronêsis is the source of all possible benefits. The foremost benefit, therefore, is phronêsis.*[39] The supposition or suspicion, which Socrates' *logos* undertook to test and to verify, was that the domain of knowledge (*epistêmê*) completely encompasses the domain of goodness (*agathon*). The argument maintains that the domain of wise judgment (*phronêsis*) completely encompasses the domain of the beneficial (*ôphelimon*). And hence the final conclusion is reached that excellence, a good and beneficial thing in itself, is either the exercise of wise judgment in its fullness or, at least, "in part."

3. This last distinction between the "whole" (*sympasa*) of *phronêsis* and "some part" (*meros ti*) of it has its difficulties.

With regard to the underlying supposition, we may picture the domain of knowledge as a circle "encompassing" another circle representing the domain of "goodness." Two cases are possible: either both circles coincide or the circle of "knowledge" merely contains the circle of "goodness." In the latter case there is knowledge severed from goodness. These two cases correspond to the two predicates *epistêmê* and *epistêmê tis* which, in turn, reflect the distinction, hazily preserved throughout the argument, between the "what" and the "how." For the first case stipulates an identity between "goodness" and "knowledge" and amounts to a definition, while the second case merely describes what "goodness" is like or what "property" it has.

But it is not clear whether both cases are possible in the relation of the circle of *phronêsis* to either the circle of the *ôphelimon* or the circle of *aretê*. How can only "some part" of *phronêsis* be involved here? The exercise of wise judgment cannot be "partitioned." A man either has good judgment (which does not preclude the possibility of his being occasionally mistaken) or he does not have it (which does not preclude the possibility of his proving occasionally right). And the exercise of wise judgment can never be detached from the consideration of the beneficial.

It seems that the shift from *epistêmê* to *phronêsis* permits Socrates to circumvent the problem of the "whole" that

39. See Aristotle, *Met.* V, 11, 1019 a 2–4. Cf. also *Laws* I, 631 c 5–6 and *Protag.* 352 b 1 – d 4, where φρόνησις replaces ἐπιστήμη once (c 6–7) and decisively: . . . ἀλλ' ἱκανὴν εἶναι τὴν φρόνησιν βοηθεῖν τῷ ἀνθρώπῳ. (In the next sentence Protagoras mentions σοφία but not φρόνησις.) For the *Phaedo* see above pp. 130 f.

knowledge poses.[40] The wisdom underlying the exercise of
wise judgment is always present—although not manifestly so
—as a "whole."

In the exuberant Palinode of the *Phaedrus*[41] it is said that
Beauty as it is in itself (*auto to kallos*), somewhere in the
nowhere "above heaven," *alone* among the intelligible models
can be *seen* by us, its splendor shining, rarely enough, we
must add, through a clearly visible phantom (*enarges ei-
dôlon*) down here on our earth. Not so Justice or Moderation
(*sôphrosynê*) or Knowledge.[42] But it is neither *dikaiosynê* nor
sôphrosynê nor *epistêmê*, it is *phronêsis*[43] which is suddenly
conjured up to provide a vivid contrast to Beauty: there are
no shining images of *phronêsis* nor of those others that
can be perceived through our senses; if such images could
ever be seen, the desires they would arouse in us would be
dreadful.[44] But why is *phronêsis* singled out for that contrasting role? Is it just an arbitrary choice of words? Does
phronêsis simply stand here for *sôphrosynê*, which in the *Phaedrus* is of paramount importance? (Or is the mention of
sôphrosynê avoided because its very nature seems to preclude
the arousing of dreadful desires?) Is not the choice of *phronêsis* rather made because, like beauty, it can be found, rarely
enough, *amongst us,* with this difference that beauty, when we
see it, has lost its wholeness though it never loses its splendor,
while the wisdom of *phronêsis,* when it affects us, lacks splendor though never wholeness? *Phronêsis* is what makes men ex-
cel, but it itself remains inconspicuous. Its splendor, its color,
is a beauty "within," as Alcibiades once at least, in a wild
moment of insight, without distinguishing *phronêsis* from
sôphrosynê, clearly saw.[45]

4. Before shifting from *epistêmê* to *phronêsis,* step three of
the argument enumerates certain qualities of the soul and
asks us to distinguish between those that are "knowledge"
and those that are "different" (*allo*[46]) from knowledge. The
examples given of the latter are courage, self-control (*sôphrosynê*) , docility, all of which *may not* be accompanied by *phronêsis.* (It is at this point that the shift from *epistêmê* to *phronêsis* occurs.) Memory and loftiness could presumably serve

40. P. 86.
41. 250 c 8 ff.
42. 250 b 1–5; 247 d 5 – e 2.
43. 250 d 4.
44. 250 d 3–6.
45. *Symp.* 216 d 1–7 (cf. *Phaedr.* 279 b 8–9).
46. Cf. ἀλλοῖον – p. 211.

as other examples, considering the kind of "memory" and "loftiness" Meno exhibits. (They seem to be listed, in fact, along with docility, to underscore the lack of *phronêsis* in Meno, the docile pupil of Gorgias.) Justice, too, is conceivable without the exercise of *phronêsis*.[47] As to "everything else of that kind," we may take as examples the qualities listed in the seventh book of the *Republic*.[48] They seem to be undoubtedly "good" qualities, oriented, on their own, towards knowledge (*epistêmê*) and guided by *phronêsis*. But they "are" not knowledge, nor for that matter wisdom (*sophia*). It is indeed questionable, in terms of the argument itself, whether there are any qualities of the soul which are not in need of being led by *phronêsis:* step five of the argument contrasts *phronêsis* with "the rest of the soul" (*têi allêi psychêi*).

The initial supposition about the relation of "knowledge" to "goodness" is left in suspense. The *logos* cannot quite cope with it.[49] And this holds also for the "simple" statement that human excellence is knowledge, although it may be safe to say that it is "some kind" of knowledge, namely *phronêsis*. Was not that precisely[50] what Socrates "suspected"? In any event, the supremely beneficial role of *phronêsis,* of the exercise of wise judgment, has been asserted and made plausible.

We have to note that *phronêsis* has *one* advantage over *epistêmê:* we do forget knowledge once acquired, but wise judgment, once we are able to exercise it, is a "whole" that can hardly be lost or "forgotten."[51]

5. Step three of the argument tells us in what happiness (*eudaimonia*) and its "opposite" consist or, at least, what their respective sources are: the exercise of wise judgment in the conduct of our lives makes these lives happy ones, the lack of that exercise brings misery. This telling is as inconspicuous as the appearance of *phronêsis* itself.

4.

[89 a 5 – c 5]   Socrates' *logos* had reached the conclusion that human excellence is *phronêsis,* either "all" of it or "some part" of it. It

---

47. As, for instance, in the story told about Xerxes' justice, reported by Herodotus (VIII, 118–19), who does not believe it, and, above all, in the case of Socrates' own trial.
48. See p. 187.
49. Pp. 86, 168 f.
50. P. 212.
51. Cf. Aristotle, *Nic. Eth.* VI, 5, 1140 b 28–30.

is at this point that Socrates takes up Meno's original, and repeated, question about the way excellence accrues to man.

Socrates makes Meno accept a consequence that apparently flows directly from the conclusion reached: if what has been said stands, then men who possess excellence—that is, as we understand, are able to exercise wise judgment—could not be born with it, "good men" could not be "good" "by birth." "It does not seem to me [that they could]," says Meno. And to show the absurdity of the opposite view, namely that good men are born "good," that is, endowed from birth with the ability to exercise wise judgment, Socrates goes on to describe the wonderful prospect that, with this view, would open to mankind.[52] Citizens everywhere would in that case be able, wouldn't they, to find people capable of discerning who among the young ones are "good by nature"; we, the citizens, would take over all the excellent youths designated by those experts, would have them sealed up in our treasuries and watch over them far more carefully than over our gold, lest anyone corrupt them; and thus, when they came of age, they could become useful to their respective cities. "Very likely so, Socrates," says Meno. Whereupon Socrates leaps to what seems to follow as the only possible alternative, by asking: Since, then, good men are not good men "by nature," do they not become "good" through learning (*mathêsei*)? The implication is that not only knowledge (*epistêmê*) but also *phronêsis* can be learned and taught. (This implication need not contradict Socrates' previous intimation[53] that nothing but *knowledge* is taught to man, since *phronêsis* can be understood as *epistêmê tis*.) Meno replies: "It seems to me that follows of necessity, and it is also obvious, Socrates, from the supposition that, if indeed excellence is knowledge, it is something teachable (*didakton*)."[54] "Perhaps so, by Zeus," says Socrates.

This exchange requires some scrutiny.

1. The wonderful state of affairs, envisaged on the assumption that *phronêsis* might be a natural gift and playfully presented to our consideration, poses problems of a most serious kind.

a) The two implicit assumptions, one, that, under the given circumstances, people could be found capable of dis-

52. For the grammar of this passage see Thompson, pp. 162–63 (28, 32, 33).
53. P. 210.
54. *Ibid.*

cerning excellence in youths, that is, of discerning youths possessing the gift of *phronêsis*, and, two, that the rest of the citizens would be willing to appoint those people for that purpose and to accept their judgment, presuppose not only a great deal of perspicacity[55] on the part of the experts but also, and what is more, a predominance of *phronêsis* among the citizens themselves. The question how such a predominance could be secured is not touched upon.[56]

b) That the excellent youths confined to a special spot should be guarded against corruption, seems to presuppose, on the other hand, that *phronêsis* itself can be deprived of its integrity, something rather difficult to reconcile with the main assumption about *phronêsis*.

2. Socrates' leap from the absurd alternative to the "positive" one, that "good men" (men possessing *phronêsis*) become "good (acquire *phronêsis*) through "learning," seems to confirm that he has abandoned his recollection thesis and is now considering the benefits of teaching and learning as divorced from what is given to us "by nature."[57] For the leap becomes necessary only on the further, unstated, assumption that the selected and isolated young men need not "learn" anything to emerge fully prepared for their future tasks. Meno, from habit, we suppose, makes that assumption. Must we follow him? Should we not rather assume that, like knowledge, *phronêsis* must still be acquired through a laborious process of "learning,"[58] not restricted to any special science or sciences, but *can* only be acquired if the learner is predisposed "by nature" towards this kind of learning.[59] Such a predisposition is indeed susceptible of corruption, the more so the richer the natural endowment of the learner.[60]

3. From Meno's positive reaction to the final consequence to which Socrates' *logos* has led we gather (without surprise) that he has not quite kept pace with the argument. He does not seem aware of the shift from *epistêmê* to *phronêsis*, or is perhaps not used to differentiating between them. But, on the other hand, he well remembers (not surprisingly either) the

55. Theodorus, in the *Theaetetus,* seems to have it. Can that also be said of Critias in the *Charmides?*
56. A large part of the *Republic* is required to deal with it (cf. Thompson, p. 162).
57. P. 210.
58. Cf. *Rep.* VI, 488 b 7 f., 489 e 4 f., 492 a 1–3 and the respective contexts.
59. Cf. pp. 93 f., 187 f.
60. Cf. *Rep.* VI, 491 d 7 – e 7. Who would not think of Alcibiades and Charmides as most pertinent examples?

"supposition" introduced by Socrates and he repeats it in its "simplest" form: if excellence *is* knowledge, it *is* teachable.[61] We note Socrates' ironically emphatic and qualified endorsement of this formula. As to Meno, he is clearly satisfied that the truth of the protasis—"excellence is knowledge"—has now been established.

5.

Meno's original and persistent question has thus also been [89 c 5 – e 9] answered to his satisfaction: human excellence, be it wholly or partly either knowledge or the exercise of sound judgment, comes into being through teaching. Yet Socrates has his doubts: what if they were wrong in agreeing about this answer? Meno refers to the impression he has just had: it seemed (*edokei*) to him a beautiful answer. Socrates corrects Meno: if anything is to be sound (*hygies*) about it, a past, and perhaps fleeting, impression cannot decide the matter; the impression, and the opinion based on it, must persist, now and hereafter. This correction foreshadows more extensive discussions of the way in which a true statement can be made and accepted. The word "sound" takes us back to the link between its meaning and that of "whole."[62]

But Meno seems genuinely puzzled: what is it that makes Socrates feel qualms about what was said, makes him have misgivings lest excellence not be knowledge?[63] Socrates explains: he does not retract and claim that there is something wrong about the proposition "if excellence is knowledge, it is a thing teachable"; but what he is apprehensive about is that excellence may *not* be knowledge, and he invites Meno, and us, to consider whether his apprehension might not be well founded.

We have to observe:

1. Socrates has shifted from *phronêsis* back to *epistêmê*. Moreover, he now uses, following Meno, the "simple" way of identifying excellence with knowledge to bring up his doubts.

2. Socrates' explanation is somewhat incomplete. He reaches the point of doubt by "inverting" the hypothetical proposition "if excellence is knowledge, excellence is teachable," the validity of which he does not deny;[64] he changes

61. Pp. 210, 219.
62. Pp. 71, 80.
63. See Thompson, p. 167 (14).
64. Cf. *Protag.* 361 a 6 – b 7.

that proposition into this new one: "if excellence is teachable, excellence is knowledge," and he is going to question whether the condition stated in the new protasis is realizable. Were the apodosis now to read "excellence is *phronêsis*," the content of the protasis could still be called in question in the same way. Socrates' being apprehensive lest excellence not be knowledge, or *phronêsis* for that matter, that is, Socrates' concern about the truth of the new apodosis, arises from his misgivings about the truth of the new protasis.

His question is: if there is anything teachable in the world, not just excellence, must there not be teachers and learners of it? Meno agrees. And conversely (*tounantion*), if there are neither teachers nor learners of a subject matter, would not the guess that it cannot be taught be a fair guess? If the subject matter is human excellence, this guess, this new suspicion,[65] has a shattering effect. Meno, accepting Socrates' inference, feels compelled to ask: "Is it really your opinion that there are no teachers of human excellence?" Can we avoid asking the same question?

Socrates' reply is that he often tries and does everything he can to find out whether there are such teachers, but that he is unable to come upon one; and this in spite of his undertaking the search not alone, but together with many other people, and especially with those who, he would think, are most experienced in the matter.

At this point the searching, hypothesizing, and guessing comes to an end. The dialogue takes a new turn: a new personage, one of authority, appears on the scene.

65. Cf. pp. 212 ff.

IX

1.

It is Anytus. Just as Meno's, Anytus' name must have been rather well-known to Plato's contemporaries, as we can infer from the writings of Plato himself,[1] as well as from remarks made by Xenophon,[2,3] Lysias,[4,5] Isocrates,[6] Andocides.[7] Aristotle[8,9] is a witness to this too. Anytus is mentioned as being in the tanning business[2] (not highly regarded in Athens), as responsible for the poor upbringing of his son who later became a drunkard,[2] as a versatile political leader,[2-8] chosen (by lot) to be grain-superintendent, and entrusted with military command,[8] whose otherwise solid reputation[9] seems to have been tarnished by his being considered the first Athenian citizen to have bribed a court,[8] and, above all, as one of the accusers in Socrates' trial.[1,2,6] Some of these data are also preserved in later authors.[10-21] Diodorus[11] reports, in addition, that Anytus, together with Meletus, was put to death by the Athenians, while according to Plutarch,[17] the accusers

[89 e 9 – 90 b 4]

1. Plato, *Apology*, passim, esp. 29 c 1–5, 36 a 7 – b 2.
2. Xenophon, *Apology of Socrates*, 29–31.
3. Xenophon, *Hellenica* II, 3, 42 and 44.
4. Lysias, XIII, 78, 82.
5. Lysias, XXII, 8, 9.
6. Isocrates, VIII, 23 (and XI, Hypothesis).
7. Andocides, I, 150.
8. Aristotle, *Athenian Constitution*, 27, 5.
9. Aristotle, *Athenian Constitution*, 34, 3.
10. Diodorus Siculus, XIII, 64, 6.
11. Diodorus Siculus, XIV, 37, 7.
12. Harpocration, *s.v.* δεκάζων.
13. Dio Chrysostomus, LV, 22.
14. Plutarch, *Life of Alcibiades*, IV, 4.
15. Plutarch, *Life of Coriolanus*, XIV, 4.
16. Plutarch, *Moralia, Amatorius*, 17, 762 c – d.
17. Plutarch, *Moralia, De invidia et odio*, 6, 538 a.
18. Maximus Tyrius, III, 1 ff.; XII, 8 a; XVIII, 6 d – e (Hobein).
19. Athenaeus, XII, 534 e – f (quoting Satyrus).
20. Diogenes Laertius, II, 38–39, 43; VI, 9.
21. Themistius, *Orationes*, XX, 239 c.

of Socrates (Anytus is not specifically named) were driven to hang themselves. Diogenes Laertius,[20] on the other hand, informs us that, after Socrates' trial and death, Anytus was exiled from Athens and also from Heraclea (on the Pontus) where he had sought refuge. Themistius[21] has the story that Anytus was stoned in Heraclea. Furthermore, Plutarch[14,16] as well as Athenaeus,[19] quoting Satyrus (3rd century B.C.), and the scholium on Plato's *Apology* 18 b[22] speak of Anytus as a—presumably—frustrated "lover" of Alcibiades. It is worth noting that, as in Meno's case, the reports disagree merely on the point of Anytus' death, if they mention it at all.

Who Anytus in the present Platonic dialogue is, can, of course, not be derived from all that information, which gives us, at best, only an image of his character in accordance with the opinions and rumors current about him in Plato's time.

Socrates introduces him as—to begin with (*prôton*)—the son of a wealthy and able father, who acquired his fortune by his own skill and diligence, not just by chance or because somebody else presented him with a gift (like, for example, quite recently, that Theban Ismenias who became so rich[23]); a citizen, furthermore (*epeita*)—we expect Socrates to add some description of Anytus, but he continues to speak about Anytus' *father*—who, in other respects, is reputed (*dokôn*) not to have been arrogant or inflated and offensive but to have been, on the contrary, an orderly and restrained man; one, furthermore (*epeita*), who, in the opinion of the majority of the Athenians, gave his son, Anytus, a good upbringing and education, for they do choose that son, this much is certain, for high offices.

This introduction, we see, does not say anything about Anytus himself. It says a great deal about his father and also about the reputation Anytus, at the present moment, enjoys among his fellow citizens. Besides, Anytus and his father cannot be total strangers to Meno who is characterized as Anytus' "guest" (*ho sautou xenos* – 90 b 5) and "family friend" (*patrikos hetairos* – 92 d 3[24]); presumably, therefore, Anytus need not be introduced to Meno. The introduction is in-

---

22. Additional sources: scholium on Plato, Apology 18 b (Hermann VI); scholium 87 to Aeschines' Κατὰ Τιμάρχου (F. Schultz, p. 270); Horace, *Satires* II, 4, 3.
23. Cf. Thompson, p. 171 (40); J. S. Morrison, "Meno of Pharsalus, Polycrates, and Ismenias," *Classical Quarterly*, XXXVI (1942), esp. 58, 76–77; Bluck, pp. 345–47.
24. We cannot help wondering about these ancestral bonds of hospitality (cf. J. S. Morrison, *op. cit.*, p. 76, note 1 – Bluck, p. 349). Yet, in terms of the dialogue, these bonds might be deeply "real."

tended for our ears: the anacoluthon[25] hints, we discern, at a
great disparity between father and son, and this hint seems
only to be amplified by the mention of the favorable opinion
current in Athens concerning the latter. The irony of this introduction matches the irony of Socrates' words in which he
informs Anytus a little later on (91 a 1–6) about Meno's
longing for that wisdom and excellence which makes men
take good care of their houses and cities, do honor to their
parents, know how to receive citizens and strangers and how
to bid them farewell in a manner worthy of a good man, a
longing that Meno has been talking about to him, Socrates,
for quite a while now (*palai*). But the irony reaches far beyond both Anytus and Meno.

Anytus' appearance is as sudden and unexpected as Meno's
original question at the very beginning of the dialogue. Anytus has just sat down[26] close by, at an opportune moment:
he[27] may be given a share, Socrates says, in the search in
which he, Socrates, as he has just confessed, is thoroughly
failing. And Socrates adds the remark that it would be appropriate (*eikotôs*) for him and Meno to let Anytus share in
that search. In support of this remark, Socrates gives Anytus
that ironic "introduction," which he concludes by saying: "It
is fitting to search with men like him for teachers in the matter of excellence, [and to see] whether they exist or do not
exist, and [if they exist] who they are." Indeed, Anytus might
be able to untie the knot, like a god in a tragedy who, at the
opportune moment, is suddenly made visible to the audience
and is then made to disappear suddenly again (*epi mecha-
nês tragikês theos*[28]). And with the appearance of Anytus, the
city of Athens, spoken about by Socrates in the earliest exchange of the dialogue,[29] the city of Athens in all its glory and
splendor and wealth, in all its pettiness and depravity and
corruption, makes its entry, too.

2.

It is Anytus, then, an Athenian citizen, whom Socrates, another Athenian citizen, addresses now. Meno and his crowd

25. Is it enough to say, as Thompson, p. 172 (42) does, that "the
    structure of the whole sentence is loose" and leave it at that? Cf.
    Robin, *Platon* (Pléiade), I, 1293, note 63.
26. See Thompson, p. 170 (34); Friedländer, *Platon II*, 1957, p 324,
    note 1; Bluck, p. 343, note to 89 e 8–9.
27. Cf. Liddell-Scott, *s.v.* ὅς B, III, 1.
28. *Clitophon* 407 a 8; cf. *Cratyl.* 425 d 6.
29. Pp. 40–41.

listen to the ensuing conversation—and so do we, trying to understand how the preceding exchanges relate to the present one. It is not much of a conversation, Socrates doing most of the talking and Anytus replying to Socrates' questions, on the whole, in a brief and summary manner, with some reluctance, it seems, and some condescension.

The theme is not, as before, the search for human excellence but the search for "teachers" (*didaskaloi*) of human excellence. The entire conversation between Socrates and Anytus, together with the exchange between Socrates and Meno, which concludes the Anytus episode, can be divided into five parts as follows: (1) a prologue dealing with "technicians" as teachers, (2) the crafty ones, the "knowledgeable ones" (the "sophists") as teachers, (3) the distinguished citizens (*hoi kaloi kàgathoi*) as teachers, (4) the great statesmen as teachers,[30] (5) an epilogue summarizing what has been said and also touching on opinions of a poet concerning the teachability of human excellence.

[90 b 4 – e 10]   *Part 1.* Socrates asks Anytus to join with him and Anytus' own guest Meno in the search they are engaged in, the search for an answer to the question, who the teachers of human excellence might be. A quick succession of rather lengthy questions on Socrates' part and short answers on Anytus' part makes it certain that, if they both wanted Meno to become a good physician or cobbler or flute-player, they would send him to be taught by physicians or cobblers or flute-players respectively. And the same would hold in all other cases of this nature. In saying this, they would imply that the teachers in question claim and declare themselves to be competent in their particular skills and ready to teach, for a fee, anyone who wants to learn from them. It would be folly (*anoia*), it would be absurd (*alogia*) to refuse to send a man who wants to learn a certain art to those who undertake to teach it for a fee and instead to trouble other people by asking them to do the teaching, people who neither pretend to be teachers of that art nor, in fact, have any pupils at all desirous of learning it. Anytus, at this point, agrees emphatically and even makes a "weighty" contribution on his own: it would be stupidly ignorant to boot (*kai amathia ge pros*). "Right you are" (*kalôs legeis*), says Socrates, with some sar-

---

30. Cf. *Apol.* 23 e 5 f.: . . . Ἄνυτος δὲ [ἀχθόμενος] ὑπὲρ τῶν δημιουργῶν καὶ τῶν πολιτικῶν . . . .

casm,[31] we presume. Agreement is thus reached as to how to go about making a man acquire all sorts of skills (*technai*) which involve some knowledge and experience: recognized "teachers" are always available to whom one can turn for that purpose.

Part 2. Socrates now calls Anytus' attention to the alleged case of Meno. "There is the opportunity for you now," he says, "to deliberate jointly with me about this stranger here, Meno." And he goes on describing Meno as someone desirous of becoming a "good man. . . ."[32] The "wisdom and excellence" (*sophia kai aretê*) Meno is supposed to be longing for are understood as the means of behaving properly with regard to one's own house and city, one's parents, fellow citizens, and strangers. The acquisition of wisdom and excellence seems thus to mean the acquisition of a *technê*, the possession of which makes a man a "good man." To whom, then, should Meno be sent to learn such excellence? Is it not obvious, from what has just been said and agreed on, that he should be sent to those who profess to be teachers of excellence and declare themselves impartially[33] available to anyone among the Greeks who wants to learn, provided he pays in return a fixed fee?[34] "But whom do you mean, Socrates?" asks Anytus. And Socrates replies: "Surely you know as well as I do that they are the men whom people call [the 'crafty ones', the 'knowledgeable ones', the 'sophists',] *the* 'teachers'." Anytus erupts: "O no, Socrates, not that! Hold your tongue! May no one who is close to me,[35] kinsman or friend, citizen or stranger, be ever seized with such madness as to be disgraced by frequenting these fellows; for they are patently the disgrace and the corruption of those who keep company with them."

Socrates expresses some surprise at Anytus' outburst. Why should these men be an exception? Why, among all the others who claim to know how to be of good service to us, should they alone not only not live up to their claim but, on the contrary, have an injurious effect on us? And how can they, on top of that, dare demand openly to be paid for what they are doing to us? Socrates, for one, cannot quite believe

---

31. Which Buttmann and Thompson, in the best Prodican manner, seem to miss: Thompson, p. 178 (34).
32. P. 225.
33. κοινούς – 91 b 4.
34. Thompson, p. 179 (15).
35. Burnet: γ' ἐμῶν.

that. He conjures up the memory of that grand old man, Protagoras, the wise, who amassed more money by this "sophistical" craft (*apo tautês tês sophias*) than did the illustrious Phidias with his splendid works (of "imitation") and ten other statue-makers. How can one believe that for forty years all Greece failed to see that Protagoras, being in this business of practicing his art (*en têi technêi ôn*),[36] was corrupting those who listened to him and that his pupils when leaving him were worse off than when they first approached him, while no mender of old shoes or clothes could stay in business for thirty days and escape death from starvation if he had a similarly deteriorating effect on the things he was supposed to repair! The reputation Protagoras enjoyed in his lifetime is intact even today, and the same can be said of many, many others like him, who preceded him or are still living.

Now, if Anytus is right, must we not conclude that these men either deceive and corrupt the youth deliberately or do so remaining themselves, too, completely unaware of what they are doing? And, in the latter case, must we not regard them, whom some call the wisest of men, as plain mad?

Anytus is adamant: it is not they who are mad, far from it; it would be much more correct to say that the young men who pay them money are mad, and still more, that the families which entrust their sons to the care of such people are mad, and most of all, that the cities are mad which allow those fellows to come in and do not expel anyone, stranger or citizen, who attempts this kind of business.

Socrates asks: "Come now, Anytus, has any one of the sophists wronged you? Or what makes you so bitter about them?" Anytus swears that he has never had any dealings with any of them, nor would he permit anyone close to him to have anything to do with them. Socrates asks: "So you are altogether unacquainted with these men?" Anytus: "And may I remain so forever!" But how could Anytus possibly know, Socrates inquires, whether there is anything good or bad in a matter which is totally outside Anytus' experience? "No difficulty about that (*rhaidiôs*)," Anytus replies, "I just know what these people are, whether I am acquainted with them or not." Socrates concludes: "Perhaps you are a diviner (*mantis*), Anytus, for how else *do* you know about them, I wonder, considering what you yourself are saying."

36. Cf. *Protag.* 317 c 1–2.

Part 3. Be that as it may, Socrates is willing to grant that the sophists are not the teachers of excellence whom Meno needs. He is willing to assume, with Anytus, that they would convert Meno into a knave. (Has not perhaps Gorgias done just that?) But the point is not to find teachers of knavishness. The service Anytus is requested to render Meno, his family-friend, is to tell him *to whom* he should turn in this great city of Athens in order to achieve distinction and acquire excellence, the kind of excellence Socrates has just been describing. Socrates invites Anytus to tell Meno that. Whereupon Anytus says rather rudely: "Why don't you tell him yourself?"[37]

[92 c 8 – 93 a 6]

Socrates replies that he already mentioned those whom he thought to be the appropriate teachers, the sophists, that is. But there was apparently nothing in that, if Anytus is to be believed. "And perhaps there is something in what you are saying (*kai isôs ti legeis*)," Socrates adds. Now it is Anytus' turn: he ought to tell to whom of the Athenians Meno should go. "Name him, anyone you please." There is no need to name just one man, Anytus retorts. No one among the distinguished Athenians (*Athenaiôn tôn kalôn kàgathôn*) whom Meno may happen to meet and to whose care he might be willing to entrust himself would fail to make him a better man than the sophists ever could.

Socrates wants to know whether these distinguished men (*houtoi hoi kaloi kàgathoi*) became what they are just by themselves, unaccountably so, and whether, not having learned their excellence from anyone, they are, nevertheless, able to teach others what they themselves did not learn.

Anytus' answer is: "I imagine, don't you, that they, too, learned from other older, also distinguished, people." And then comes something of a challenge: "Or don't you think that there have been good people, and many of them, in this city of ours?"

"I do, Anytus," is Socrates' reply, "I do think that there exist here people good at dealing with matters of public concern (*ta politika*) and, moreover, that such people have existed in the past in no less a degree than now." But Anytus' challenge is met by a much graver challenge on Socrates' part.

Part 4. Those distinguished men who possessed excellence, were they also good teachers of their own excellence? That

[93 a 6 – b 6]

37. Cf. Thompson, p. 189 (31).

is the question. What has been under consideration for quite a while now (*palai*) is not whether good men exist or do not exist here, in Athens, or whether they have existed in the past, but whether excellence is teachable. And thus we have to examine, Socrates insistently and elaborately repeats, whether good men, in addition to being good men, know now and have known in the past how to transmit excellence to another man, to transmit their particular excellence with regard to which they were (or are) good (that is, respected as good men), or whether this kind of thing is not transferable at all nor susceptible of being received by one man from another. That is what Socrates and Meno have been trying to find out for quite a while now (*palai*).

[93 b 6 – 95 a 6] Socrates sharpens this question to the utmost, taking his clue from what Anytus has just said (*ek tou sautou logou*). Some of the best known men among the distinguished Athenians are introduced by him into the discussion, famous statesmen, whose names helped shape Athens' glory and have not been forgotten to this very day: Themistocles and Aristides, Pericles and Thucydides. And it is about these men specifically that Socrates asks his question.

Each of them was a man of excellence. Anytus agrees heartily as far as Themistocles and Aristides are concerned. As to Pericles and Thucydides, Socrates apparently does not envisage the possibility that Anytus might question their merits. Anytus, at any rate, is not given an opportunity to disagree.

If ever there were excellent men who were also good teachers of their own excellence, those great men must have been that. The case is argued only with regard to Themistocles, but the outcome of the argument is clearly meant to be applicable to all of them.

Asked whether Themistocles was a good teacher of his own excellence, Anytus replies: "I think he was, provided he wanted to be one." How could he not have wanted some other people, above all—presumably—his own son, to become distinguished men (*kaloi kagathoi*), is Socrates' rejoinder. Is it conceivable that he could have been jealous of his own son and could have deliberately decided not to transmit his excellence to him, that excellence which made him himself, Themistocles, a good man? Anytus does not seem to conceive of that as a possibility, and Socrates proceeds to describe, in some detail, and with an inordinate amount of sarcasm, the kind of education all these great men provided for their sons.

Themistocles saw to it that his son had good teachers in horsemanship who made him amazingly proficient in that art. Thus, as far as his native qualifications, his "nature," were concerned, nobody could have alleged that there was something wrong with the young man, Socrates intimates, rather maliciously, we suspect. Anytus does not notice the irony; he is inclined to agree. But, Socrates continues, did Anytus ever hear anybody, young or old, say that Themistocles' son acquired that excellence and skill which his father had? No, Anytus did not.

Aristides gave his son the best possible education available in Athens, letting him be taught whatever could be taught, but this young man, as Anytus, having known him personally, can see for himself, has not turned out a better man than anyone else.

Pericles, a man "so loftily wise," had his two sons taught horsemanship and had them also educated in music and in athletic exercises and in everything else that pertains to art (*talla . . . hosa technês echetai*). And in the exercise of all these arts they were, indeed, not worse than any other Athenian, as Anytus knows. But did not Pericles want to make his sons good men? Socrates implies that, as far as that goes, he did not succeed,[38] and there is no objection on Anytus' part.

Finally Thucydides! He also brought up two sons and, in addition to giving them a good education in other things, he made them the best wrestlers[39] in Athens, employing, as one hears, the best known practitioners and teachers of the art of wrestling. Yes, Anytus did hear about that. But apparently the sons of Thucydides did not become "good men" either.

In this survey of paternal accomplishments and failures Socrates gives special attention to the last of the four. He introduces Thucydides and his sons for Anytus' consideration "so that you [Anytus] may not think only a few Athenians and those of meanest stature (*kai tous phaulotatous*) proved incapable in the matter."[40] And a little later on again: "But perhaps Thucydides was of mean stature (*phaulos*)! and did not have the greatest number of friends among the Athenians

38. Cf. Thompson, pp. 184 f.
39. See H. T. Wade-Gery, "Thucydides, the Son of Melesias: A Study of Periklean Policy," *The Journal of Hellenic Studies*, LII (1932), 205–27 (Bluck, p. 378).
40. Considering the way Socrates speaks of Aristides in the *Gorgias* (526 a – b), these words must refer, at least, both to Themistocles (which is not too surprising) and to Pericles (which seems "shock-

and their allies! Of a great family he was and of mighty influence in this city of Athens as well as everywhere else in
Greece. . . ."[41]

What is to be deduced from all these extraordinary case
histories?

It is hardly to be believed that Themistocles intended to ed-
ucate his son the way he did and yet did not intend to
make him a better man than his neighbors with regard to
the craftiness (*sophia*) in which his father, Themistocles himself, excelled, *if* indeed excellence is a thing teachable. Anytus
is compelled to admit that, even with some emphasis on his
part. So much for Themistocles, one of the outstanding men
of the past, as a teacher of excellence.

Aristides does not fare better in this respect, but the conclusion about excellence being perhaps not a teachable thing is
not stated explicitly in his case.

Pericles did not succeed in making good men out of his
sons. That he wanted to achieve this result appears likely, but
he could not achieve it, and this failure again gives Socrates
the opportunity to weigh, apprehensively, the possibility that
excellence may not be a thing teachable.

As for Thucydides, Socrates argues, it is clearly unlikely
that he should have made his children learn things, the
teaching of which involved expenditure of money, and should
not have made them learn how to become good men, which
would not have cost him anything, *if* that sort of thing were
at all teachable. For, *if* it is teachable, given the stature of the
man, he could have done the teaching himself; or, lacking
leisure to undertake such teaching because of his preoccupa-
tion with affairs of state, he could have found a man among
his fellow-countrymen or among foreigners who was likely to
make those sons of his good men. (The implication seems to
be that Thucydides, luckily enough, would not have needed
to remunerate such a man.)

In summing up all the evidence, Socrates concludes: we
really cannot help facing seriously, friend Anytus, the likelihood that human excellence may not be a teachable thing.

Anytus is incensed. He issues a warning. "To speak evil of
people—that is something which seems to come easily (*rhai-*

---

ing"). The emendations proposed by Stallbaum, Madvig, Vermehren,
Ast, Schanz, as well as the version of codex T (Burnet) "δυνατούς"
have hardly any merit. (Cf. Thompson, p. 247.)

Does not Socrates use this "shocking" phrase deliberately? (Cf. also
Dig. Laert. III, 63.)

41. Cf. Aristotle, *Athen. Const.* XXVIII, 5.

diôs) to you, Socrates. Now, if you will listen to me, I should like to advise you—be careful. Elsewhere, too, it may be easy (*rhaidion*)[42] to do evil to people or [for that matter] to do them good, but in this city of ours this is very definitely so, and I believe you know that yourself."

With these words Anytus seems to disappear, as suddenly as he had come in.

We hear Socrates speak to Meno: "Anytus appears to be angry, Meno. I am not at all surprised. For he thinks, in the first place, that I am speaking evil of those men, and, further-more, that he himself is one of them. Well, some day Anytus will know what 'speaking evil' means, and when that day comes he will stop being angry—but now he does not know."[43]

Part 5. With Meno substituting for the apparently departed [95 a 6 – 96 d 4] Anytus, Socrates continues the discussion concerning the teachability of human excellence.

He is assured by Meno that in Thessaly, too, there are dis-tinguished men (*kaloi kágathoi*). But asked whether these men are willing to offer themselves as teachers of the young and whether they agree among themselves that human excel-lence has its teachers and is, in fact, something teachable, Meno demurs: sometimes one may hear them affirm that it is and sometimes that it is not. Socrates draws the inference: if they themselves are in disagreement about no less an issue than that one, it is hardly possible to acknowledge them as teachers of the matter in question. Meno accepts the infer-ence.

Next, what does Meno think of the sophists, the only ones who profess to be teachers of human excellence? Does Meno think that they are? Meno confides to Socrates that he is filled with wonder—very much so—at never hearing Gorgias promise anything of the kind; when Gorgias hears others making such promises, he just laughs at them. (Apparently, he never made such a promise to Meno.) His task is, Gorgias thinks, to make people expert orators. Does that mean then, Socrates insists, that in Meno's opinion the sophists are not teachers of excel-lence? Meno confesses that he cannot tell: sometimes he thinks that they are, sometimes that they are not; he is wavering about that, he says, just like everybody else.

42. Burnet's text has ῥᾷον, according to Buttmann's conjecture (cf. Thompson's judgment pp. 247 f.). Bluck, pp. 385–88, argues for re-taining ῥᾴδιον.
43. Cf. Diog. Laert. II 35, Thompson, pp. 203 f., Bluck, p. 388.

Tacitly, Socrates interprets this wavering as uncertainty about the main question, the teachability of human excellence. He wants Meno to realize that this uncertainty is shared not only by other people in public life, but also by a poet, the poet Theognis. This man, too, sometimes regards human excellence as teachable and sometimes as not teachable. Socrates refers to some of his verses. It appears that Theognis at one point says: "From the good ones you will win lessons about the good"[44] (the "good ones" are identified with those who have "great power") ; and then again: "If understanding (*noêma*) could be fashioned and put into a man," those who are able to achieve that "would have received much in high re- compense" (the implication being that this feat cannot be done) ; and again: "Never would a bad son have sprung from a good father, for he would have listened to wise words: but not by teaching will you ever make the bad man good." Meno can see that the poet, too, in these passages, contradicts himself on one and the same subject.

It is a remarkable situation. On the one hand, those who claim to be teachers of excellence (the "crafty ones," the sophists) are not universally acknowledged (*homologountai*) to be what they claim to be, as the teachers of any other sub- ject matter are; the consensus is rather that they themselves do not even have the knowledge they allege they have (*oude autoi epistasthai*) and thus are corruptive (*ponéroi*) with regard to the very matter, human excellence, of which they claim to be teachers. (This was said by Anytus, not by Meno. As to Gorgias, he does not claim to be teaching human excel- lence.) On the other hand, those who by common consent are acknowledged (*homologoumenoi*) to be themselves distin- guished and excellent men (*kaloi kàgathoi*) sometimes say that excellence is a teachable thing and sometimes that it is not. (This was said by Meno, not by Anytus. The poet Theognis, a distinguished man himself, can be cited as an example.) People so confused about a subject matter could, strictly speaking, not be called its teachers, Socrates suggests, and Meno emphatically agrees. And that would hold, we un- derstand, specifically, if the subject matter were "human ex- cellence."

The situation thus described prevails, we gather, in Attica no less than in Thessaly, and presumably everywhere at all times. Socrates and Meno are about to reach a most disturb- ing conclusion.

44. Cf. Thompson, p. 248.

If neither the sophists nor the men who possess excellence themselves (*kaloi kàgathoi ontes*) are teachers of that subject "excellence," obviously no others, as far as one can see, are. And if there are no teachers, there can be no learners either. And it has been already[45] agreed—it was a fair guess at that time—that a subject matter of which, for any reason, there are neither teachers nor learners would not be a teachable matter.

The sequence is repeated: nowhere are teachers of excellence in sight; if no teachers, no learners either; human excellence, therefore, is hardly a teachable thing.

Meno closes the discussion: "It does not seem to be, if indeed we examined the question properly. And now I cannot help wondering, Socrates, are there ever any good men at all? Or, if so, in what possible way can they come to exist?"

3.

We have to remind ourselves of the "inverted" hypothetical proposition on which the entire preceding discussion with Anytus and Meno rests: "If excellence is teachable, excellence is knowledge."[46] Socrates had misgivings about the protasis of that sentence, but he had them only because of his concern about the content of the apodosis, to wit, that human excellence is knowledge (be it in the sense of *epistêmê* or of *phronêsis*).[47] Since those misgivings appear to have proved justified, since therefore human excellence can apparently not be identified, either wholly or partly, with "knowledge" (although this conclusion is not stated explicitly either by Socrates or by Meno), the question about the nature of human excellence, which has, in fact, been answered before,[48] must, so it seems, be faced again.

How does Meno face it? Since human excellence appears not to be teachable, for the good reason that no teacher of it can be found, Meno is led to wonder how men of excellence could ever come or have come to exist. Two additional and crucial premises underlie this wondering. They need not be stated because one was agreed on before[49] and the other was implicitly[50] kept as a premise all along. One is: men of excellence do not possess their excellence as a "natural" gift; the

45. P. 222.
46. Pp. 221 f.
47. *Ibid.*
48. Pp. 214, 218.
49. P. 219.
50. P. 220.

other is: the benefits of teaching and learning are divorced from what is given to us "by nature." Meno's *aporia* is thus based on the commonly accepted view of teaching and learning, which Socrates, too, seems to have adopted.[51] If, indeed, men, on the one hand, cannot acquire excellence by "learning" it from a teacher *and,* on the other hand, do not possess it "from birth," there is no way for a man to be an excellent man.

But the reliance on common and familiar views is not confined to Meno's concluding remark. The shadow of Meno's *amathia* provides the background for the entire Anytus episode.[52] We shall have to look at it carefully from that point of view.

1. Part one of the episode ends with Anytus' remark that to ask people who are not recognized as competent teachers of a given subject to instruct somebody in that subject would be a sign of stupid ignorance, of *amathia,* in addition to being an act of folly (*anoia*) and absurdity (*alogia*), as Socrates had said.[53] The comical character of this remark is put in full relief by Anytus' subsequent behavior (end of part two) with regard to the sophists, more exactly, with regard to the appellation "sophist" that labels certain people. He has never met anyone of this class; yet he claims ferociously that he knows what sort of people they are and that there is no difficulty about his knowing them.[54] Socrates likens this kind of knowledge to the clairvoyance of a diviner, a playfully polite but far from flattering comparison. For the power of divination is a divine gift to human thoughtlessness (*aphrosynêi anthrôpinêi*); no one in his senses (*ennous*) can have a share in it.[55] If Anytus is a "diviner," he cannot be a sensible man, cannot exercise wise judgment, cannot have *phronêsis.* What is more, the very lack of judgment manifested in Anytus' contention that he *knows* the sophists without ever having had the opportunity to *learn* anything about them, shows his own *amathia,* his own "ignorant" way of looking at things. But still, how is it that he can claim with such certainty to know them?

2. Although he has to admit everything that is said by Socrates about the sons of Athens' great statesmen (part four), he is angry with Socrates and accuses him of reviling the famous

51. Pp. 209 f., 220.
52. Cf. p. 211.
53. P. 226.
54. Cf. ῥᾳδίως in 92 c 4 with ῥᾴδιον, οὐ χαλεπόν and οὐκ ἀπορία in 71 e f. (p. 46; cf. p. 88) and with ῥᾳδίως in 84 b 11 (p. 174).
55. *Tim.* 71 e 2–4 (cf., on the other hand, p. 13 and note 32).

fathers of those insignificant sons. That is how Socrates interprets Anytus' accusation. But why should Anytus feel so
strongly about Socrates' words? Socrates gives at least one
reason for Anytus' feeling: Anytus thinks that he himself is
one of those men (*hêgeitai kai autos einai heis toutôn*). That
is to say, Anytus, in Socrates' understanding, regards himself
not only as one of the distinguished men, the *kaloi kàgathoi*,
of Athens (part three), but also as one of its foremost leaders.
If that is the case, there is good reason for Anytus to suspect
that he himself may also be a target of Socrates' abusive way
of speaking. Is not the upbringing of his own son, if Xenophon's account[56] is to be believed, liable to being added to
Socrates' list of educational failures?

Anytus' anger, inasmuch as it is based on his own high opinion of himself, points again to his *amathia*. For, in Diotima's
words,[57] ignorance, stupid ignorance (*amathia*), is precisely
this irksome thing which strikes us when a man who is neither
distinguished nor capable of the exercise of wise judgment
thinks of himself as quite self-sufficient. Does not this description fit Anytus? His father, according to Socrates' "introduction," was an orderly and restrained man, not arrogant, not
inflated and offensive.[58] Are we not supposed to infer, by way
of contrast,[59] that the son, Anytus, has all those undesirable
qualities and none of the paternal good ones? Is not his in-
temperate outburst against the "sophists" a case in point? Are
we not thus *shown*, even before the great examples have been
brought up, that one good father gave his son a good upbringing and education,[60] and yet was not able to transmit his
own moderation to his offspring? Anytus surely does not see
himself in this light. According to Socrates' verdict,[61] Anytus
considers himself a man of worth, on a level with Athens'
greatest. This is just what constitutes his lack of *sophrosyne*
as well as of *phronêsis*, his *amathia*.[62] But Anytus has something important to fall back on to bolster his self-appreciation:
his fellow citizens hold him in high esteem.[63]

3. Still, do Socrates' words warrant so acute an anger on
Anytus' part?

56. P. 223.
57. *Symp.* 204 a 4–6: αὐτὸ γὰρ τοῦτό ἐστι χαλεπὸν ἀμαθία, τὸ μὴ ὄντα καλὸν
κἀγαθὸν μηδὲ φρόνιμον δοκεῖν αὐτῷ εἶναι ἱκανόν.
58. P. 224.
59. P. 225.
60. P. 224.
61. P. 233.
62. Cf. *Phileb.* 48 c – 49 c.
63. P. 224.

Socrates pointed out that excellent men do not seem to be able to transmit their own excellence to their sons. That in itself is hardly an abusive statement. It might be offensive to Anytus because he could well understand it as applying also to himself in relation to his own son. He might have been more shocked by Socrates' characterizing as *phaulotatoi*[64] those famous Athenians whom Anytus chooses to regard as his peers. He might also have felt insulted by Socrates' reminding him of Thucydides' high stature and, by implication, of his, Anytus', own low origin. But is not the primary source of his anger the impression, which neither he nor we can avoid having, of Socrates' hardly disguised contempt for *all* the celebrated political figures that made Athens the great city it is in the eyes of the world?

In the *Gorgias* the condemnation of Miltiades and of his son Cimon, of Themistocles, and above all of Pericles, is made explicit,[65] while Aristides and other unnamed men are treated as exceptions.[66] The Athenian statesmen to whose reputation Callicles appeals[67] are condemned by Socrates because they did not live up to the only proper task of a good citizen (*monon ergon agathou politou*) [68]: they did not improve their fellow citizens but rather contributed to their corruption. In Socrates' conversation with Anytus on this very subject, the focal point is, however, not just the sweeping condemnation of Athenian statesmen and of political practices in Athens, but precisely Anytus' *anger*. We have to understand the meaning of this anger as provoked by Socrates' expression of contempt for Athens' famous statesmen.

A human community, and especially a political community, has to protect its members in one way or another; it has, at least, to provide the minimal conditions under which the immediate needs of its members can be met. But it must also provide the conditions under which it itself may be preserved. It cannot dispense with institutions, customs, traditions. Whatever changes it may undergo, whatever "innovations" it may originate or accept, it lives by memories. Cities with their sanctuaries, public buildings, monuments, memorials, burial grounds, harbor memories of all kinds. Those of us who share, to whatever degree, in the community's memories are "at

64. P. 231.
65. 515 c ff.
66. 526 a – b.
67. 503 c 1–3.
68. 517 c 1 f.

home" in it; those who do not, are "strangers" regardless of
their legal status. One might well live in a city unaware of
the intangible links between its present and its past and thus
be merely its guest. On the other hand, the sharing of the
community's memories may be quite "superficial," a habitual
reliance on a shadowy past. This, in fact, is what happens to
be the case more often than not.

Those memories include the names of men considered responsible, in one way or another, for the conditions which determine the life and the acknowledged status of the political
community in question. The reputations of those men are
among the most cherished *mnêmeia* of the *polis*. This, at any
rate, is how Anytus seems to regard such reputations.[69] To
question the validity of those monumental *mnêmeia* means
to attack the very existence of the *polis*. To hold them in contempt means to deny the ultimate authority of the *polis*.

Of such a denial the "sophists," who travel from city to city
and are nowhere "at home," can be found guilty—that Anytus
(and not only Anytus) indeed "knows." To know that, one
does not need to be acquainted with any one of them: their
reputation is well-established. And has not Socrates, although
an Athenian citizen and one who almost never leaves Athens,
just given ample evidence of his sharing the sophists' nefarious
attitude?

Anytus' anger is rooted in his firm reliance on the prevailing opinion (*doxa*) concerning the respectability (the
kalokagathia) or the unworthiness of people, that is to say,
in his firm reliance on the good or ill repute (*doxa*) of those
people. The *mnêmeia* of the *polis* fill *his amathia*. He is the
counterpart of Meno. But in this role he represents above all
the *polis* of Athens itself, where it is easy to do evil to people
or, for that matter, to do them good, as he himself says.[70]

Anytus' anger and menacing warning parallel Meno's anger
and veiled threat.[71] But Anytus, unlike Meno, can rely on
Athens powerful popular support. The unveiling of Anytus'
amathia amounts to an indictment of an entire *polis*. The
polis of Athens is on trial. The soul of Athens is Anytus'—
and thus also Meno's—soul in large script.

4. We can thus understand the full significance of the inversion which transformed the hypothetical sentence "If excellence is knowledge, excellence is teachable" into the one

69. Cf. *Rep.* IV, 426 d 1–6.
70. Pp. 232 f.
71. P. 89.

under consideration: "If excellence is teachable, excellence is knowledge." The new protasis poses a *political* problem. In Socrates' understanding, it poses the ultimate political problem. For it can well be denied that the presence or absence of "teachers" of excellence decides the question whether excellence is or is not teachable. But in the absence of genuine teaching—and learning—of excellence the *polis* is bound to shrink[72]: the mingled and mangled *mnêmeia* of the *polis* will become its ghostly heroes.[73]

The problem of "teachers" is not confined to Athens, just as the phenomenon of *amathia* is not restricted to Meno and to Anytus, though, in the dialogue, Meno as well as Anytus and Athens play paradigmatic roles. Three times during his conversation with Anytus Socrates refers to the clearly imaginary fact that Meno "for quite a while now" (*palai*) [74] has been talking about his desire to learn excellence and about the problem whether there are teachers from whom excellence can be learned. No, Meno has not been doing that, but the problem is indeed an ancient and ever new one, one which is applicable to any political community and one which Meno could not ignore had his *phronêsis* not been perverted into *panourgia*.[75]

5. Blind as Anytus is in his raging against the "sophists," his point that these men do not qualify as teachers of human excellence provokes Socrates' remark: "And perhaps there is something in what you are saying."[76] Gorgias, according to Meno's testimony, considered the claim of others to teach excellence a laughable matter.[77] In what sense might Anytus be right? Human excellence is not a *technê* which can be taught and learned like medicine, shoemaking, or flute-playing. But even if it were, the teachers of excellence would have to be "experts" concerning *aretê* in the same manner in which the teachers of medicine, shoemaking, and flute-playing must be themselves expert physicians, cobblers, and flute-players. That is to say, the teachers of human excellence would have to be themselves excellent men. Anytus and Socrates seem to agree that the professed teachers of *aretê* do not possess any genuine *kalokàgathia*. But Anytus assumes as self-evident that if that one condition for being able to teach excellence obtains—the

72. P. 192.
73. Cf. *Gorg.* 518 e – 519 a.
74. 91 a 2; 93 b 1; b 6 (cf. pp. 225, 230).
75. P. 188.
76. P. 229.
77. P. 233.

condition that the teachers themselves possess excellence—the teaching will be done and done successfully, as past experience has shown. That is why he regards any one reputed to be a *kalos kàgathos* as a potential teacher of *aretê*.[78] He thus clings to the view that the teaching of *aretê* is comparable to the teaching of any art. He does not notice that this view puts the reputed *kaloi kàgathoi* on the level of the "sophists."[79] Nor does he notice, in his state of *amathia,* that Socrates' argument about the inability of excellent fathers to transmit their excellence to their sons is a spurious one, intended, at best, to stir up his, Anytus', anger: the ability to learn depends, in the case of *aretê* as in any other case, decisively on the quality of the learner's soul,[80] as Socrates, with some malice,[81] implied in the case of Themistocles' offspring.

It is noteworthy that Socrates does not make any use of the "father" argument in his concluding conversation with Meno.

---

78. P. 229.
79. Cf. *Gorg.* 519 c 2–3 and the context, also *Rep.* VII, 492 a 5 ff.
80. Cf. pp. 106, 187 f., 220.
81. 93 c 9–10 (cf. p. 231).

X

1.

This time Meno appeared to have reached a state of perplexity: he was wondering (*thaumazô* – 96 d 2) whether good men can exist at all and, if they did, how they could possibly have come to exist. For excellence turned out to be something *not teachable,* and it had been "agreed" quite a while ago that no man possesses excellence "from birth." So much was Meno puzzled by this outcome that he was not even certain whether the question had been properly examined. Was Meno finally "learning"?

[96 d 5 – e 6]   But in all that wondering Meno seemed to have forgotten the apodosis of the hypothetical proposition under consideration. If excellence is not teachable, excellence cannot be knowledge of any kind. It is Socrates who leads him back to this conclusion.

The conversation with Anytus, however, has brought the theme of *doxa,* of opinion *and* reputation, to the fore and with it the problem of statesmanship. Socrates takes up both this theme and Meno's new problem.

Human excellence cannot be knowledge of any kind because no teachers of excellence can be found. The lack of such teachers and the resulting lack of good men seem to be confirmed by what Socrates now, comically enough, claims to realize. Both he and Meno, Socrates discovers, also find themselves among people lacking any excellence (*phauloi*) and this must be the fault of their respective teachers, Prodicus and Gorgias. For their teaching has turned out to have fallen short of what it ought to have been (*ouch hikanôs pepaideukenai*); otherwise he, Socrates, and Meno would not have ridiculously failed to notice in their preceding search that men conduct their affairs well and in the right way (*orthôs te kai eu*) not merely under the leadership of knowledge (*ou monon epistêmês hêgoumenês*); and that is probably also why he,

Socrates, as well as Meno, being "no good" themselves, are
unable to discern in what possible way good men come to
exist. Above all, then, they will now have to attend to themselves and look for the right teacher who would find *some*
way of making them better men. Meno does not understand
what Socrates is talking about and what is supposed to have
escaped their notice. Socrates explains.

He reminds Meno of what had been "agreed" on, and [96 e 7 – 97 c 5]
agreed on "rightly" (*orthôs* – 97 a 1), while they were discussing Socrates' *logos* concerning *aretê* and *phronêsis*[1]: good
men must do us good for it could not be otherwise.[2] Socrates
and Meno were also agreed with good reason (*kalôs*), weren't
they, that these good men will do us good if they lead us "in
the right way" (*orthôs*) in the conduct of our affairs.[3] But
Socrates' and Meno's agreement on the point that it is not
possible to give the right (*orthôs*) lead when one does not
exercise wise judgment (*ean mê phronimos êi*)[4] looks like
an agreement which was not right (*ouk orthôs*). Meno asks:
"What *do* you mean by 'right'?"[5] Socrates goes on explaining.

If a man, knowing (*eidôs*) the road to Larisa or to any
other place he may want to reach, should take that road and
lead others along, he would certainly lead them well and in
the right way (*orthôs kai eu*). But what about another man
who had never taken that road and *does not know* it (*mêd'
epistamenos*), yet *has a right opinion* (*orthôs doxazôn*) as to
which one it is? Would he not also lead others along that road
in the right way (*orthôs*)? Meno cannot deny that.

That second man, then, it appears, will not be a worse
leader than the first, "as long, at any rate, one would think,
as he keeps his right opinion" (*heôs g'an pou orthên doxan
echêi*) about that of which the first man has knowledge
(*epistêmên*); while the first man knows, in this case, the
truth and is fully aware of this (*phronountos*), the second

1. Pp. 211–14.
2. Pp. 212 f. (step one) and p. 215 (1 a).
3. ὡμολογήκαμεν (97 a 1) – ὡμολογοῦμεν (a 4) – cf. Thompson, p. 215 f.
   (7) and Bluck, p. 403.
4. Pp. 213–14 (steps three, four, five) and p. 215 (1 b).
5. There seems to be no compelling reason to bracket ὀρθῶς, as Schanz
   has done. Burnet in the text, Thompson, p. 250 (12), and Bluck,
   p. 404, uphold Schanz. Compare, on the other hand, Robin, *Platon*
   (*Pléiade*). I, 1294, note 85: "Y a-t-il lieu, avec la plupart des
   éditeurs, de suspecter le mot «droitement»?"
   It is precisely its "frequency" in the passage (cf. Thompson, *loc.
   cit.*) which prompts Meno to ask his question.

man is not: he only believes something which happens to be true without knowing that it is true (*oiomenos men alêthê, phronôn de mê*). It follows that "true" opinion (*doxa alêthês*) is not a worse leader with regard to the right way of conducting our affairs (*pros orthotêta praxeôs*) than the exercise of wise judgment (*phronêsis*). That is what Socrates thinks he and Meno had neglected to take into account when they were considering what sort of thing (*hopoion ti*) [6] human excellence might be and were saying that only the exercise of wise judgment provides the lead for acting rightly (*tou orthôs prattein*) : they had overlooked "true opinion" (*doxa alêthês*). "So it seems," says Meno. Socrates concludes: Right opinion (*orthê doxa*) does us no less good than knowledge (*epistêmê*).

We observe:

1. In the example of the road, the man who has a right opinion about it, without ever having traversed it, will have that right opinion presumably because somebody else had instructed him reliably on the subject. (That also holds if he has gained his information from a drawing or from a map.) Whether he himself had walked that road or had been told about it, he must have committed what he had learned to his memory. But the "learning" is different in the two cases: if he had been on that road before, he knows it now at "first hand"; if he relies on what he had been reliably told, he has a right opinion "from hearsay." [7]

2. There is an abundant use of the term *orthôs* in Socrates' explanation leading to the expression *orthê doxa*. At the same time "right opinion" is used synonymously with "true opinion" (*alêthês doxa*). [8] The term *orthôs* seems to be attuned to the world of human affairs (*tôn pragmatôn* – 97 a 4), to the right way of conducting them (*pros orthotêta praxeôs* – b 9), to the right way of acting (*orthôs prattein* – c 1). An *orthê doxa* is primarily an opinion which is responsible for a right action, that is to say, for an action beneficial to us, to others, or to the community as a whole. Its "rightness" is its "truth." By the same token, the exercise of wise judgment, *phronêsis* or *phronein* (97 b 7; b 10; c 1), is now understood without any qualification as a state of knowing, of *eidenai*, *epistasthai*, or *epistêmê* (96 e 2; 97 a 9; b 2; b 6; c 4 f.) : the man who exercises wise judgment (*phronimos esti* – cf. 97 a 6 f.) is a

6. Cf. 208–11.
7. Cf. p. 45.
8. ἀληθὴς δόξα is first mentioned in 85 c 7: cf. above pp. 174–79. (See also V, 6.)

man who is "knowledgeable" (*epistamenos* – cf. b 2) about
the affairs of the world.

In the *logos,* in which Socrates identified human excellence
with the exercise of wise judgment, we already saw the shift
from *epistêmê* to *phronêsis* taking place.[9] And the comprehensive conclusion reached there[10] was one centering on man
(*tôi anthrôpôi* – 88 e 5). But that *logos* spoke in the main of
phronêsis as providing the right "lead" in a man's soul. There
was actually no explicit agreement[11] as to the role "good men"
play in the *polis,* no explicit agreement about the role of good
statesmanship. Now, after the intervention of Anytus, the
emphasis is on this very point, on the way the "right" kind of
leadership can be exerted among men. "Right opinion"—no
more—seems to be required for the purpose.

3. The question arises whether Socrates, in his *logos* about
phronêsis, had really neglected to take "right opinion" into
account. Does not a man who exercises wise judgment in
various situations which require some decision on his part
assent to, or reject, a variety of "propositions" correctly?[12] Is
not, therefore, a man who is *phronimos* a man who on the
whole[13] opines rightly (*orthôs doxazei*)?

Meno has a reservation to make about the conclusion So-   [97 c 6 – 11]
crates has just reached, to wit, that right opinion does us no
less good than knowledge. The man who is in possession of
knowledge, he submits, has the advantage of always hitting
the mark, while the man who has but a right opinion will
sometimes hit it and sometimes not. Socrates disagrees: How
could a man who is always (*aei*) in possession of a right opinion ever (*aei*) miss the mark, "*as long indeed as he opines
the right thing*" (*heôsper ortha doxazoi*)? Meno concedes the
point, too rashly, though.

Where was he wrong? He did not see that a "right opinion"
is not simply an "opinion" which, no doubt, can be either
right or false.[14] We note in passing that "false opinion"
(*pseudês doxa*) is nowhere mentioned in the argument.[15] It

---

9. Cf. p. 215.
10. P. 214 (step six).
11. Cf. p. 243, note 3.
12. Cf. p. 105.
13. Cf. p. 216.
14. Cf. pp. 159 ff.
15. The connotation of "unforgotten" (cf. p. 176) is no longer associated with "ἀληθής" in this entire passage either. There is no
ἀνάμνησις myth at this juncture to help preserve it (cf. pp. 208 ff.).

is rather amusing to observe that Meno, in keeping with his character, lumps "right" and "false" opinions together. Yet Meno seems to have a point, too, although he does not know how to make it.

Since right opinions depend, for the most part, on hearsay, it is indeed a matter of chance whether one is told the right thing or not. It is conceivable, furthermore, that one might even hit the mark without being told about the right thing at all: one might just happen to take the right road on the strength of a "hunch" or of a lucky guess. Could not such a correct, if haphazard, guess be also called a right opinion? Socrates himself limits the infallibility of a man who has a right opinion about something by the phrase: "as long indeed as he opines the right thing." This phrase repeats the condition mentioned before (97 b 5): "as long, at any rate, one would think, as he keeps his right opinion. . . ." The condition is now put in a more definite way. Does not this conditional phrase take care of all possible cases of correct opining? And does it not, by implication, make the point Meno was trying to make?

2.

[97 c 11 – 98 a 9]   Meno, to be sure, does not pay any attention to that conditional phrase. He is wondering again. He is wondering why, granted the truth of what Socrates just said, knowledge is held in so much higher esteem than right opinion and why they should be distinguished at all. For, in Meno's understanding, Socrates had just shown that right opinion cannot, of necessity (*anankê moi phainetai*), differ from knowledge. Socrates adds to Meno's bewilderment by asking him whether he, Meno, knows why he is in this state of wonder. Or would Meno prefer to be *told* by Socrates the reason why he, Meno, is in this state (*ê egô soi eipô?*)? Meno definitely does. He prefers, as we shall see in a moment, to be merely opining about his own wondering.

The reason is, says Socrates, that Meno has not paid enough attention to Daedalus' statuary![16] "But perhaps there is none of it in your country," Socrates adds, as if any of the kind Socrates means existed in Athens. Meno's bewilderment must be complete. Socrates proceeds to explain what he means.

16. Cf. *Euthyphro* 11 b – c, 15 b (also *Hipp. maj.* 282 a and *Laws* III, 677 d).

He likens "right opinions" to the statues built by the legendary Cunning Worker, because these statues, too, have to be fastened with chains to make them stay; otherwise they run away and escape. Meno does not understand. Socrates goes on with the simile.

To own a work of Daedalus in its unchained state is not worth very much; it is like owning a slave inclined to run away, for a statue wrought by Daedalus does not stay put. But in its chained state it is worth a great deal, for Daedalus' products are most excellent works.

All that is applicable to "true opinions." For they, too, are a possession to be highly treasured as long as they stay put: they make for all that is good and beneficent (*panta tàgatha ergazontai*). Unfortunately, they by themselves do not want to stay for any length of time but run out of the human soul. Thus they are not worth very much until one "binds" them. This binding consists in finding *reasons* for them in one's own thinking (*aitias logismôi*). "And this, Meno, my friend, is 'recollection', as was agreed between us in what was said before."

Whenever true or right opinions are thus "bound" they become "knowledges," first of all, and furthermore they become stable and lasting (*monimoi*). That is why knowledge is held in higher esteem than right opinion: it differs from right opinion by its being bound fast (*desmôi*).

The questions Meno raised appear to have been answered now. Meno need not wonder any longer. Meno is indeed impressed. It really must be something like that, he opines. It is doubtful, however, whether Meno understands the complexity of the picture presented by Socrates.

Let us consider Socrates' words.

1. The right opinions Socrates is talking about are primarily those which determine praiseworthy actions of men. Socrates' new contention arose out of his conversation with Anytus about the teaching of human excellence and the role the great Athenian statesmen have, or have not, played in this teaching. The right opinions are also those which we entertain with regard to the men responsible for the conduct of human affairs on a larger scale. The good reputation of these men is a matter of *our* opinion and, if our opinion about them is right, *their* good reputation, *their doxa*,[17] is deserved.

---

17. It is worth noting that this is the sense of δόξα throughout the speeches of Glaucon and of Adeimantus (especially of the latter) in the second book of the *Republic*.

Furthermore, their good reputation can persist only if our opinion about them remains stable.

2. In contrasting "right opinion" with "knowledge," Socrates assigns instability to the former and permanence to the latter. In what sense can a right opinion be said to be unstable? Opinions of men do change; they seem by their very nature fickle, easily reversed. A man who has a right opinion about something may change his mind too. But, then, will he still have a *right* opinion? Is not that the point of the conditional clause: "as long indeed as he opines the right thing . . ."? If it is, "knowledge" provides the proper counterbalance to "right opinion." For to know something means to know what and *why* this something unchangeably is what it is and, therefore, this knowledge itself cannot be subject to change. But knowledge, like right opinion, can be lost, can be forgotten, can "run out of the human soul."[18] In that sense knowledge is no less unstable than right opinion. Only knowledge of the kind *phronêsis* is seems immune to forgetfulness. The exercise of wise judgment can hardly be "forgotten."[19] Is not a man who *keeps* opining rightly, relying on what he was reliably told, a man known for exercising wise judgment simply because his wisdom consists in recognizing the wisdom of others? Does not such a man, too, possess human excellence and is he not indeed able to guide us in our actions?

3. The theme of recollection reappears stripped of all mythical connotations. Recollection is now identified with the "binding" of right opinions to which we subscribed "from hearsay." To "bind" them means to find reasons for them in one's own thinking. The process is described in the crucial argument between Socrates and Cebes in the *Phaedo*, where this description "envelops" the—not quite successful—attempt to find the reason for the deathlessness of the soul.[20] The finding of reasons for something in one's own thinking is precisely what we mean by *understanding* and *learning*. The goal is knowledge (*epistêmê*). Should this goal be attained, that which was formerly opined (*doxaston*) and merely remembered will stand firmly and stably on its ground: it will be something "known" (*epistêton*).[21] The known itself by itself is removed from the vicissitudes of time.[22] The term

18. Cf. p. 157.
19. Cf. p. 218.
20. Cf. pp. 136–37, 147.
21. Cf. *Theaet.* 201 c 9 – d 4.
22. Cf. pp. 150, 157.

"recollection" refers now directly to the effort (*meletê*) of understanding and learning, an effort which anticipates the final, perhaps unattainable, stage of knowledge.[23] Again, does not this effort embody all excellence man can attain?[24]

4. The simile of Daedalus' statuary does not dissolve the difference, and perhaps tension, between *phronêsis* and *epistêmê*. A Daedalic statue which stands fast can serve as an image of "knowledge" as well as of *phronêsis,* both of which are constant and lasting, though in a different sense, compared with "right opinion" which lacks firmness and stability. But the decisive feature of the image is that it presents to our sight *statues,* and statues which can *move.*

A statue, an *agalma* (97 d 6), is a monument erected to honor a god or a man. It is a lasting "memorial," a *mnêmeion,* a visible manifestation of somebody's glory or "reputation" which we venerate or cherish in our opinions and memories. Such a statue is human *doxa* and *mnêmê* made visible and tangible. The legend of Daedalic statues capable of "running away" seems, in Socrates' understanding, to mirror the inconstancy of both human opinions and human reputations. To eliminate our false opinions and to find a firm, a "sufficient" foundation for our "right" opinions is the task of learning. And should not the reputation of a man be measured by *more* than an opinion, even a "right" one, about what constitutes human excellence?

Meno has not taken Socrates' words literally. He has not, [98 b 1–6] we presume, noticed the implications these words carried, but he certainly has understood that Daedalus' statuary was no more than a simile. Socrates, on his part, assures Meno, once more, that he, Socrates, is not speaking as one who possesses knowledge: he too, like Meno, Socrates claims, does not *know what* the difference between "right opinion" and "knowledge" is (*kai egô hôs ouk eidôs legô*); he is just groping for the truth about this difference by using images (*eikazôn*). But *that* "right opinion" is something different (*ti alloion*) from "knowledge" is not at all a matter of imagery for him: "If there is anything else I should claim to know (*eidenai*), and there are few things of that sort, one thing, this one, I would certainly put among those I do know." "And right (*orthôs*) you are, Socrates," says Meno with touching innocence.

It is the second time in the dialogue that Socrates so force-

23. Cf. pp. 86 f., 124, 149, 168, 171 f.
24. Cf. pp. 183 f., 201.

fully takes a definite stand. Just before Meno expressed his preference for going back to the problem he had raised at the very beginning of the dialogue rather than for considering the question "what is human excellence," Socrates had stated that he was not prepared to maintain anything he said about "recollection" except one thing only: that it was *better* to rely on his recollection story and to make an attempt to learn (or to "recollect") than to give credence to Meno's contention concerning the impossibility of any learning and thus to become slothful. As far as this *one* point was concerned, Socrates was willing to fight for it, in word and deed, as much as he could.[25] What he asserts now is the fundamental and "sufficient" supposition on which that first forceful statement rests. The effort of learning is meaningful only if there be possible a state of knowledge *different* from the state of right opinion. For the "rightness" of any opinion presupposes the existence of truth which only *epistêmê*—or *phronêsis*—can reach.

3.

What follows is a quick and yet strangely involved summary of almost all that has been said after, and even before, Anytus had appeared on the scene. This summary is given by Socrates with a view to a new and better understanding of human excellence. But what he says is completely overshadowed by Meno's and Anytus' *amathia*. Accordingly, no more light is brought to bear on the subject. *Epistêmê, phronêsis* and *sophia* are used interchangeably. Opinion, and mostly false opinion, reigns supreme. Only occasionally does Socrates pierce that curtain. And in the wake of this cursory and, in part even incoherent, recapitulation the argument made about "right opinion" appears curiously modified.

[98 b 7 – e 13]   Let's see (*ti de?*), says Socrates, this is still right (*orthôs*), isn't it, that "true opinion," in guiding the performance of any action, is no less efficacious than knowledge? In Meno's opinion Socrates is still saying something true. "Right opinion," therefore, is by no means worse than knowledge and will do us no less good with regard to our actions; nor is a man who has a "right opinion" worse off than a man who possesses knowledge. Meno agrees. Furthermore, it had been agreed that the good man is beneficial to us. "And since men

25. P. 183.

would thus be good men and beneficial to their cities, should
such men happen to exist, not by virtue of their knowledge
only but by virtue of their having right opinion as well"
—Socrates does not finish the sentence; instead of supplying
the consequence, he adds another preliminary clause—"and
since neither of these, knowledge and true opinion, belongs
to men by nature, and since they aren't acquired either
. . ."[26]—Socrates still does not state the consequence; he in-
terrupts the sentence altogether, and never finishes it, seeking to assertain whether Meno agrees with the first part of
that second clause. "Or do you think that either of them
[knowledge or true opinion] is [given to us] by nature?"
Meno does not. Socrates presses the point: if neither is given
by nature, good men cannot be good from birth. Meno
fully agrees.

As far as knowledge (*epistêmê*), or *phronêsis,* is concerned,
this has been Meno's premise all along.[27] What is remarkable,
and new, is that this premise is now, with Socrates' help, extended to include "true opinion." Why should it not indeed?
Does not Meno cling to the correlative assumption that one
acquires both knowledge and true opinion by being *told*
about the truth?[28] Socrates' example of the road to Larisa
supports that assumption. The case of correct guessing[29] is
not brought up.

What would the end of the sentence have been, had Socrates finished it after the first causal clause? Presumably this:
there is nothing to prevent those good men from being good
by virtue of their right opinions. The second clause, however,
does not permit this conclusion. Socrates has to continue his
"summary" in a different vein.

"Since, then, [knowledge as well as right opinion are] not
[given] by nature"—as we see, Socrates does not care to
state explicitly that either may account for excellence in man
—"we considered after that (*meta touto*) whether it is something that can be taught" (we have to understand that "it"

26. 98 d 1: οὖτ' ἐπίκτητα. Thompson, p. 252 (23), and Bluck, pp. 416–17,
    discuss the various views advanced with regard to these words. Bluck
    mentions Verdenius' reference to Kühner-Gerth, *Ausf. Gramm. d.
    griech. Sprache* II, 228–29, and Denniston, *The Greek Particles,* pp.
    509–10, in favor of οὖτε (as against Bekker's conjectural οὐδέ). Why,
    then, as Robin, *Platon* (Pléiade), I, 1294–95, note 90, points out,
    alter or remove the phrase? It anticipates the conversation with
    Meno up to 99 b 10, but not beyond that.
27. Cf. pp. 219, 235.
28. Cf. pp. 40, 58, 65, 67, 93 f., 97, 184.
29. P. 246.

refers to human excellence). If now human excellence consists in *phronêsis* (*epistêmê* is abandoned), it appeared to us as something teachable, didn't it? Meno agrees.[30] And should it be something teachable, excellence would be, so it seemed to us, didn't it, *phronêsis*. Meno agrees. This "inversion" of a hypothetical sentence repeats the inversion made some while ago.[31] This time it is made more explicit, with *phronêsis* substituting for *epistêmê*. The legitimacy, or illegitimacy, of this inversion does not bother Meno. Socrates continues his "summary."

"And if there were really teachers [of human excellence], it would be teachable, if not, not, so it seemed to us, didn't it?" "But we had definitely come to agree that there are no teachers of it?" "We had thus agreed that it is neither teachable nor [therefore identifiable with] *phronêsis?*" Meno keeps confirming what Socrates says. "And we do definitely agree that this thing, human excellence, is a good thing?" Meno: "Yes."[32] "And that which leads us in a right way (*to orthôs hêgoumenon*) is something good and does us good?" Meno agrees. A new "conclusion" comes into sight.

[99 a 1 – b 10] About this much there is agreement, so far: only these two things, true opinion (*doxa alêthês*) and knowledge (*epistêmê*), lead us in a right way (*orthôs*), and a man who has either of them provides the right lead. What comes about by chance (*apo tychês*) is not the result of *human* leadership (*anthrôpinê hêgemonia*). (This definitely appears to eliminate haphazard, if correct, guessing as a case of right opinion.[33]) Socrates repeats: a man is a leader towards that which is right (*epi to orthon*) by virtue of these two, true opinion and knowledge. That seems right to Meno. Now, since human excellence (as has been found) is something which is actually not teachable, it cannot be taken any longer to be knowledge (*epistêmê*). It does not appear to be possible, says Meno. (This conclusion was not stated explicitly before.[34]) One of the two things which is good and beneficent having thus been discarded, namely knowledge, it could hardly be the leader in the affairs of a city. It does not seem to be that to Meno, either. Men like Themistocles and those others

30. Pp. 209–10, 219.
31. Pp. 221 f.
32. Cf. pp. 211 f.
33. Pp. 246, 251.
34. Pp. 234–35.

"whom Anytus here has just mentioned" (*hous arti Anytos hode elege*) were therefore leaders in their cities *not* by virtue of any wisdom (*sophia*), *not* because they were wise (*sophoi*). And that is why such men, being what they are *not* through knowledge (*di' epistêmên*), are unable to make others their peers. Meno: "That's how it is, it seems, Socrates, as you say."

We note:

1. It was not Anytus, it was Socrates who first mentioned those men and spoke about them rather extensively.

2. Anytus has reappeared! He is perhaps listening to the conversation, fearful perhaps lest his guest Meno be corrupted by Socrates. There is something phantom-like about his presence now. We wonder, however, whether his first, seemingly god-like appearance had not been rather phantom-like, too.

3. The sons of those famous leaders are not referred to any longer. The reputedly great statesmen are said now to be unable to make simply "others" (*allous*) resemble themselves. But do they not set examples emulated by others, by Anytus, for instance?

4. Since knowledge has been discarded as a source of leadership, we can expect "true opinion" to fill its place.

Socrates, however, continues as follows: since those leaders are not what they are through knowledge (*epistêmêi*), the only remaining possibility is that they are what they are through "good opinion," through *eudoxia*. [99 b 11 – c 6]

Does Socrates mean that statesmen are guided by sound and good opinions in their counsels and actions? Or does he mean that statesmen are reputed to be thus guided in the opinion of their fellow citizens? The term *eudoxia* is chosen with care. It is strikingly *not* synonymous with either "true opinion" or "right opinion," in spite of its affinity to both of them.[35] It means "good repute." It points indeed to the kind of "opinion" generally opined to be "true" or "right," because those who hold or utter an opinion of that kind are themselves held in high esteem and said to be "true and good." It points to the all-pervasive medium of trust and belief in

---

35. It is hard to understand why Thompson, p. 225 (15), writes: "I do not think Plato intended any play on the ordinary meaning of the word 'good repute,'" and it is amazing to see Liddell-Scott, *s.v.*, εὐδοξία ignore the context. (Cf. Bluck, p. 424.) See also *Apol.* 22 a 3, *Rep.* II, 363 a and IV, 426 b–d.

which we live and cannot help living, to the habitually accepted and acknowledged opinions and reputations by which, to a more or less high degree, all of us, and, in a most conspicuous and decisive way, Meno and Anytus are swayed.

Socrates proceeds to clarify what he means by *eudoxia*. Men whose business is the affairs of public concern (*politikoi andres*) and who guide their cities in the right manner (*orthousin*) are related to wise judgment (*pros to phronein*) in no other way than soothsayers and diviners are: these people, too, "speak true" and do so often enough, but they know not what they say. That may well be the case, says Meno.

We observe that there are many ways of interpreting soothsaying: if soothsayers or prophets happen to say or to predict the truth, divinity itself may speak through their mouths; or they may be told by divinity to say what they say; or they may be told, and bribed, to say what they say by clever men; or they may just guess correctly. In the latter case "chance" (*tychê*) would be involved. This case was eliminated by Socrates a short while ago: "Human leadership" (*anthrôpinê hêgemonia*) cannot be equated to the intervention of "chance."[36] But "divine leadership" could. Whatever the ways of soothsayers and diviners, it is their "reputation," deserved or undeserved, which makes others listen and accept what they say. We remember that Socrates had rather maliciously likened Anytus to a diviner.[37] The occasion had been provided by Anytus himself, when he based his harsh opinion of the sophists on nothing but the reputation these fellows enjoyed among the reputable citizens of Athens.[38] In this particular case, Socrates intimated, Anytus might well have hit the mark.[39]

[99 c 7 – e 4] Socrates suggests, and Meno agrees, that men who accomplish successfully many great things in deed and in speech while lacking sense (*noun mê echontes*) are worthy of being called "divine." It would be right, too, to call the soothsayers and diviners just mentioned as well as the entire "creative" tribe (*tous poiêtikous hapantas*[40]) "divine." And why should we claim that statesmen are less divine and less possessed by a god than those other people? They are breathed upon and

36. P. 252.
37. Pp. 228, 236.
38. P. 239.
39. P. 229.
40. Cf. *Symp.* 205 b 8 – c 3; *Laws* III, 682 a 3.

held from on high (*ek tou theou*) whenever they bring many
great affairs of state to a successful end by making speeches
without knowing what they are talking about. Quite so, says
Meno imperturbably. Socrates has a last trump to play. He
can adduce excellent authorities to justify the epithet "divine"
bestowed upon such men: women certainly, too, as Meno must
know, call good men "divine"; and Spartans, too, when they
praise some good man, are wont to say (in their sibilant manner[41]) : *"This* is a man divine."* Meno approves of this way
of speaking: "And clearly, Socrates, they are right," he says.
He does not seem to be aware at all of the extreme sarcasm
which flavors Socrates' words. But Anytus is still about, presumably listening, and Socrates[42] takes the opportunity to remark: "You are perhaps offending Anytus here (*Anytos
hode*) , though, by what you are saying." "It does not matter
to me," is Meno's[43] rather contemptuous reply. Socrates:
"With that man we shall converse again at some future time,
Meno."

Socrates restates briefly the conclusion just reached and   [99 e 4 – 100 c 2]
presents it as the result of the entire dialogue we have been
witnessing. Let us not forget: he is talking to Meno.

If, says Socrates to Meno, *if* their manner of searching and
speaking[44] had been faultless throughout this entire conversation, human excellence would appear to be something
neither given "by nature" nor capable of being taught; it
seems rather to accrue to men, whenever that happens, by
"divine allotment" (*theiai moirai*) ,[45] good sense being absent
(*aneu nou*) in such cases, unless, Socrates adds, *unless* among
the statesmen, among the men concerned with public affairs,
there should be *one* capable of making a statesman of another
man. Should there be such a one—in the course of the conversation with Anytus and Meno on that subject none was
found—*should* there be such a one, he could well be said to
be among the living what Homer says Teiresias is among the
dead. This is what Homer says[46]: among those in Hades,
Teiresias alone is in his senses, the others are flitting phan-

---

41. σεῖος instead of θεῖος – see Bluck, pp. 142–43, 430–31, and esp. Aris-
    totle, *Nic. Eth.* VII, 1, 1145 a 28–29.
42. Cf. Friedländer, *Platon II*, 1957, p. 324, note 2, and Bluck, pp. 431 f.
43. *Ibid.*
44. For the grammar cf. Thompson, pp. 77 f. (22).
45. Cf. Aristotle, *Nic. Eth.* I, 9, 1099 b 10 and the context.
46. *Odyss.* X, 494–95: τῷ καὶ τεθνηῶτι νόον πόρε Περσεφόνεια, οἴῳ πεπνῦσθαι,
    τοὶ δὲ σκιαὶ ἀίσσουσιν. (Cf. *Rep.* III, 386 d 7.)

toms. As far as excellence is concerned, such a man would indeed be among us here like a true being surrounded by phantoms.[47] Meno appears highly pleased by Socrates' words.

Socrates repeats once more, this time categorically: It manifestly follows from all this figuring that human excellence accrues to men, whenever that happens, by "divine allotment" (theiai moirai). This time, after the mention of Teiresias, the phrase theia moira may not imply any sarcasm at all.[48] We shall know the clear truth (to saphes), however, about all that has been said, Socrates continues, when, and only when, we shall have attempted to find what excellence all by itself is before searching out the way it might accrue to men. It is doubtful whether Meno understands the simplicity and immensity of the task set before him. Socrates urges him, and us, to embark upon the enterprise of learning.

Socrates has to leave now. By way of parting, he has a suggestion to make: Meno should persuade his host Anytus (ton xenon tonde Anyton) of the very same things of which he, Meno, has been persuaded in the course of the preceding conversation. The purpose of this persuasion, Socrates indicates, is to make Anytus less angry, more amenable to reason (hina praioteros êi).

We note: Anytus is apparently still there, phantom-like. We wonder: has Meno been persuaded of anything?

There is a last "addition" on Socrates' part: should Meno succeed in persuading Anytus, the polis of the Athenians also might derive some profit from it.

Here the dialogue ends. The prospect of a conversation between Meno and Anytus has its charms. But we, the readers and witnesses of the dialogue, have to continue the search for human excellence on our own.

---

47. See Gorg. 521 d 6–8.
48. Cf. Rep. VI, 493 a 1–2; 499 c 1; IX, 592 a 8–9; and also Aristotle, Nic. Eth. X, 9, 1179 b 21–23 and the context. It seems fair to assume that the range of meaning of θεία μοῖρα is coextensive with the range of meaning of καλοκἀγαθία. (Cf. also Leo Strauss, On Tyranny. An Interpretation of Xenophon's Hiero, 1948, pp. 22, 90.)